PENGUIN BOOKS

THE GURKHAS

Byron Farwell served as an officer in the North African and Italian campaigns in the Second World War and also in the Korean War. Since then he has lived in Switzerland, England and the United States. He has travelled in more than one hundred countries and is a Fellow of the Royal Geographical Society. He is author of *The Man Who Presumed* (a biography of Henry M. Stanley), *Burton* (a biography of Sir Richard Burton), *Prisoners of the Mahdi, Queen Victoria's Little Wars, The Great Boer War* and *For Queen and Country* (a social history of the Victorian and Edwardian Army). His latest book, *Eminent Victorian Soldiers*, will be published by Viking in early 1986. Mr Farwell was elected a Fellow of the Royal Society of Literature in 1964.

THE
GURKHAS

———

BYRON FARWELL

———

PENGUIN BOOKS

Penguin Books Ltd, Harmondsworth, Middlesex, England
Viking Penguin Inc., 40 West 23rd Street, New York, New York 10010, U.S.A.
Penguin Books Australia Ltd, Ringwood, Victoria, Australia
Penguin Books Canada Ltd, 2801 John Street, Markham, Ontario, Canada L3R 1B4
Penguin Books (N.Z.) Ltd, 182–190 Wairau Road, Auckland 10, New Zealand

First published by Allen Lane 1984
Published in Penguin Books 1985

Made and printed in Great Britain by
Richard Clay (The Chaucer Press) Ltd,
Bungay, Suffolk
Typeset in Aster

For my children:

Joyce Lewis

Byron John Farwell

Lesley Farwell

Contents

Map appears on pages 18–19.
Plates appear between pages 154 and 173.

Acknowledgements

———————

I am grateful to a great many people in a great many places for information. In particular, I must mention Major-General D.K. Palit, Vr.C., and Lieutenant-Colonel A.A. Mains. Both have been exceptionally generous and have devoted much time to answering my floods of questions. In addition, I want to thank Major-General J.L. Chapple, C.B.E., Major-General Brigade of Gurkhas; Mr A.C. Gould; Lieutenant-Colonel H.C. Gregory, O.B.E.: Brigadier C.R.L. Guthrie, M.V.O., O.B.E.; Colonel R.C. Jackman, O.B.E.; Mr David Gwynne Jones; Lieutenant-Colonel David Morgan, M.B.E., who commanded the 1/7th in the Falklands War; Lietenant-Colonel R.W.C. Reeves; Mr Angus MacLean Thuermer; Major T. Watts; and Major Edward F. Wells, U.S.M.C.

Foreword

Kaphar hunnu bhanda marnu ramro
('It is better to die than be a coward' – motto of Gurkhas)

I saw my first Gurkha soldiers in Italy during World War II: two little men with Mongolian features, probably from the Second Battalion of the 4th Gurkha Rifles. I remember being struck by the jaunty angle of their hats and by their confident, self-assured swagger. Their uniforms and patches proclaimed them members of Britain's Indian Army. Later I heard stories of their prowess in battle, particularly with their short curved knives, called *kukris*, with the cutting edge on the inside and the notched phallus on the blade. I did not see their like again until many years later in Nepal.

On a narrow, crowded street in Katmandu one day in 1967 I saw a man moving slowly and heavily toward me. From his dress one could see he was a *parbatiya*, a man from the high hills west of Katmandu where recruiters find most of their soldiers. He was small, perhaps not more than five feet two inches tall, but his bare legs were knotted with outsized muscles. He was bent forward from the weight on his back, supported in part by a *doko*, a kind of headband which *parbatiya* children begin to use at about the age of seven. He plodded steadily in a straight, undeviating course, expecting me and all others to move from his path – and we did. As he drew level I saw his load: an old-fashioned safe that could not have weighed less than three hundred pounds. He may have been destined to carry this burden several miles. It is possible that he was a physical reject from the British or Indian Army, turned away as a youth not fit enough to be a recruit.

This is the story of those volunteers from selected tribes in Nepal who are declared fit enough to serve as mercenaries in Gurkha regiments: who they are; why they have maintained such a close relationship with the British for 165 years; how they are recruited, organized and employed; and something of their customs, personalities, characters and characteristics. It is also the story of the men who lead them.

There is no agreement as to who is or is not a Gurkha, and there is no agreement as to how the name of such people should be spelt in English. There are some who would call all Nepalese 'Gurkhas' regardless of their origin, tribe or social class. Others would limit the term to those who live in the hills around the town of Gurkha, some twenty-five miles north-west of Katmandu, primarily Magars or Gurungs. However, to soldiers and, I would guess, to most others, Gurkhas are those people of Mongolian origin from tribes which British and Indian officers regard as the military tribes or the fighting classes of Nepal who are enlisted and called by that name – and, of course, their families. This generally is the meaning used here.

There are today (1984) eleven Gurkha infantry regiments in two units, each calling itself the Brigade of Gurkhas, in two national armies. The regiments are numbered consecutively, as though they all belonged to the same army, but the 2nd, 6th, 7th, and 10th are in the British Army while the rest are in the Indian Army. The 2nd likes to use the spelling 'Goorkhas'. There is also a variety of other spellings such as Ghoorka, Ghorkha, Ghurka and Goorka. The word is more correctly pronounced as it is now spelt in the Indian Army: 'Gorkha'. It comes from *go*, meaning 'cow', and *rakh*, meaning 'protector'; thus Gurkhas are 'protectors of cows', and they are Hindus. To British soldiers the Nepalese hillmen are affectionately known as 'Johnny Gurkhas' or simply as 'Johnny Gurks'. Indian Army ranks (used by Gurkhas before 1948) are explained in Appendix A.

Perhaps it is as well to mention here that there are alternative spellings for every place name, proper name or other Nepali word. I have tried to use the versions most frequently encountered. The battle cry of the Gurkhas is 'Ayo Gurkhali!', which is generally rendered in English as 'The Gurkhas are upon you!' Literally translated, it is 'Coming the Gurkhas'.

A word on sources is necessary. Mr V. Longer, an Indian military historian, has maintained that British source material is tainted with imperialist notions and that modern Indian sources are 'chauvinistic and flamboyant in their braggartism'. While there is certainly some truth in this, to discard all Indian and British sources is impossible, for no Gurkha ever wrote a book about his experiences in any language; no collections of Gurkha letters are extant; no Nepalese records are available; until the middle of this century there were not even short articles written by Gurkha soldiers. Historians must, therefore, rely heavily upon other sources, primarily British, though statements by those who were neither British nor Indian have been particularly valued. However, in the evaluation of the Gurkha soldier all sources are in agreement. Yuji, a Japanese officer in World War II who fought the Gurkhas and was guarded by them when he was a prisoner of war, certainly had no reason to flavour his opinions, yet he had this to say:

> The Gurkhas were transparently honest men, very brave sticklers for regulations – the very model of sturdy, honest and simple soldiers – and as front-line troops during the war they had given the Japanese army a really rough time.

I have relied much upon regimental histories and the autobiographical works of officers who served with Gurkhas. Unfortunately, there are no regimental histories for Gurkha units which passed into the army of the new India on 1 January 1948, and only one history of a British regiment since that time. There have been regimental journals, and the Indian Army publishes in English an annual called *The Gurkha;* the British Army publishes a similar work called *The Kukri.* I have relied upon these and the kindness of serving and former officers.

Even regimental histories are not always as informative as one would like. To illustrate: a history of the 8th Gurkhas contains this item concerning a soldier in the 3/8th (Third Battalion of the 8th Gurkha Rifles): 'Particular mention must be made of the courage of 86600 Rifleman Punaram Pun. Unfortunately he died.' That is it. There is no further mention or comment. In what way Rifleman Punaram Pun distinguished himself we will never know.

Mercenaries have been in bad odour in recent years, but the trade is an ancient and enduring one. A.E. Housman had praise for them in 'Epitaph on an Army of Mercenaries':

> What God abandoned, these defended,
> And saved the sum of things for pay.

Nearly every European power except Switzerland has used them. Switzerland, however, like Scotland, has always been an exporter of mercenaries, and today supplies the Swiss Guards to the Pope and is well represented in the French Foreign Legion.

France's legionnaires are renowned for their toughness and admired for their fighting skills, but few have ever loved them. The Gurkhas, too, are noted for their toughness, but for their *physical* toughness; they lack the brutish traits of the legionnaires, and the harsh discipline of the Legion is absent in Gurkha regiments. Their military skills and bravery are rightly admired; in addition, they charm all who come into contact with them – except those declared to be enemies.

Throughout all British military literature of the past 165 years I have found only one man who ever said a disparaging word about the Gurkhas: the eccentric Orde Wingate. With this single exception, the opinions of every British officer who ever served with Gurkhas and every general who ever had the good fortune to have Gurkha battalions under his command form a long, loud paean of admiration and praise.

It has been said that the average Englishman considers all other countries to be mistakes; that he sneers at Europeans, Americans and 'colonials'; that his greatest disdain is for those whose skin colour is different from his own. Yet all prejudice is set aside in his admiration for the sterling qualities of these Mongolian hillmen. Perhaps none knew them better than Field-Marshal Lord Slim, who served with Gurkhas as a regimental officer and commanded them as a general in battle:

> The Almighty created in the Gurkha an ideal infantryman, indeed an ideal Rifleman, brave, tough, patient, adaptable, skilled in field-craft, intensely proud of his military record and unswerving loyalty. Add to this his honesty in word and deed, his parade perfection, and his unquenchable cheerfulness, then service with Gurkhas is for any soldier an immense satisfaction.

For British officers, one of the Gurkha's endearing qualities is his strict obedience to orders. Major-General L.E.C.M. Perowne has told of his days with Gurkhas in Malaya. When one of his men lay in hospital seriously ill, the medical officer told Perowne that he would soon die unless he showed some determination to live. Perowne went to his bedside and sternly gave him a direct order: 'Do not die!' According to Perowne, 'from then on he recovered'.

Field-Marshal Lord Birdwood said that 'no soldiers in the Indian Army have been more valued than our ever-gallant and hard-fighting comrades from Nepal'. Kitchener, when he first came to India, asked General William Hall if Gurkhas could stand hardship. General Hall told him that 'they'll stand anything, except abuse'. Kitchener, ever reserved, later referred to them as 'some of our bravest and most efficient soldiers'. Tim Carew, who as a young officer in World War II won a Military Cross fighting with Gurkhas, called them 'the bravest, most cheerful and most loyal mercenaries to fight under any flag'. And Mrs Dunbar

Mutter, wife of a British officer who lived in India during the Mutiny, spoke affectionately of 'our allies, the good little Goorkhas'.

The most poetic and moving tribute to the Gurkha soldier is found in the introduction to *The Dictionary of the Nepali Language* by Professor Sir Ralph Turner, M.C., who had been adjutant of the 2/3rd Gurkhas in World War I:

> My thoughts return to you who were my comrades, the stubborn and indomitable peasants of Nepal. Once more I see you in your bivouacs or about your fires, on forced marches or in trenches, now shivering with wet and cold, now scorched by a pitiless and burning sun. Uncomplaining you endure hunger and thirst and wounds; and at the last your unwavering lines disappear into the smoke and wrath of battle.

An anonymous author of a history of the 5th Gurkhas, after extolling the cheerfulness, simplicity, straightforwardness, vigour, courage and endurance of the Gurkha, adds that: 'None who has ever known him but has felt a very genuine affection for the sturdy little man from the hills, and those to whom he has given his confidence, he has never failed'. General Sir Francis Tuker spoke of the Gurkhas' 'selfless devotion to the British cause, which can hardly be matched by any race to another in the whole history of the world . . . Why they should have thus treated us is something of a mystery'. Indeed; and a mystery which needs to be explored, for while the British undoubtedly had enormous affection for the Gurkhas, they failed in the event to match their loyalty.

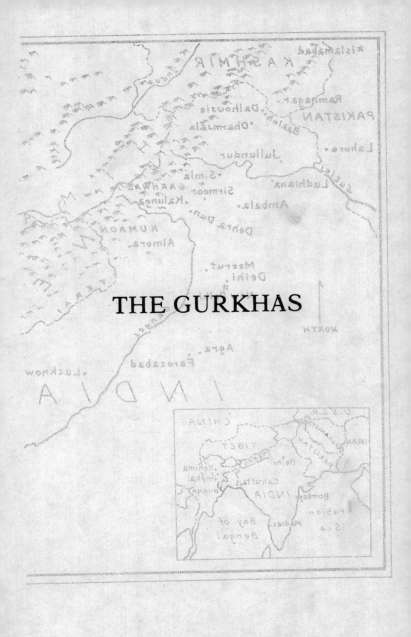

THE GURKHAS

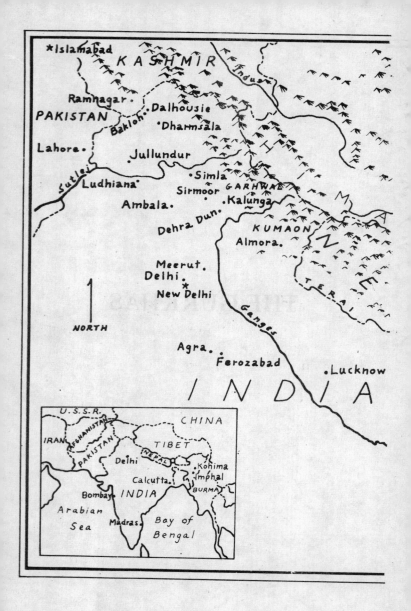

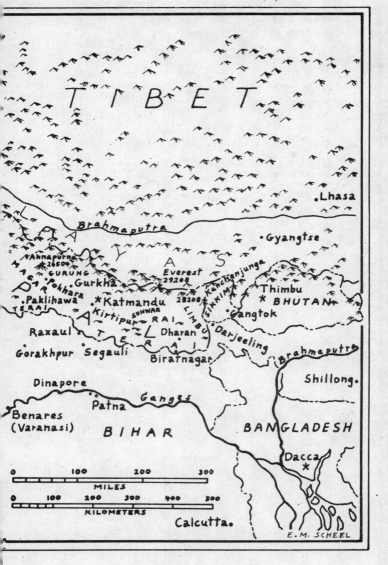

TIBET

.Lhasa

Brahmaputra

.Gyangtse

H I M A L A Y A S

Annapurna
26504
GURUNG
Pokhara .Gurkha
.Paklihawa
TERAI
Raxaul
Gorakhpur .Segauli

Everest
29208

Kanchanjunga

SIKKIM
Thimbu
★ BHUTAN

*Katmandu
28208
Kirtipur
SUNWAR
RAI
L Dharan
T E R A I
Biratnagar

LIMBU
Gangtok
Darjeeling

Brahmaputra

Dinapore
Patna
.Benares
(Varanasi)
Ganges

BIHAR

Shillong.

BANGLADESH

Dacca
★

| 0 | 100 | 200 | 300 |
MILES

| 0 | 100 | 200 | 300 | 400 | 500 |
KILOMETERS

Calcutta.

E.M. SCHEEL

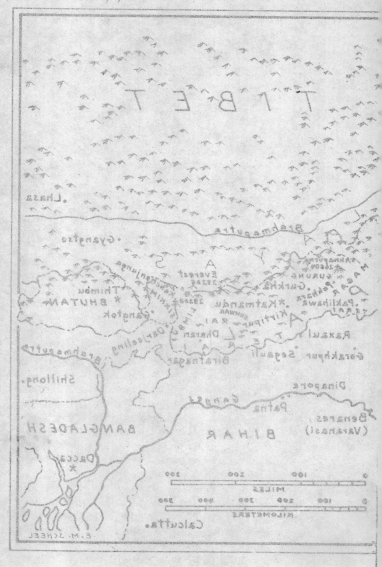

Introduction

> For the warrior there is no thing more
> blessed than a lawful strife.
> Happy the warriors who find such a strife
> coming unsought to them as an open
> door to Paradise.
>
> – Bhagavadgita, II, 31 and 32

The lives of the hill people of Nepal are difficult to describe, not only because of the complex way in which their social, religious and economic strands are interwoven, but also because they are entwined in different ways in different parts of the country and among different tribes and castes. The Gurkha mercenaries, with the exception of those who are enlisted in the 9th Gurkha Rifles, are not of the *Kshatriya* or warrior caste, in spite of generations in which sons have followed fathers to become soldiers (see Appendix B). Instead they are classified as *Vaisiya*, the caste of traders, cultivators and herdsmen. Given the reputation of the Gurkha as a soldier this classification seems peculiar, yet the Gurkha soldier in his homeland is either a shepherd or a cultivator; he ekes out a meagre existence from uncooperative soil on terraced hills at eight to ten thousand feet above sea level.

The term 'tribe' makes anthropologists wince. It seems imprecise to them and they often go through remarkable circumlocutions to avoid the word. However, almost everyone except an anthropologist knows its meaning, and if it is defined simply as a body of primitive people who describe themselves by a common name, it is a useful term. In Nepal, most tribes are divided into a number of clans, which are in turn subdivided into complex kindreds.

Of the dozens of tribes in Nepal, the best known is the Sherpa because of Tenzing Norkay, who in 1953, with Edmund Hillary, became one of the first two men to reach the summit of Mount Everest. Although Sherpas are strong and seemingly impervious to physical hardship, they are not sought after as soldiers and have been enlisted only in very small numbers, mainly as mess servants. According to C.J. Morris, an authority on the tribes of Nepal, the Sherpas when left to themselves 'are extremely lazy, and will spend the whole day in gambling for drink, of which they are inordinately fond . . . they lack that standby in times of stress – an innate sense of discipline – which makes the Gurkha the wonderful fighter he is'.

Very little is known for certain of the origins of the Nepalese tribes. There is little recorded history of the land before the eighteenth century and most of that concerns only the small area within a fifty-mile radius of Katmandu. Tibetans, Mongolians and Aryans have merged in varying degrees in different tribes and some intelligent guesses can be made as to origins, but there are distinct differences in features, characteristics and customs. Most tribes even have their own language; the *lingua franca* of Nepal is Nepalese (or Gurkhali, as it is called in the army), but prior to the mid 1930s many recruits could not speak it, and even today there are a few who speak only their tribal language and must learn Gurkhali in the army. In the hills and highland valleys of the Himalayas, generation after generation have lived and died and been forgotten, their history as individuals and as a people unrecorded, and so dissolved into myth and legend, conflicting, unreliable, undecipherable.

Most of the Gurkha mercenaries have traditionally come from four tribes which have markedly Mongolian features; a comparatively fair, clear skin; little, if any, hair on the face or body (young men usually pluck out any facial hairs); and the most characteristic feature of all, the epicanthic fold which creates the almond-shaped eyes. Magars (pronounced 'muggers') and Gurungs are *parbatiya;* Limbus and Rais are *kiranti* from eastern Nepal. Only one regiment, the

9th Gurkha Rifles (now in the Indian Army) recruits Rajputs. Of the eleven regiments in the two armies, only three (7th, 10th and 11th) recruit *kiranti* and seven *parbatiya*, though in recent years an increasing number of recruits have come from the low-lying Terai on India's border. (For more on Gurkha tribes, see Appendix D.)

A Gurkha calls himself by his given name followed by the name of his tribe or clan. Gurungs usually use 'Gurung' as a last name; Limbus and Rais also generally use their tribal name as a last name; but Magars use the name of their clan. There are a limited number of first names, the most common being Bahadur (Brave), usually linked with another such as Man (Spirit) or Dil (Heart) or Bhakta (Loyal). Thus, Manbahadur Thapa would be a Magar named Brave-in-Spirit. Gurkha parents do not call their children by their given names but by the order in which they were born: Jetho (Eldest), Mainlo (Second Eldest), Sainto (Third Eldest), and so forth. Because so many names are alike, the regimental serial number, or the last three digits of the number, commonly precede the name in the records of the Gurkha battalions. As a result, a man often acquires the name of his number as a nickname; thus, Bhaktabahadur Ale might be better known to his friends as Battis (Thirty-two). Wives also learn the army numbers of their husbands. Limbus never speak the name of their spouse, so a wife, when asked her husband's name, will give his number.

Because names usually revealed tribal origins, men from tribes not usually recruited would sometimes change their names in order to enlist. Gyamsu Lama was not even Nepalese but came from Sikkim. He changed his name to enlist during World War II when the British, eager for men, became less particular about inquiring into tribal origins. His true identity was not revealed until he won the Victoria Cross.

The land inhabited by these tribes is rugged and inhospitable. Nepal is 520 miles long and about 100 miles wide, about the size of Florida or slightly larger than England. There are four distinct zones:

1. *Terai.* A low-lying land, jungle and swamp at about sea level. It is hot and has been described as 'one of the most malarious spots on the face of the earth'. It lies on the border of India and Nepal.

2. *Duns.* The valleys at the foot of the hill country.

3. *Hills.* Small mountains, between four and ten thousand feet high.

4. *Alpine region.* This extends from the hills into Tibet and includes the main Himalayan range. (Mount Everest lies partly in Nepal and partly in Tibet.)

Until 1956, there were only 160 miles of all-weather roads in the whole of Nepal; Katmandu, the capital of the country, was isolated, with no modern transport. Coolies and pack animals are still the major form of transport in the hills and mountains, with more coolies than animals. Outside the Katmandu Valley, high technology is represented by the ox cart. Even today, wheeled transport, electricity, window panes, hospitals, telephones and most tools are unknown to the majority of Nepalese. Everything is carried on men's backs – grain, tools, stones, clothing, soil. And it is carried over winding, precipitous tracks, across swaying, flimsy bridges flung over gorges through which cold rivers roar. Travel is slow, difficult and dangerous. In this hard land two out of three children do not survive infancy, and as late as 1960 the average age of a Nepali peasant was twenty-six.

Isolation was, and to a certain extent still is, the deliberate policy of the Nepalese government and special permission is required to leave the Katmandu Valley. Until the 1950s no tourists were allowed and only a few officials and foreigners invited by the Maharajah were allowed to enter the country. Field-Marshal Birdwood, writing in 1941, said: 'It is the ambition of many, but the good fortune of few, to visit Nepal, the land of the Gurkhas.' The first genuine tourists (ten Americans and two Brazilians booked by Thomas Cook & Sons) arrived in 1955, their visas good only for the Katmandu Valley in east-central Nepal.

Travel in rural Nepal is hindered by the lack of accurate

maps and difficulty in calculating distances. The unit of
linear measurement often fluctuates according to the time
of day, the season of the year or the idiosyncrasies of men
and beasts. One measure, for example, is the *rumale-kosh*
(handkerchief mile), which is, according to Major Bhaktabahadur Gurung, 'the time taken by a wet handkerchief
fluttering from a walking stick to dry'.

CHAPTER
1

War and Peace
in Nepal

The history of Nepal until quite recently has been a long, sad tale of brutality, greed, cruelty, betrayal, barbarity, treachery, rebellion and assassination. Public affairs were conducted with the aid of intrigues, torture, bribery, intimidation and other unsavoury techniques; plots and conspiracies were part of everyday life. Lawrence Oliphant, a nineteenth-century resident of Katmandu, once remarked that 'if you do not associate with assassins, you must give up the pleasures of Nepal society'. Sir Francis Tuker later wrote: 'It is hardly possible for those who have been brought up in the belief that murder is a deadly sin ... to have any but the dimmest understanding of a society, a circle, a community in which to murder makes no impress whatsoever on the conscience of the being who commits it, who abets it or who orders it.'

The concept of Nepal as a nation is a recent one. For most of its history it has consisted of dozens of tribes and petty kingdoms. Even the Katmandu Valley possessed three tiny monarchies in its 205 square miles. In the hills to the north – west of this valley was a tiny state called Gorkha where in 1742 a man named Prithwi Narayan became king. Colin Simpson, a modern Australian writer, has described him as 'a hillbilly Napoleon, a savage in silk pants'. Ambitious and ruthless, he conquered the petty kingdoms of the Kat-

The Durbar or royal palace, Katmandu, c.1852 (*British Library*)

mandu Valley and before he died in 1774 he laid the foun-
dations of the present state. In the process he did such things
as promising the townspeople of Kirtipur that they could
surrender to him without fear of retribution, then cutting
off the lips and noses of all males over the age of twelve.
Only flute-players were exempt. The present king is a direct
descendant of Prithwi Narayan, whose statue stands in
Katmandu – noble founder of the nation.

Prithwi Narayan's successors continued to conquer
neighbouring states, even taking in the present-day Indian
provinces of Garhwal and Kumaon, and what later became
the Simla hill states. Before the end of the eighteenth century these warlike people had reached the zenith of their
power and were rubbing the edges of territory conquered
by another warlike people: the British.

The boundary between the territories of Nepal and those

of the Honourable East India Company was ill-defined and the Court of Directors in London fretted about it. They complained that there must be a 'want of vigilance' or a 'defect in the system of management' for their agents in India to have 'permitted boundaries to elude definition and anarchy to persist'. The Nepalese (Gurkhas) were happy to exploit the situation by seizing villages and committing minor depredations. Finally, on 29 May 1814 they attacked three police posts in the Butwal District and killed a score of Indian policemen as well as an Englishman, who was put to death in an unpleasant fashion. In November 1814 Lord Moira (perhaps better known by his later title of Marquess of Hastings), Governor-General of Bengal, declared war.

A British force of 22,000 men was divided into four columns to invade Nepal. This was the first of a number of invasions into the great hill ranges of northern India. Of the four generals in charge of the columns, two were completely incompetent; they failed to reach even the outer ramparts of Nepal and were subsequently sacked. A third general, Rollo R. Gillespie, appears to have been not entirely sane. He had received head wounds in earlier battles and it was said that his mind was unsettled by alcohol and megalomania; he was vain and impetuous, and harboured an intense desire for glory. He was also a martinet and his soldiers hated him for his strictness in dress and drill. He found glory and a permanent peace for his fevered brain at a place called Kalunga.

Gillespie's force, starting from Meerut with 4,000 men and twenty guns, captured Dehra Dun but was soon held up for more than a month by a fort at Kalunga, a few miles further east. The fort, isolated on a jungle-covered hill about 500 feet high, was protected by outer defences of twelve-foot high double palisades of rough-hewn logs filled with stones. It held about 600 men and women, mostly Magars and Gurungs, under the command of a Gurkha named Balbahadur. At Kalunga the British encountered a foe as brave and determined as themselves – perhaps somewhat more so. One English officer, James Baillie Fraser, said of the

Gurkhas that 'they fought us in fair conflict like men, and, in the intervals of actual combat, showed us a courtesy worthy of a more enlightened people'.

The first major assault on the fort was badly coordinated and it failed because the 53rd Foot, irked by orders of Gillespie which the soldiers regarded as capricious, shirked their duty. This failure so enraged Gillespie that he dashed forward with demoniac enthusiasm, brandishing his sword and screaming. He seemed to expect his men to follow. None did. A musket ball in his chest killed him at the foot of the ramparts. He was not lamented.

The siege dragged on and, as it did, the British admiration for the outnumbered defenders of Kalunga increased. All agreed that the Gurkhas were brave. John Ship, then an ensign in the 87th Foot, wrote in his memoirs:

> I never saw more steadiness or bravery exhibited in my life. Run they would not, and of death they seemed to have no fear, though their comrades were falling thick around them, for we were so near that every shot told . . .

It was during this battle that a curious incident occurred. In the middle of a British bombardment a Gurkha came out of the fort and approached the British lines waving his hands; the first surrender, thought the British. A cease-fire was ordered and he was welcomed into the lines. His lower jaw was shattered and he was happy to be patched up by the surgeons, but this done, he asked permission to return to the fort and continue the fight.

At last the British guns battered the crude fort into rubble. Still it did not surrender. A handful of the defenders, perhaps sixty or eighty, fought their way clear and escaped. The fort itself, with those no longer able to defend themselves or flee, was simply abandoned. Captain Henry Sherwood, paymaster of the 53rd Foot, one of the first to enter the battered fort, described the shambles he found there in a letter to his wife. The wounded were in 'a most wretched state'. One man, wounded in the head, lay on a cot 'making figures in the bloody dust with his fingers'. A Gurkha woman clutched a bleeding child to her breast. Two little girls, one a mere toddler, wandered about, their parents dead. 'This day I saw the horrors of war,' wrote Sherwood, 'and indeed horrible it is.' Kalunga was a bloody affair, and the British suffered greater casualties than the Gurkhas. Balbahadur lost about 520; the British lost 31 officers and 750 other ranks.

The British temporarily called off their campaign. Of the four columns only one, under General David Ochterlony, had experienced any success. A second campaign in 1815 did not do much better than the first. It was only in the third attempt, begun in 1816, when Ochterlony was in sole command of an army numbering 17,000, that the war was brought to an end. Ochterlony defeated the Gurkha General Amar Sing at Jaithak and again in a decisive battle at Malaun. (Among the slain heroes of the final phase of the war was Lieutenant Thomas Thackeray of the 26th Native Infantry, killed near Jaithak, an uncle of four-year-old William Makepeace Thackeray.) British admiration for their enemies grew and after the Gurkha surrender of Malaun, Amar Sing was allowed to march out with his arms, accoutrements, colours, two guns, and all his personal property – a rare surrender ceremony in this part of the world.

The Nepalese were forced to sue for peace, and on 4 March 1816 a treaty was signed at Segauli (now an unimportant little junction about twenty miles from Rexaul). Nepal had to give up the provinces of Kumaon and Garhwal as well as the lowland Terai. A provision of the treaty specified that no Briton, European or American could take service with Nepal without the consent of the British authorities. To this the Nepalese Durbar (government) readily consented, for they distrusted and resented foreigners and the most hated provision of the treaty was that by which the Nepalese agreed to accept a British Resident. The most curious and perhaps the most important clause in the Treaty of Segauli was that which gave the British the right to recruit Nepalese subjects. Actually, the British admiration for their Nepalese enemies had been such that they could hardly wait for the

war to end before enlisting Gurkhas into their own forces.
Indeed, four battalions of Gurkhas had already been
formed – three of which exist to this day.

Philip Mason, in his splendid history of Britain's Indian
Army (*A Matter of Honour*), said that the Nepalese war was
one of the few which 'left each side with an increased respect
for the other'. At Kalunga today there are still two small
obelisks which were erected by the British after the war.
One is dedicated to General Rollo Gillespie and his British
and Indian dead. The other is dedicated to their gallant
adversaries: 'They fought in the conflict like men and, in
the intervals of actual conflict, showed us a liberal courtesy.' The love affair between the British and the doughty
little Mongolian hillmen had begun. It has lasted for more
than 165 years.

A soldier of fortune, Captain Hearsay, who had served
under the Mahrattas before fighting for the Honourable East
India Company in the Nepalese war, was one of the first to
recommend enlisting Gurkhas into the Company's army:

> They are hardy, endure privations, and are very obedient,
> have not much of the distinction of caste, and are a neutral
> kind of Hindoo, eating in messes almost everything they meet
> with, except beef. Under our government they would make
> excellent soldiers.

Ochterlony also recommended that Gurkhas be enlisted –
and this when he was still fighting them. As a result, permission was given to raise some levies of irregulars, and
Lieutenant Robert Ross of the 6th Native Infantry and
Lieutenant Frederick Young of the 13th Native Infantry
formed a corps which contained many men from Garhwal,
Kumaon and elsewhere in India who were not, strictly
speaking, Gurkhas, though they had many Gurkha features
and characteristics. In the event they proved unreliable:
Young's men deserted him at the first sight of the Nepalese
army, and Young, who refused to run, was captured. He
was surrounded by grinning Gurkhas who asked why he
had not bolted with his men. Young replied that he had not
come so far in order to run away. Such reasoning was

admired by his captors, who told him approvingly: 'We
could serve under men like you.' Young was well treated
and while in captivity he learned something of the Gurkhas' language, manners and customs. The more he learned
the more he admired them.

On 24 April 1815 the Governor-General authorized the
formation of the first Gurkha battalion. Lieutenant Young
went to the prisoner of war camps for the first recruits and
gleefully recorded: 'I went there one man and came out
3,000.' From these volunteers he raised a battalion at Sirmoor, near Dehra Dun, and became its first commandant.
It was called the Sirmoor Battalion and eventually became
the 2nd King Edward VII's Own Gurkha Rifles. It serves
the British still.

Frederick Young was at this time thirty years old and an
experienced soldier. He had received his commission in the
Honourable East India Company's Army in 1800 after
appearing before a board in London which asked him only
two questions:

'How old are you?'

'Fifteen on 30th November last.'

'Are you ready to die for your king and country?'

'I am.'

'That will do.'

And so the fifteen-year-old boy went out to India and
served his sovereign and country for forty-four years. At
seventeen he fought in the Central India Campaign under
General Lord Lake; later he took part in the Java Expedition, returning in 1813 in time for the Nepal War, where he
served for a time as aide-de-camp to General Gillespie, who
died in Young's arms at Kalunga. He is rightly regarded as
the father of the Brigade of Gurkhas, serving for twenty-
eight years as the commandant of the Sirmoor Battalion.

Two other battalions, called the Nasiri ('Friendly') battalions were raised at Subathu in the Simla Hills. These
were soon amalgamated into a single battalion which
became the 1st Gurkha Rifles. Another, the Kumaon Battalion, which became the 3rd Gurkhas, was raised at Almora
in Kumaon in 1815. A Gurkha battalion, like other battal-

ions of infantry in the Indian Army at the time, consisted
of eight companies, each of about 120 men; the battalion
was commanded by a British officer, called the commandant, and had a British adjutant. Later other British officers were added.

Although the expense of maintaining these battalions was
small and the quality high, the Court of Directors of the
Honourable East India Company, ever preaching economy
to its agents in India, told Lord Hastings: 'We therefore
trust that no impediment will arise to their [the Gurkha
battalions] being disbanded at an early period.' They never
were.

CHAPTER
2

Dacoits
and Small Wars

The Sirmoor became the first of the Gurkha battalions to see action under the British, being present at the battle of Sambhar in the Pindari War of 1817 and taking part in the Mahratta War of 1817–18, but the first battle honour was won by elements of both the Sirmoor and Nasiri battalions at the siege of Bhurtpore in 1825–6. It was at the end of this six-week siege that the Gurkhas were heard to pay their British comrades in arms a compliment: English troops, they said, were 'very nearly the equal to us'.

Most of the work of the Gurkha battalions in the first thirty years of their existence consisted in chasing bandits, a hard and bloody business, for many of these dacoit bands were large and powerful. In 1824, one led by a man called Kulwa and his brother, Bhoora, launched a daring and successful attack upon a convoy, guarded by 200 police, carrying treasure from Jawalpur to Saharanpur.

On 2 October 1824 Mr Grindall, the magistrate at Saharanpur, asked Mr Frederick Shore, the superintendent at Dehra Dun, for military aid: a band of some 800 dacoits under Kulwa and Bhoora had seized the fort at Koonja in the south-east part of the district and were 'committing every species of atrocity'. The message arrived at Dehra Dun at eight o'clock in the evening and six hours later Shore and Captain Frederick Young, with 200 Gurkhas of the Sirmoor Battalion, were on their way. At Saharanpur they were joined by Grindall with some civil police and another 150 Gurkha soldiers. Lieutenant Debude, R.E., and twenty-five-year-old Doctor John Forbes Royle (later to earn fame as a botanist) also went along as volunteers.

At two o'clock on the afternoon of 3 October, having marched thirty-six miles in twelve hours, they came in sight of Koonja and found the dacoits waiting for them. They were drawn up in line of battle along the outskirts of the village and in front of a fort of thick, high mud walls on slightly rising ground at the north end of the village. They at once opened fire on the advancing Gurkha soldiers and the police. Young ordered his men to drop their knapsacks and form up for a charge. With himself at their head and Shore on the left flank, they advanced smartly. The dacoits at once withdrew into the fort.

Although outnumbered at least three to one, and with neither ladders nor guns to breach the walls which were now manned by matchlock men ('a determined band of ruffians'), Young and Shore, with unbounded confidence in themselves and their men, decided to attack at once 'before the enemy could escape'. A tree was cut down and its branches lopped off by the ever-handy *kukris*. Slung from rope on a stout frame, it made an effective battering ram. Shore and Debude supported the front ropes; Gurkhas manned each side. An extended company provided covering fire while with a 'one, two, three and hurrah' the ram crashed through the stout iron-bound door, making a gap large enough for two men abreast to pass through, crouching. Young and two Gurkhas pressed through, closely followed by Shore and the storming party.

There was at once fierce hand-to-hand fighting. A dacoit swung his sharp, curved *tulwar* at Young's neck, but Shore sabred him just in the nick of time. A few minutes later Young repaid the favour when Shore, the corded handle of his shield gone, faced a giant of a man. Young's double-barrelled Menton missed fire once, but the second shot downed the dacoit just as he was delivering a powerful slash that passed under Shore's precariously held shield and cut a gash in his side.

Meanwhile the Gurkhas had set to work with their bayonets and *kukris*, and many of the dacoits were trying desperately to escape over the walls. One, cornered and disarmed, begged for his life in the most humiliating manner known to a Hindu. On his knees he stuffed grass into his mouth while crying, 'I am your cow!' A Gurkha cut him down with his *kukri*.

With most of the fort seized, Young left a hundred men to deal with those still holding out while he organized a beat through the fields of sugar cane, flushing out and killing about twenty. Inside the fort there were 153 dead dacoits and thirty prisoners, of whom twenty-nine were wounded. The Gurkhas lost five killed and thirty-three wounded, several of whom later died. Kulwa, the dacoit chieftain, was killed in the fight, but his brother, Bhoora, escaped, though it was later learned that he had been badly wounded and that the wound mortified and eventually killed him. For several years after the battle, Kulwa's severed head swung in a cage over the entrance to the Dehra Dun gaol. Two small cannons taken from the fort are still trophies of the 2nd Gurkhas and are today posted outside the quarter guard in Hong Kong. The fort at Koonja is no more, but its outlines can still be distinguished.

Young found it worthy of note in his report that his Gurkhas had not molested any of the women in Koonja or in its fort.

In recognition of its feat with the battering ram, the battalion was given the privilege of wearing a ram's head on its crest and cross-belt badge.

Frederick Shore, incidentally, was an artist of considerable ability who became famous for his paintings of Indian birds. He also came to be regarded as an amusing eccentric, for he often wore 'Mohammedan clothes' and went about accompanied by two tame bears with silver collars.

The next opportunity for the Gurkhas to distinguish themselves came with the First Sikh War of 1845–6, when

Gurkhas rifling dead Sikhs during the First Sikh War, 1846.
Ascribed to B.D. Grant (*National Army Museum*)

the Khalsa army of the Sikhs in the Punjab, following the
death of Ranjit Singh, crossed the Sutlej and invaded British India. This was a four-battle war and the Nasiri and
Sirmoor battalions fought in two of them: Aliwal and
Sobraon. Lieutenant-Colonel John Fisher, who commanded the Sirmoor Battalion at Aliwal, said: 'My little
fellows behaved beautifully; we were first into the
entrenchments and spiked the first gun.' At one point the
Sirmoor Battalion lost its regimental colour when the
Gurkha officer carrying it was killed. At once a squad under
Havildar* Badal Sing Thapa sprang forward and recovered
it, earning Badal Sing the Indian Order of Merit. Another
havildar, Lachhiman Sarki, was promoted to subadar for
spiking a gun, but unfortunately sustained wounds that

* See appendix A for an explanation of Indian Army ranks.

proved mortal and he did not live long enough to enjoy his new rank.

It was at Sabraon that General Sir Hugh Gough, when told that his guns were running out of ammunition, exclaimed, 'Thank God! Then I'll be at them with the bayonet!' Here four Gurkhas won the Indian Order of Merit and Lieutenant-Colonel Fisher lost his life. General Gough, in his colourful after-action report on the battle, had this to say:

> I must pause in this narrative especially to notice the determined hardihood and bravery with which our two battalions of Goorkhas, the Sirmoor and Naseree, met the Sikh whenever they were opposed to them. Soldiers of small stature and indomitable spirit, they vied in ardent courage in the charge with the Grenadiers of our own nation and, armed with the short weapon of their mountains, were a terror to the Sikhs throughout the great combat.

In spite of the praises they garnered whenever they went into action, the Gurkhas were not seen as a *corps d'élite*, a distinct race with special qualities quite separate from the martial races of India. It was the part played by a reduced battalion at Delhi during the great mutiny in the Bengal Army that established the Gurkhas as being not only exceedingly brave but also determinedly loyal.

CHAPTER
3

Gurkhas at Delhi

In 1857 all India was divided into three parts, called presidencies: Madras, Bombay and, largest and most important of all, Bengal, which included the Punjab. Each had its own army. The great Indian Mutiny, which began in Meerut, was confined to the Bengal Army. It was sparked by rumours that the cartridges issued to Indian troops (which had to be bitten before loading into muskets) were coated with pig's fat (repugnant to Muslims) and cow's fat (abhorrent to Hindus). In Bengal there were about 150,000 Indian troops, 1,000 Gurkhas and 23,000 Europeans; most of the latter were in the western Punjab and not readily available. In the 900 miles between Meerut and Calcutta there were 55,000 Indian sepoys, most of whom mutinied, and only 5,000 European troops.

As the mutiny swept through northern India, every sepoy became suspect. Many officers who had sworn that their own men were loyal and would remain so were hacked to bits by these same men. In most places the British, their backs to the wall, held their ground and fought bravely, but such was the reputation for ferocity established by the Gurkhas that when a rumour ran through Simla that the Nasiri Battalion at Jutogh, three miles west, had mutinied and were about to descend upon the town, Britons panicked and fled headlong, some men even abandoning their wives and children. It was a disgraceful scene, to be remembered later with shame.

The rumour that terrified Simla was false. No Gurkha joined the mutineers. In fact, the Gurkha mercenaries in the Indian Army, as well as the Nepal Durbar, did their best to reassure the British of their support. Shortly before the Mutiny, when stories of the greased cartridges were circulating, Lieutenant Duncan Macintyre found himself in charge of a detail composed of men from all three Gurkha battalions undergoing a musketry course at Amballa. He was surprised but pleased when one day his men, camped with Indian infantry, requested through a Gurkha officer that they be allowed to pitch their tents with those of the British soldiers. As Macintyre reported the incident:

> The reason for this was that they did not like being mixed up with the *kala log* (black folk) as they called the native Sepoys, whom they reported as showing very bad feelings in their conversations regarding the use of the greased cartridges. At the same time, they requested that these might be served out to them, in order to show the Poorbiahs* that they had no fellow-feeling with them in the cartridge question.

Permission to camp with the British soldiers was given and greased cartridges were issued to them, even though ungreased ones were available.

At noon on 14 May 1857 a weary sowar on a camel made his way through the crowded bazaar at Dehra Dun, crossed the square and stumbled into the orderly room of the Sirmoor Battalion. His news was of the mutiny that had taken place at Meerut three days before. Major Charles Reid, commandant of the battalion, at once issued orders to march. Baggage was left behind as four hours later the battalion, 490 strong, marched out of its cantonments. Each man carried sixty rounds of ammunition in his pouches and two elephants brought on the reserve of ammunition.

Major Reid started by forced marches for Meerut by way

* Men from Oudh, Benares and Behar, the provinces where most British sepoys were recruited.

of the town of Roorkee. When he reached the Ganges Canal, he ordered his tired men to eat and rest. As they did, several disaffected Indian sappers from Roorkee appeared among his men, telling all who would listen that the British had mixed ground-up bullock's bones with the flour they were using to make their chappatis. The Gurkhas laughed at them.

Reid embarked his battalion in forty-five canal boats, put skirmishers along the banks, and went on his way. Near the village of Bhola he was attacked by mutineers, but the Gurkhas drove them off and occupied the village, where they found stolen government arms and equipment. Eighteen prisoners were taken, tried by a drumhead court martial, and thirteen were quickly convicted. After dinner that evening Reid ordered them to be shot and the entire village burned. Of the unlucky thirteen, five were Brahmans. It was a test of the lower-caste Gurkhas' loyalty that they did not hesitate to kill them. Marching on, Reid came upon another village in which government property was found in three houses. Their owners were hanged. When the ropes broke on the drop of two of them, Reid simply moved forward a file and ordered them to shoot, which they did, undaunted by the fact that they were Brahmans. This refusal to allow religious scruples to interfere with duty has always made the Gurkhas more versatile in British eyes.

A few days later Reid learned that General Archdale Wilson, who was marching toward Delhi, was in danger of being attacked, so he disembarked his men and set off for Wilson's force, marching twenty-seven miles in one night. Three days later they came up with the 60th Rifles (now 2nd Royal Greenjackets), part of Wilson's force, who at first thought they were the enemy and fired on them. Fortunately, no blood was shed. When the 60th discovered that Reid had brought Gurkhas to their assistance, they set up a cheer. Thus was begun one of the most famous and long-lasting of regimental friendships, one that has endured to this day.

Higher officers still regarded the Gurkhas as of uncertain loyalty and they were put in camp alongside the artillery, which was given secret orders to open fire on them at the least hint of trouble. However, the Sirmoor Battalion soon had an opportunity to demonstrate its loyalty, for the next day, 8 June, the entire force moved forward and just seven miles outside Delhi encountered mutineers in a strong position barring the way. In two hours of heavy fighting the British and Gurkhas captured thirteen guns and drove off the mutineers. Also captured and occupied was the 'Ridge', the two-mile-long Badle-ki-Serai, a rocky elevation, soon to be famous, which dominated the city.

Now began the so-called Siege of Delhi, ancient capital of the Moguls. Strictly speaking, it was not a siege at all, for the British made no attempt to surround or blockade the city, which was seven miles in circumference, and they had too small a force to hinder the normal commerce or the movement of guns and supplies. They merely occupied the ridge outside the city walls and repulsed all efforts to dislodge them. From here, too, they from time to time launched attacks on the city's gates.

Reid and his Gurkhas, with two companies of the 60th Rifles, were assigned the southern end of the ridge and occupied a large, flat-roofed house with a broad veranda known as Hindu Rao's House, about 1,200 yards from the Mori Bastion of the city walls. Hindu Rao's House became the main picket of the force before Delhi.

No sooner were the Gurkhas in position than they were attacked by a body of mutineers who were urged on by cries from the city walls. In the dust and heat they fought, often hand to hand, for nearly sixteen hours. In his diary Reid wrote:

> My little fellows behaved splendidly and were cheered by every European regiment. I may say every eye was upon [us] . . . The General was anxious to see what the Gurkha could do, and if we were to be trusted. They had doubts about us; but I think they are now satisfied.

This was but the first of twenty-six determined attacks the Gurkhas beat back between 8 June and 14 September. They also took part in several British-launched attacks.

When the mutineers came out from behind their stone walls (twenty-four feet high with a wide and deep dry ditch in front) to erect heavy batteries closer to the ridge, the Gurkhas and four companies of the 60th Rifles fell upon them, killing or severely wounding an estimated 300 for a loss of only fifteen.

There were ample opportunities for individuals to distinguish themselves. Havildar Badar Sing, who had won the Indian Order of Merit 3rd Class at the Battle of Aliwal, captured an enemy standard in one fight and in another cleared mutineers from a building where they were in a position to enfilade the British position, killing thirty-five. He was promoted to jemadar and raised to 2nd Class in the Indian Order of Merit.

The price of glory was high. A British colonel wrote that 'the poor little Gurkhas have somewhat less than half the number of effective men that they had on the day of their arrival here, and yet they are always jolly and cheerful as ever, and as anxious to go to the front when there is an attack'. Indeed, by the end of June the Sirmoor Battalion had suffered 138 casualties out of its original 490, and by 29 July, when Reid's wounded were sent to Ambala, he was left with only 200 men in his battalion. Among the dead was Taka Rama, killed by round shot; he had been the best marksman in the battalion and had killed twenty-two tigers around Dehra Dun. Among the wounded was Subadar-Major Singbir Thapa, who forty years earlier had fought under Balbahadur against the British at Kalunga.

The position around Hindu Rao's House was also dangerous for the civilian followers: of fifteen *pipawallas* (men who carried and distributed food and ammunition) one was killed and four were wounded. In spite of these losses in the battalion, morale remained high. When Reid, suspecting an imminent attack and desperate for men, went to the hospital to see if any of his men were fit to return to duty, every patient who could move volunteered.

Early in the morning of 1 August reinforcements arrived, including the Kumaon Battalion. They were instantly thrown into action to help repulse a major attack by 10,000

mutineers. Reid, on the right flank, had a narrow escape.
As he handed his telescope to an orderly, a round shot took
off the orderly's head and wounded a *pipawalla* who, in the
midst of battle, was bringing Reid some tea. Reid's luck
held. When he and the famous John Nicholson ('The Lion
of the Punjab') were observing the action from the roof of
Hindu Rao's House, shrapnel burst over them. Three balls
struck Reid's telescope. (The telescope and a table top from
Hindu Rao's House can still be seen in the mess of the First
Battalion of the 2nd King Edward VII's Own Gurkha Rifles
in Hong Kong.) A Gurkha soldier standing beside Reid lost
an eye and another was struck in the chest. Neither Reid
nor Nicholson was touched.

There were other incidents. General Thomas Lyte was
talking with two young ensigns on the veranda of Hindu
Rao's House near the colours of the Sirmoor Battalion,
where a sentry was posted, when suddenly a round shot
crashed through the veranda and cut the sentry in half. The
officers were stunned and horrified, but the corporal of the
guard, with cool imperturbability, stepped out and calmly
posted another sentry before having the corpse removed.

The Mutiny and every subsequent conflict in which
Gurkhas participated produced its crop of Gurkha sentry
stories, most of which fastened on the sentry's keenness and
literal interpretation of orders. John Nicholson's face and
figure were familiar to every soldier on the ridge, but he
complained that although he frequently climbed the lad-
der to the roof of Hindu Rao's House, and all the Gurkhas
knew him well, he was never allowed to pass until he had
given the password.

Walking to Hindu Rao's House one day, Reid saw a
wounded Gurkha boy squatting behind a rock and holding
a rifle. The boy saluted when he saw him and Reid stopped
to ask how he came to be there. The boys said that he was
the son of a soldier and had been with his father at a forward picket helping him to load his rifle when his father
was killed. He had then gone to help a man from the 60th
Rifles, but this soldier was soon wounded. After finding a
litter to carry the wounded man to the hospital, the boy

had picked up his rifle and had himself joined the fight until wounded in both legs. 'But I am not much hurt,' he told Reid. Although he was only fourteen years old, Reid enlisted him on the spot and had him carried to the hospital. Two weeks later he was on duty as a serving soldier.

The mutineers often tried to lure the Gurkhas to their side. On one occasion they promised not to fire if they would come over. The Gurkhas took advantage of their offer to advance, and then gave them a volley and charged. They were pleased to learn that after this the mutineers were offering to pay ten rupees for a Gurkha's head – the same going price as that for an Englishman's head.

Near the end of the siege five large bales of clothing arrived, sent by the 'kindly ladies of Mussorie' who had heard that 'our Gurkhas' were in rags after three months' fighting. Mutineers, seeing the Gurkhas parading in new uniforms, thought apprehensively that reinforcements had arrived.

At last it ended. The British summoned all their strength and will, blew in the Kashmir Gate, and took Delhi by storm. By 20 September 1857 the city was again in British hands; the rebels had been dealt a serious defeat. But there were heavy casualties: Nicholson was mortally wounded and Reid, who had been lucky for so long, was hit in the head by a musket ball and was at first presumed dead. He regained consciousness as he was being carried away from the battle on the back of a Gurkha and eventually recovered. The original 490 men of the Sirmoor Battalion had been reinforced by ninety more, but total casualties for the siege were 327. Of the nine British officers, only one came through unscathed.

In 1858 the Sirmoor and Kumaon battalions were given the battle honour 'Delhi'. At Reid's request, seconded by the colonel of the 60th Rifles, the Gurkhas were officially styled 'riflemen' rather than 'sepoys' and they were permitted green uniforms with red facings like the 60th. The worth of Gurkhas was now recognized and in 1857 a fourth Gurkha regiment was raised in Almora and in the following year a fifth at Abbottabad.

Unfortunately, not every soldier received the reward his gallantry deserved. Reid's reports and recommendations for awards were written in pencil, and for this reason they were classified as 'unofficial'. No action was taken. It was some time before Reid learned of this, and by the time he had re-submitted his recommendations in ink, Lord Clyde thought it was too late. Replying to Reid, he said: 'The time is past for publishing further despatches relative to services, which, however meritorious, are now of old date.'

Not only were the Gurkha mercenaries loyal, but the government of Nepal also offered active support. As soon as the Mutiny began, Maharajah Jang Bahadur, prime minister and ruler of Nepal, offered to send troops. At first this generous offer was foolishly refused, but a few months later it was gratefully accepted and six regiments (about 5,000 men) marched into northern India and joined General Sir Colin Campbell before Lucknow. After the Mutiny a grateful East India Company returned the Terai – the strip of jungle lowland along India's northern border – to Nepal.

CHAPTER
4

Character
and Characteristics

It was only after the Mutiny that the British began to take a serious and studied view of the Gurkhas, to regard them as something more than good 'native infantry', as something special. Officers who had served with Gurkhas knew about them, of course, and admired them, but they were few and Gurkha battalions usually served in remote areas.

It was an era when British regiments of the line were filled with society's rejects and it was felt that fierce discipline was required to keep the men under control; Gurkhas, however, were enthusiastic soldiers requiring little disciplinary action. Frederick Young recorded that in one period of seven years it had been necessary to hold only one court martial; no British battalion could make such a boast, and probably such a record could not be duplicated in the nineteenth century by any battalion in any European or American army. Desertion, common in most armies, was almost unheard of in the Gurkha battalions, although nothing was easier.

'Briton and Gurkha had one quality noticeably in common,' wrote General Sir Francis Tuker; 'both were honest and incorruptible.' Not even Sir Francis could believe that all Britons were honest or that they were all incorruptible, but no Englishman could bestow higher praise, and the records and the literature, as well as personal reminiscences, testify to the Gurkha's integrity. It is difficult to believe that any large body of soldiers of any nation could be as consistently honest and truthful over such a long period as the Gurkhas, but British officers, writing of them during the past 160 years, all agree that theft and lying were rare – and apparently still are. Here is Patrick Davis, a former British Gurkha officer, writing in 1970:

> In a world where grand and petty larceny are habitual, distortion of truth and self deceit commonplace, the honesty of the Gurkha seemed unique. The quality of Gurkha honesty went beyond mere restraint from 'borrowing'. It was a quality of mind, of character, that permeated all their actions and reactions, a natural integrity, an inborn frankness. If you caught a Gurkha in the wrong he would not deny his guilt or start to shift the blame elsewhere ... They seemed to issue from a mould superior to that of most other men. Probably their honesty, their honour, like their sense of the ridiculous, was derived from an instinctive realism: they seemed able to see to the centre of things. I have not met another people with so few illusions about themselves or the world around them, or who, looking at the world with this practical, objective, unromantic eye, found it funny. It was easy to command such people. It was a privilege to be allowed to do so.

Indeed, the Gurkha's sense of humour cannot be denied, but it is earthy and often macabre – not to everyone's taste. John Masters remembered the cremation of a soldier in the 4th Gurkhas who had been accidentally killed by a sentry. One of his comrades in the cremation detail described how the corpse persisted in sitting up as the flames reached him. 'You've never seen anything so funny!' he said. They had to hack him up and burn him in pieces.

In Burma during World War II, when a high-explosive shell tore to pieces a soldier named Bhimbahadur, a witty comrade called out: 'Eh! If the colonel could not make Bhimbahadur smart when he was in one piece, what will the gods do with him in six bits?' Roars of laughter greeted this sally.

During World War I in Mesopotamia a Lewis machine gun team of the 2/4th Gurkhas was in action and the No. 1 gunner was killed by a bullet in the head. His place was smartly taken by the No. 2 gunner, but he, too, was shot. When the No. 3 gunner sprang to the gun and was in turn shot, gleeful laughter went up from Gurkhas in a trench nearby. They had hastily made book on his chances for survival and the winners were jubilant.

On a voyage from India to Iraq in May 1941, the 2/4th Gurkhas had fair weather and the men were delighted and fascinated by the sea, which none had ever seen before. They lined the rails daily, excited by the sight of flying fish and porpoises, but the greatest entertainment was provided by a despondent ship's fireman who, far out to sea, leapt overboard and drowned.

At Thabeikkyin, Burma, in January 1945, the men of the 4/4th, well dug in on a reverse slope, were pleased to see the Japanese shells passing harmlessly overhead and were absolutely overjoyed to see them hitting brigade headquarters in the rear. Even the British officers took a perverse joy in seeing the staff shelled.

Not all Gurkha humour is macabre; some is merely ridiculous. John Masters told of a lance-naik running along a long line of camels, squeezing the testicles of each as he passed, to the delight of his companions – and of Lieutenant Masters.

Gurkhas were known for their steadiness on parade and in action, but Captain John Morris once saw them break ranks. During manoeuvres near Delhi in 1923 a battalion of Gurkhas was advancing across a field when they saw a pair of camels trying to copulate. Their grotesque clumsiness was irresistible. The lines wavered and broke, and a wild, cheering circle formed around the struggling pair.

Field-Marshal Sir William Slim told a story of one day when he was a corps commander in Burma and was crossing an open field under mortar and artillery fire. All around him were men of the 7th Gurkhas crouching behind every little mound and bush:

My inclination to run for cover, not lessened by a salvo of mortar bombs that came down behind me, was only restrained by the thought of what a figure the corps commander would cut, sprinting for safety, in front of all these little men. So, not liking it a bit, I continued to walk forward. Then, from behind a rock that offered scant cover to his bulky figure, rose my old friend, the subadar-major of the 7th Gurkhas, his face creased in a huge grin which almost hid his twinkling almond eyes. He stood there and shook with laughter at me. I asked him coldly what he was laughing at, and he replied that it was very funny to see the General Sahib alone there by himself *not knowing what to do!* And, by Jove, he was right; I did not!

Discipline in its finest sense is the cheerful obedience of orders. This perfect discipline the Gurkha has always possessed, for he knows how to be obedient without being servile and he loves soldiering. A British national serviceman stood watching the Gurkha contingent which had been in England for the coronation of Queen Elizabeth II as it paraded for inspection before embarkation at Southampton for its return to Malaya. 'The little bastards look as if they like it!' he exclaimed. It was not unusual to see Gurkhas practicing or drilling each other when off duty and, as Tim Carew has pointed out, 'Gurkhas are always meticulous about marching in step in the most daunting of circumstances'.

The Gurkha characteristic which most astonished Britons was his quick adaptability and his acceptance of strange people and extraordinary circumstances. Few young soldiers in any army, facing battle for the first time, are prepared for the noise, muddle, blood, horror, and their own fear, nor are they fully aware of the physical and psychological attrition resulting from cumulative filth and fatigue, but even the newest Gurkha recruit appeared to accept with equanimity war's horrors and physical hardships, remaining cheerful, able to emerge from battle – even defeat – with his morale unimpaired.

Young Gurkhas who had never seen a European before, perhaps had never seen anyone not of their own tribe, easily adjusted to the sight and the customs of others quite different from themselves. Colonel Nigel Woodyatt was with a detachment of Gurkhas in Amritsar, holy city of the Sikhs, in the 1920s. They were received with black looks, and when soldiers went to the bazaar they were subjected to offensive remarks. But they grinned at it all and in a couple of months the Sikhs found themselves liking them. General C.G. Bruce sometimes took Gurkhas to Europe with him; they quickly made friends with French peasants, Swiss guides, Scots gamekeepers and English maidservants.

The marvels of Western civilization failed to impress most Gurkhas. In Mesopotamia during World War I the attention of a subadar-major was drawn to an aeroplane in the sky. He had never seen such a thing, but it did not surprise him; he knew the story of Rama, and so he said, 'That's nothing new. After all, the gods flew to Ceylon hundreds of years ago.'

Colonel R.B. Mullaly of the 10th Gurkhas and a staunch admirer, went as far as to admit that the Gurkha was perhaps not perfect. 'If he has a fault . . . it is a hasty temper, which sometimes leads him into trouble, but his anger goes as quickly as it comes and he seldom bears a grudge.' But Johnny Gurkha did have other faults: he was generally slow to learn and he loved rum and gambling, often to excess.

The toughness of Gurkha skulls is legendary. In 1931 at Razmak, on the North-West Frontier, when the mess mule of the 2/4th Gurkhas kicked a havildar in the head with both his iron-shod hooves, the havildar complained of a headache and that evening wore a piece of sticking plaster on his forehead. The mule went lame.

A historian of the 8th Gurkhas told of the 'most unusual and unfortunate manner' in which Lieutenant and Adjutant R.R. Swinton met his end. Lieutenant Swinton was leading a party of Gurkhas in the Lushai Hills on the North-East Frontier in September 1890 when he was attacked. During the fight Swinton was struck by a bullet which ricocheted from the head of Gorey Thapa, his orderly. Gorey was only slightly injured. Lieutenant Swinton was killed.

Subadar Jangia Thapa had been one of Lord Roberts's

A Gurkha tests the blade of his *kukri* (*Illustrated London News*)

orderlies during the Second Afghan War, and it was in the course of this war that he earned his nickname, 'Bullets'. It was said (and widely believed) that he had once been hit in the forehead by a bullet, which had completely flattened itself without penetrating his skull.

In Burma during World War II Havildar Manbahadur Limbu of the 7th Gurkhas was shot through the spleen. A Japanese officer, intending to finish him off, slashed open the back of his head with his sword. But Manbahadur lived – and walked for sixty miles before he caught up with his unit. The battalion medical officer who patched him up told him that by rights he should be dead. Manbahadur merely grinned and asked permission to go back to his platoon. He was sure it had grown slipshod during his absence.

Also legendary is the Gurkha's ability to sleep through anything. Subadar-Major Bhairabsing Thapa of the 4/6th Gurkhas went to sleep while riding on a Sherman tank one night in 1943 during a training exercise near Madras. He fell off the moving tank without awakening – neither then nor when an entire regiment of tanks rumbled past in the dark only inches from his head. When he finally awoke, it was to find himself pinned to the ground by the differential of a 3-ton truck which had been driven slowly over him in the darkness.

Although slow to learn, the Gurkha held tenaciously to what he had been taught and had absorbed, and one of the things he was taught was not to lose his equipment and particularly to guard his weapons. To lose a weapon through carelessness was a court martial offence. Brigadier Mark Taversham, when commanding 62 Brigade in India in November 1943, dived into a river to rescue a Gurkha Bren gunner of the 4/4th who had 'sunk' during a river exercise. Taversham found him anchored to the bottom by his gun, to which he clung so stubbornly that both men nearly drowned.

During the long retreat of the British Army from Burma in World War II the 1/5th Gurkhas at Shwegyin were ordered to destroy their heavy weapons, but Havildar Agam Gurung, who commanded the 3-inch mortar platoon, refused. Throughout the long, harrowing march of more than 500 miles his men carried the cumbersome mortar and all its parts and ammunition, even when, for a time, they were forced to carry casualties as well.

Lakhman Rai and two of his officers in the 4/10th Gurkhas – Major A.R. Davis and Major J.G.H. Templer – became separated from their battalion during the retreat from Burma in World War II. They spent twelve arduous and dangerous days, with more than one narrow escape, in country that was swarming with Japanese troops before finally reaching the safety of their own lines. Lakhman was a 2-inch-mortar man and for all this time he refused to throw away his useless mortar. His regimental history records that he 'triumphantly checked it in before he was sent to hospital to recover'.

In January 1945, near Thabeikkyin, Burma, A Company of the 4/4th Gurkhas ran into trouble: two men were hit and fell in the open near some Japanese bunkers. Every attempt to recover the casualties drew heavy enemy fire. Even the use of smoke grenades to cover the attempts failed. One of the wounded men was hit again and was killed. An air strike was called, but it seemed certain that when the planes arrived their bombs would kill the surviving Gurkhas as well as the Japanese. In a desperate bid, Major M.R. Strivens dashed across the open ground and flung himself down by the wounded man's side. He tore off his equipment and dragged him swiftly back to cover. It was a brave deed. But on Striven's heels was Rifleman Pasbahadur Matwala, who made the same mad, dangerous dash – to rescue the wounded man's rifle and equipment.

In 1890, during the guerrilla phase of the Third Burma War, when Lieutenant (later Major-General) George Younghusband was an intelligence officer, he made a six-month journey in disguise through hostile country with a Gurkha orderly. In a careless moment he once set his Martini-Henry carbine against a tree while he made a note of a compass bearing. When he finished and reached for his carbine, it was gone. Pursuit of the thief was rewarded by a blow on his head. Younghusband, telling of this incident much later in life, ruefully said: 'I heard a great deal about that carbine for many months, indeed years afterwards.' 'I am, of course, a mere soldier in the ranks,' his orderly would remind him, 'but one thing I do not lose, and that is my carbine.'

CHAPTER

5

On India's North-West Frontier

Not until World War I was there cause for Gurkhas to be sent outside the eastern hemisphere. After the Mutiny there was still action enough on the north-eastern and north-western fringes of Britain's Indian empire. On the North-West Frontier the British fought against the Afghans and the warlike Pathan tribes – Wazirs, Mahsuds, Yusafzais and Orakzais – and against colourful and violent people such as the Mullah Powindah, the Hindustani Fanatics, the Faqir if Ipi, the Red Shirts of Peshawar, the Mad Faqir of Swat, the Khan of Amb, and that Islamic fire-eater, the Haji Shaib Turangzai (irreverently known to British officers as the 'Hot Gospeller'); and they fought in outlandish places the – the Black Moutains, the Khyber Pass, Kurram, Gilgit and Ali Masjid.

The long stretch of tribal territory that separated British India from Afghanistan ranged from ten to one hundred miles in width and ran from Chitra! in the north to Baluchistan. It was (and is still) a rugged, mountainous land with Beau Geste forts and stone sangars, where every house is a small fortress with a rifle tower. The Pathan inhabitants of these inhospitable regions were tall, lean, hawkish men, noted for their guerrilla skills, their treachery and their cruelty. Dressed in turbans, earth-stained garments and rope sandals, they merged easily into the landscape and moved about in it with a possessive familiarity. From time immemorial they had raided the fertile plains and carried on blood feuds with each other. War was their occupation and killing their favourite pastime. In these encounters the British took few prisoners and the Pathans none at all. The Pathans not only preferred all their enemies dead, they liked to mutilate them. Common practice was to slice off the testicles and stuff them into the victim's mouth. A wounded soldier was lucky if he died before the mutilation began.

Through bribes and military force the British attempted, not always successfully, to protect the more peaceful inhabitants of the plains and to maintain some semblance of law and order. The bribes took the form of tribal allowances, road contracts and the hiring of tribesmen to be watchmen (*khassadars*). Force was represented by a succession of regular battalions of British, Indian and Gurkha troops and by several irregular corps and tribal militia. By such means a balance was maintained, a balance not between peace and war, but between the warring sides, for there were few days in which at least one side was not shooting at the other.

Although other Gurkha regiments served on the North-West Frontier, it was the 5th Gurkhas, raised at first as the 25th Punjab Infantry or Hazara Goorkha Battalion on the Frontier in 1858, which served the longest: it stayed for ninety years. It became the most famous and most decorated of the Gurkha regiments and its soldiers won seven Victoria Crosses. It was the only Gurkha regiment to be designated 'Royal' and permitted to add 'Frontier Force' to its title. And so its full title from 1923 until in 1957 it became part of India's army was 5th Royal Gurkha Rifles (Frontier Force).

The Pathans were intimately familiar with the order of battle of Britain's Indian Army and made their own evaluation, said to be better than an inspecting general's, of the quality and worth of each battalion to appear on the Frontier. When a new battalion arrived or one filled up with young, untried soldiers, they would be sure to test their mettle: to steal their rifles and give them a baptism of fire. The Gurkhas quickly earned the Pathans' respect. It was said of the Mahsud that he respected only the Prophet and a Gurkha with a *kukri*. Pathans were known to call out to Gurkhas: 'We don't want you. Where are the red turban men [Sikhs] and the white folk?'

One of the most common duties of troops on the North-West Frontier was the guarding of caravans, convoys and columns of troops making their way through the passes in the mountains. This was usually done by picketing the heights overlooking the always winding road or path down which camels, mules and horses moved. The most danger-ous moments in these operations came when the column had passed and the picket was withdrawing. Pathans would spend hours carefully crawling unseen towards a picket's position. Their favoured time to strike was just as part of the picket had left and the rest were withdrawing. For this reason the withdrawal was delicately handled: some men of the picket would swiftly leave and take up firing posi-tions below; when they were safely in place, the rest would move quickly to rejoin them. Normal practice was for the officer to retreat with the last group to leave the position, but this was not the way it was done in Gurkha regiments.

It is said that a Gurkha walks somewhat awkwardly on level ground, is better than most going uphill, and that no living thing is faster than a Gurkha leaping downhill. Cer-tainly no British officer could negotiate a downhill slope as fast as his men. If he remained with the last group to leave the position, he would either be left far behind as his men rushed past him or they would have to slow down to pro-tect him. Sensibly, therefore, British officers in Gurkha battalions joined the first party to leave a picket position. Sometimes, if it could be arranged, a mountain battery laid a few shells on the abandoned position to catch any Pathans who rushed into it.

It was while withdrawing from a picket that Lance-Naik Lilbahadur Gurung of B Company, 2/6th Gurkhas, bound-ing down a hillside, heard the sharp click of the lever on a grenade he was carrying in his pack and the noise of the burning fuse. Yelling for his men to stay clear of him, he ran off to the side as far and as fast as he could. The grenade exploded and he fell mortally wounded.

On the North-West Frontier even minor affairs could be bloody. In May 1917 two companies of the 1/4th Gurkhas (about 250 men) in Waziristan fought a battle with hostile Mahsuds and suffered 124 casualties, of whom one British officer, one Gurkha officer and ninety-two other ranks were killed. Sniping at British troops in camps was endemic but, though often annoying, it was seldom serious. The 1/6th Gurkhas in Waziristan in 1940 were for a time sniped at by a Pathan they nicknamed Horace. Every evening he took up a position in the hills at extreme range and fired exactly five bullets from his ancient rifle. He was never known to hit anyone.

Britain fought three wars with Afghanistan, and Gurkhas took part in the last two. Indeed, in the Second Afghan War of 1878–80 their reputation as soldiers was enhanced and they earned no less than five battle honours. It was in this war, too, that the 5th Gurkhas formed their firm and enduring friendship with the 72nd Highlanders (later the 1st Seaforth Highlanders), with whom they were brigaded throughout the campaign. When General Frederick Roberts, who established his own reputation in this war, was raised to the peerage, he chose as supporters for his arms a representation of a 72nd Highlander on one side and a rifleman of the 5th Gurkhas on the other.

Lord Roberts's admiration for the Gurkhas was widely shared. Captain Ernle Money of the 11th Bengal Lancers wrote home to his parents: 'You have no idea what fine little fellows the Goorkhas are. They actually do not know what fear is. They have throughout the campaign behaved gloriously. Everyone admits that they have as a body . . . marched and fought better than anybody – no matter who.' His admiration for Gurkhas was passed on to his son, who grew up to be Lieutenant-Colonel E.F.D. Money, D.S.O., a commandant of the 4th Gurkhas.

One of the important results of the Second Afghan War for the Gurkhas was the elevation of Roberts to power, for he authorized second battalions for each of the five regiments. Three of these new second battalions – those of the 2nd, 3rd and 5th Gurkhas – took part in the expedition to raise the siege of Chitral in 1895. The Second Battalion of the 2nd Gurkhas (commonly written 2/2nd and spoken of as the 'second second') also took part in the now almost forgotten Tirah Campaign of 1897–8, as did the second battalions of the 1st and 4th Gurkhas and the first battalions of the 3rd and ever-present 5th Gurkhas.

It is generally agreed that 25 August 1895 was the blackest day in the history of the North-West Frontier for the British: on that day they lost the Khyber, the main pass linking India with Afghanistan.

British military prestige sank to its nadir. Authorities therefore decided on a major campaign to regain the Khyber, punish the Afridis and Orakzais, and invade the Tirah, an unexplored area south-west of the Peshawar Valley that was the southern home of these tribes. An army of 44,000 was assembled – a larger army than was sent to the Crimea in 1854 – with 60,000 transport animals: camels, donkeys, elephants, mules and bullocks. It was as a part of this force that the Gurkhas were again able to distinguish themselves.

The most dramatic episode in the campaign was a spectacular charge by the Gordon Highlanders against Pathans ensconced on the heights of Dargai. It is still remembered on 20 October of each year, celebrated as Dargai Day by the Gordons. It was indeed a gallant charge, but the first man into the Pathans' position was Subadar Kirparam Thapa of the 2/2nd Gurkhas. It was during this campaign that the Gordons and the 2nd Gurkhas became such fast friends, a regimental friendship which persists to this day. The Gordons volunteered to carry the Gurkha wounded down from the Dargai heights and the Gurkhas never forgot it.

There were few pitched battles in the Tirah. The Pathans preferred to snipe continually and to make rushes at rearguards. The British had to be content with destroying villages and crops, burning stores of grain and cutting down

Awaiting the order to advance. Men of the 5th Gurkhas beside those of the 72nd Highlanders, 1878 (*Illustrated London News*)

fruit trees. These were not activities calculated to win the hearts and minds of the Pathans and their response was to make the rear of any marching column their primary target. The British rotated this duty, unpleasant as well as dangerous, for it meant being last to make camp and last to eat the evening meal. On 24 November 1897, when the 2/2nd Gurkhas came into camp after an exceptionally long and particularly trying day as rearguard, they found that the Gordons had pitched their tents for them and had taken over their night-time duties.

When the campaign was over and the 2/2nd Gurkhas were on their way back to their home at Dehra Dun, their train stopped briefly at Rawalpindi, where the Gordons had assembled to cheer them and bid them farewell. Later, gifts were exchanged. The Gordons gave the 2/2nd a silver shield and a statuette to serve as a musketry trophy; the Gurkhas gave the Gordons two specially made *kukris*, one for the officers' mess and one for the sergeants' mess.

The Tirah campaign had a calming effect on the turbulent tribesmen. For fifty years prior to the campaign the Frontier had been in constant turmoil; the fifteen years after the campaign were the most peaceful the Frontier had ever known.

Troops operating in such inhospitable regions faced dangers other than the musketry of the Pathans. There was always much sickness, and cholera was a constant threat. Simply moving about in such rugged country was perilous. During the cold weather of 1924–5, when the 1/4th Gurkhas were attempting to cross the Beas river near Mirthal, three men and two camels were washed away in the swift current. Captain F.E.C. Hughes, the adjutant, leapt into the river in an unsuccessful attempt to rescue the first two victims, and, in spite of the fact that he could not swim, Rifleman Lalbahadur Mal followed him and was drowned. Lalbahadur was posthumously awarded the silver medal of the Royal Humane Society for his foolhardy and fatal effort. It was the first such award ever made to an Asian.

CHAPTER
6

The North-East Frontier

Peace was almost as rare on the North-East Frontier, between India and Burma, as on the North-West Frontier. From 1860 until the end of World War II one or more Gurkha battalions was stationed in Assam or north-east Bengal. The terrain in which they lived and fought was as rugged in its way as that of the North-West Frontier, yet the North-East Frontier never captured the public imagination; its name has never been wreathed in the romantic images of the North-West Frontier and its wars and campaigns have been largely ignored. Even in World War II, when action there was as dramatic as anywhere else and where for a time the fate of India hung in the balance, General Sir William Slim, certainly one of the best generals of the war, and his Fourteenth Army did not get the attention in the world's press that they deserved. The Fourteenth was called the 'forgotten army' and its hard-fought campaigns a 'forgotten war'.

The Abors, Nagas and Lushais with whom the British fought were – and are still – more primitive than the Pathans (they fought with spears and bows and arrows) but they were not as bloodthirsty or as cruel. However, the hills and jungles in which they lived were even more difficult to negotiate than the barren lands of the Pathans. Colonel Leslie W. Shakespear of the 2nd Gurkhas described it:

Throughout the entire region there is no level ground beyond the small stretches of a few hundred yards, the rivers are mountain torrents, the lower hills covered with the densest bamboo jungle, which in the higher ranges gives place to evergreen trees, oak and pine, and the only communications are along narrow goat trails leading from village to village.

When little Mary Winchester was carried off by the savage Lushais and many months of peaceful overtures failed to procure her release, the Lieutenant-Governor of Bengal declared that a punitive expedition was 'absolutely necessary'. So in 1871, in spite of the difficulty of pushing an army through such inhospitable country, a military expedition was mounted to push into the Lushai hills and rescue her.

Both the 2nd and the 4th Gurkhas contributed a battalion for this expedition and the future Lord Roberts served as a staff officer to General C.H. Brownlow, the expedition's leader. The three-month campaign was deemed a success: the tribe was forced to hand over little Mary and not too many soldiers were killed or died of disease. As for Mary Winchester, she was found to be a beautiful child of about six or seven years of age, with hazel eyes and delicate features, who by this time smoked a pipe and spoke only the language of the Lushais, whom she ordered about with an air of authority which General Brownlow admired and took as a sign that she had been well treated. Indeed, the Lushais appear to have adored the child: before they reluctantly turned her over they cut her long hair in order to have something to remember her by. Mary was 'saved' but seems to have become an instant problem for the army, whose officers appear not to have given much thought to what was to be done with the child after she was rescued. She could not be returned to her parents, for they had died since her capture. Eventually she was shipped off to grandparents in Elgin, Scotland, and disappeared from history. As for the Gurkhas, their attitude seemed to be that if the sahibs wanted to spend months crashing about in the jungle to find a little white girl with hazel eyes, well, that was *thik chha* (OK) with them, and it was all soldiering.

Manipur was a protected state, somewhat larger than Wales, in south-eastern Assam. In 1890 a revolution there led by the Senapati (commander-in-chief of the army) overthrew the Maharajah. The British decided that they did not like the Senapati and set about deposing him. Frank St Clair Grimwood was the political agent at Manipur and he had with him only 100 men of the 43rd (Goorkha)* Regiment of Bengal (Light) Infantry (later 2/8th Gurkhas), an inadequate force to attempt the arrest of the Senapati. He appealed to Mr James Wallace Quinton, Chief Commissioner of Assam, who sent 400 Gurkhas under Lieutenant-Colonel Charles Skene. They reached Imphal, the Manipur capital, on 22 March 1891, with only forty rounds of ammunition per man in their pouches. Two days later, Skene launched an attack on the Senapati's palace. The attack failed.

Grimwood, Skene and two other officers foolishly agreed to meet the Senapati. All four were promptly murdered. The troops withdrew to the British Residency, where the Manipuris attacked them. When the Residency was shelled, the senior British officers remaining, Major Louis Boileau and Captain George Butcher, with the widowed Mrs Grimwood and a handful of men, managed to escape the Residency and head for the safety of Cachar a hundred miles to the west. They left behind about 270 leaderless Gurkhas, all of whom were eventually captured or killed. The young and beautiful Ethel Grimwood, dressed in a white silk blouse, patent leather shoes and a long blue skirt, guided the group. They had marched for two days and climbed 3,000 feet above the plain; they were exhausted and without food; hostile Nagas with spears followed them, watching for stragglers. Mrs Grimwood had just sprained her ankle. At this moment they encountered 200 Gurkhas who, oblivious of events in Manipur, were on their way for a normal tour of duty at Imphal. Only then did Ethel Grimwood break down and cry.

While the débâcle at Imphal was in progress, a detach-

* See Appendix C.

ment of thirty-three Gurkhas under Jemadar Birbal Nagarkoti, stationed at Langthobal four miles from the Residency,
became aware of their danger. Birbal Nagarkoti realized
that he would be of little help to those at the Residency
with his tiny force, but he knew that Lieutenant Charles
Grant was at Tamu, about sixty miles away; he made his
way there, cutting a path through the Manipuris who were
already beginning to surround him.

Lieutenant Grant was a brave, resourceful and energetic
officer. He had with him only a subadar and fifty sepoys of
the Madras Native Infantry, of whom thirty were recruits.
Nevertheless, with the Gurkhas, his own men and three
elephants loaded with supplies and ammunition, he set out
to fight the entire Manipuri army. He won two small battles and was only fifteen miles from Imphal when he
received a message from the enemy, announcing that they
were holding fifty Gurkhas and fifty-eight Indian civilian
clerks (*babus*) who would be killed if Grant continued his
advance. Grant then opened communication with the Manipuris but, feeling more rank was called for, signed all his
letters 'Colonel A. Howlett, Commanding 2nd Burma Regiment'. When a parley was agreed upon, he decorated himself with badges of rank borrowed from his subadar. In his
dealings with the Manipuris, he told them that he did not
care a damn about the *babus*, but he wanted the release of
the Gurkha prisoners.

The Manipuris assured Grant (falsely) that the prisoners
were on their way to Cachar and, assuming he had a regiment with him, sent to his camp 500 pounds of *atta*, fifty
pounds of *dhal*, and fifty pounds of *ghee*.* Although in fact
he was running short of supplies, Grant returned the food
in a cavalier manner and boldly demanded hostages for the
safe arrival of the Gurkhas at Cachar. A subadar was
actually offered as a hostage, but the audacious Grant
demanded a member of the Durbar (government). He had
now gone too far. The Manipuris refused and launched an
attack. Grant's men were armed with Sniders and Martinis

---

* *Atta* is a cereal (maize, buckwheat or millet). *Dhal* consists of split peas,
beans, lentils, etc. *Ghee* is clarified butter.

and he was down to his last fifty rounds for each Snider and twenty-five rounds for each Martini when he received an order from his superior, Captain Edward Presgrave, to retreat.

Eventually the British organized 4,000 men into three columns and invaded Manipur, to accomplish what Lieutenant Grant and his little party had almost achieved by themselves. The first column arrived at Imphal on 27 April 1891 and found the place deserted. Regarding this as a clean slate on which they could write their own prescription, the British proceeded to tell the Manipuris how they should be governed. They decided that the most fit and proper person to rule the land was the six-year-old grandson of the former Maharajah, and he was duly enthroned.

Men and women do not always get their just deserts in life, so it is always pleasant to note when this does occur. Major Boileau and Captain Butcher, who deserted their Gurkha soldiers at the Residency, were court-martialled and cashiered. The treacherous Senapati, who was eventually apprehended when disguised as a coolie, was speedily tried and efficiently hanged. The plucky Lieutenant Charles Grant was awarded a well-deserved Victoria Cross, Jemadar Birbal Nagarkoti was decorated with the Order of British India, and other ranks in both the Gurkha and Madrasi units were awarded the Indian Order of Merit and given six months' pay and allowances.

The courageous Ethel Grimwood was given the Royal Red Cross and a pension for life. The Royal Red Cross was then a new decoration, having been instituted by Queen Victoria in 1883. It was intended as a form of recognition for women who nursed sick and wounded soldiers under trying conditions. The award of this decoration to Mrs Grimwood for her feat was unique – and has remained so.

Gurkhas at this date were not eligible for the Victoria Cross. (Other ranks of the Indian Army did not become eligible until 21 October 1911.) The Order of British India, which Jemadar Birbal Nagarkoti received, was the highest available to him. This order for 'native officers' was instituted on 17 April 1837 and came in two classes: the first class of the order entitled the recipient to the title of 'Sirdar Bahadur', to be used following his name, and a pension of two rupees per day; the second class of the order gave the title 'Bahadur' and a pension of one rupee per day. The titles could be somewhat confusing when awarded to Gurkhas whose given name was Bahadur, for if Bahadur Pun received the second class, he became Bahadur Pun, Bahadur, the first 'Bahadur' being the name given him by his parents and the second being a title awarded him by the Government of India. The order was originally given to exceptional officers for long and faithful service, so the award to Birbal was also exceptional.

The Indian Order of Merit (I.O.M.), the first official British award for gallantry, was instituted by the Honourable East India Company in 1837. The medal was in three classes and was for 'natives' only. The first award was always the 3rd Class; if there was a second award, the 3rd Class medal was replaced by the 2nd Class medal; if a man won the award three times, his 2nd Class medal was replaced by the 1st Class. A gratuity was given with the medal.

Kishenbir Nagarkoti of the 1/5th Gurkhas won the 3rd Class of the I.O.M. in December 1878 for his gallantry at Mangiar (Monghyr) Pass; less than a year later in October 1879, at the Battle of Charasia during the Second Afghan War, he won a second award and so exchanged his 3rd Class medal for a 2nd Class; scarcely more than two months later, at Takht-i-Shah, he won the award for the third time and was awarded the 1st Class medal. Then in 1888 he performed a fourth act of great gallantry during operations in the Black Mountain Expedition, but government had no higher honour to bestow on him. It was finally decided to increase his pension and to present him with a special gold bar to be worn on the ribbon of his medal, bearing the date of his last heroic act: 18 June 1888. It was a unique decoration.

At a later date the awards given the Gurkhas for their actions in Manipur would have been medals of a lower order: the Indian Distinguished Service Medal (I.D.S.M.), instituted in 1907, or the Military Medal (M.M.), instituted in 1916 and lowest on the totem pole of gallantry decorations.

In the decade and a half preceding the Great War of 1914–18 there were few opportunities for Gurkhas to distinguish themselves. There were only two military expeditions of note. One was that led by Francis Younghusband (the brother of George, who lost his carbine in Burma) into Tibet in 1903–4 and the other was an expedition into the Bazar Valley on the North-West Frontier. Of these, the Tibetan expedition was the most exotic and six companies of the 8th Gurkhas went along. Probably the least equestrian race in Asia, Gurkhas served as mounted infantry on this occasion.

The Gurkhas were delighted suddenly to find themselves cavaliers, but there were initial problems: they knew nothing of horses, and proper animals and saddlery were unavailable. Their first chargers were pack ponies, twelve or thirteen hands high. The mule girths (the only kind available) were eighteen inches too long and bridles did not fit. The serge infantry trousers chafed the Gurkhas' legs and there was many a bruise and sprain before Gurkha and horse looked as if they belonged together. Fortunately they had a long cold winter in which to practise; riding breeches were eventually supplied and a better breed of riding animal was procured. In April, when the expedition started its advance towards Gyantse, the Gurkha cavalry – a 'jolly, swashbuckling crew' – was reasonably proficient. It proved itself invaluable as a reconnaissance unit and as a relentless pursuer.

The expedition encountered a bitterly cold winter in the Himalayan uplands. It was often so cold that rifle bolts froze in the breeches. The Maxim machine guns were even more prone to malfunction. Lieutenant A.C. Hadow, who was in charge of them, removed sensitive parts at night and slept with them. The guns were water cooled, but water froze in the jackets; rum was mixed with the water, and to prevent gunners from taking swigs some kerosene was also added. One day in mid March a blizzard struck a supply column

A Gurkha sentry on Phari keep, Tibet. Sketched by N.V.L. Rybot, a member of Younghusband's expedition (*British Library*)

and there were seventy cases of snow-blindness among the Gurkhas, who had also gone thirty-six hours without food.

On 6 July 1904 a major battle was fought with the Tibetans at Gyantse, and here Lieutenant John Duncan Grant (no relation to the hero of Manipur) of the 8th Gurkhas won a Victoria Cross and Havildar Karbir Pun won the Indian Order of Merit. Grant led the storming party that charged the Gyantse fort. On emerging from the cover of the village, the forlorn hope had to advance up a bare, precipitous rock face with little or no cover. It came under heavy fire from the fort's curtain and the flanking towers on both sides. At the same time showers of rocks and stones came hurtling down on them, thrown from the fort above. A breach had been made in the curtain, but it was only large enough to admit one man at a time, crawling on hands and knees.

Both Grant and Karbir Pun tried to reach it. As Grant came near, he was wounded and thrown off the rock; Karbir Pun was also thrown back and fell thirty feet. In spite of their injuries, they again scrambled up to the breach and through it, the havildar shooting one Tibetan as he came through. The rest of the Gurkhas quickly followed them and the fort was taken.

The Tibetans did not again attempt to contest the advance of the invaders and Younghusband marched unopposed into Lhasa on 3 August 1904.

John Grant lived on for sixty years after winning his Victoria Cross in Tibet, retiring in 1921 as Colonel J.D. Grant, V.C.,C.B. After he died in 1967, his widow donated the £25 honorarium given to the widows of holders of the Victoria Cross to the Walker Scholarship Fund for Gurkha Children.

CHAPTER
7

Recruiting

The process by which Gurkhas were formerly recruited was unique, and although the process has changed in the past thirty years, it is still unique. Before 1886 there were only five single-battalion regiments of Gurkhas and no centralized system of recruiting. Each battalion made its own arrangements. Because British officers were not then allowed into Nepal, the recruiting had to be done by the Gurkhas themselves. Recruiting parties of Gurkha officers and non-commissioned officers were sent off into the Himalayan hills, to return with young men eager to be soldiers.

British officers never saw the fields, hills, mountains, valleys and villages of their men, for Nepalese rulers were ever suspicious of foreigners, particularly Europeans. King Prithwi Narayan, cruel but canny, said of the British: 'First the Bible, then the trading station, then the cannon.' Missionaries, traders and soldiers were kept beyond the frontiers. (To this day, Christian missionaries are not allowed to proselytize in Nepal. They can establish and run hospitals and schools, but they must not, by law, preach.) There was only one small crack: each year the British chief recruiting officer was allowed to confer with the British Resident in Katmandu and to pay his respects to the Maharajah. In practice it was not really necessary for British recruiters to go to Nepal; the system of using Gurkhas to recruit Gurkhas was somewhat cumbersome, but it worked. Besides, soldiers returning from leave would frequently return with a brother, a cousin or a friend. Sometimes young men would find their own way down from the hills to the regimental depots in India.

Apart from the provisions of the Treaty of Segauli, which stated that Gurkhas (except for the members of the Royal Bodyguard) 'will be at liberty to enter into the service of the British Government, if agreeable to themselves and the British Government choose to accept their service', no real agreement on recruiting in Nepal was reached until the British decided to double the number of Gurkha battalions. The Nepal Durbar had not always looked with favour on British recruiting and there had been times when recruits had to be smuggled over the border. When recruiting parties were turned back at the frontier, they wandered around the border area attending fairs and picking up such young men as they could. However, in 1886 when Maharajah Sir Bir Shamsher Rana Bahadur became prime minister and his brother, General Chandra Shamsher, was appointed commander-in-chief of the Nepalese army, Nepal agreed to cooperate and actually assisted the British in finding the men for the second battalions of the five Gurkha regiments. In the same year the British established a recruiting depot at Gorakhpur in the United Provinces (Uttar Pradesh). This depot was the base for all recruiting parties looking for Gurung and Magar recruits in west-central Nepal.

Captain C.A. Mercer of the 1/4th Gurkhas wrote a report on 30 July 1886 in which he evaluated the results of the first recruiting season – that is, from October 1885 until May 1886 – under the new system, during which 854 young men were examined, of whom 788 were accepted and despatched to regiments for training. This was a net increase of 150 recruits over the number taken in during the previous recruiting season. The Nepal Durbar supplied many of the potential recruits, but Captain Mercer was not satisfied with their quality and he concluded that 'the system

of Regimental Recruiting, with all its drawbacks, is infi-
nitely superior to that of recruiting through Durbar officials'.

Most of the men enlisted by Mercer were Magars and
Gurungs, but he was the first officer to recommend exten-
sive recruitment of Limbus and Rais from western Nepal.
His report gives a picture of the typical recruit of the period:
'The average physique of these men was decidedly good –
average age, 17–23; average height, 5 ft 2 ins.: altogether a
remarkably good stamp of man.' Today it is unlikely that
a man as old as twenty-three would be accepted; most are
closer to seventeen. The average height today is not more
than an inch taller.

Mercer approved of Gorakhpur as the chief centre for
recruiting men from western Nepal, for it was 'within a
few days' reach of the principal "Ghats" or fords connecting the British and Nepal border. It is the headquarters of
the Bengal North-Western Railway . . . so recruits can be
despatched to their respective stations or to within easy
distance of them in a very short space of time.'

Gorakhpur had been used as a recruiting station before it
was made into a major centre. But then recruits were
housed in *serais* in the town, many of which were 'filthy
dens', according to Mercer, in which healthy young men
contracted diseases, many dying of cholera. In 1885 the
government purchased 'Goorkha Village', which was close
to the railway station and was capable of accommodating
several hundred recruits until they could be processed.
Mercer sealed off the area so that 'none but recruiting parties, recruits and the small bazar [sic] establishment were
on any account to be allowed to reside within the limits of
the village'. In 1903 plague caused the depot to be moved
to Pharenda, but seven years later the depot was back in
the same area, at Kumraghat, three miles from Gorakhpur.

When the British began deliberately to recruit Kiranti
for the 7th and 10th Gurkhas, a recruiting station was
opened at Darjeeling. At first this was only a single room
located in the bazaar and recruits and recruiters lodged
wherever they could find accommodation, but in 1902 barracks which formerly housed an artillery battery were taken

Rifleman of the 2/4th Gurkha Rifles wearing drill order of 1886.
Sketch by G.G. Borrowman, *c.* 1938 (*National Army Museum*)

over. Later, a central depot for eastern Nepal was established at Ghoom. There was also a part-time depot at Purnea, later moved to Sakri. In 1890 the police battalions of Assam and Burma were also recruited from eastern Nepal and later the Burma police and the Assam Rifles similarly came under the control of the Recruiting Officer for Gurkhas.

The addition of second battalions in 1886 doubled the strength of Gurkha infantry. By 1908 the Gurkha Brigade, as it now came to be called, reached its highest peacetime strength of twenty battalions formed into ten regiments. The number of recruits required annually to maintain the twenty Gurkha battalions at full strength was about 1,500 young men. In spite of the fact that recruiting was confined to a very small area in a very small country, recruiting sufficient numbers was never, in peacetime, a major problem.

In the first forty years of their existence, Gurkha regiments were not too discriminating in the class of recruit they took in. Some were Garhwalis, Kumaonis and others who were not, strictly speaking, Gurkhas. However, as time passed the regiments became increasingly particular about the men they recruited. British officers believed – and some still do – in the 'martial races', and there was a decided preference in the Indian Army for Pathans, Jats, Dogras, Sikhs and others who are considered more military-minded and more likely to make good soldiers. By General Order dated January 1883 the Government of India ordered that Gurkhas be enlisted only in Gurkha regiments. This included not only the five consecutively numbered regiments of Gurkha infantry, but also the 42nd, 43rd and 44th regiments of Bengal Native Infantry. In 1903 the 42nd became the 6th Gurkha Rifles; in 1901 the 43rd became the 2/8th Gurkhas, and the 44th became the 1/8th Gurkhas.

The social class of the recruits always had to be taken into consideration. Captain H. Bingley, who wrote three handbooks for the Indian Army, said:

> Fighting capacity depends not only on race but also on hereditary instinct and social status; therefore it is essential that every effort should be made to obtain the very best men

of that class which a regiment may enlist . . . Men of good class will not enlist unless their own class be well represented in the regiment.

So more and more recruits tended to come not only from the same tribes, but the same clans, kindreds and families. Sons followed fathers into the same profession. Soldiering was considered an honourable profession, and soldiers and former soldiers acquired through arms a standing in their village or valley. This was true in the last century and it is true in this one. Kulbahadur Gurung enlisted in the 5th Gurkhas in 1898 and retired in 1921 as an honorary captain. Thirty years later he came into the recruiting depot at Lehra, India, to talk with the recruiting officer. He had lost his two sons – but he was quick to add that he had two grandsons who would soon be old enough to enlist.

In 1973 Major P.H. Ridlington, Gurkha Signals, went to the village of Gurkha Captain Lalbir Thapa, formerly of the 1/6th Gurkhas, to pay him the Gurkha Dependents Fund grant for his son, Rifleman Kosbahadur Thapa, who had drowned. Lalbir was asleep in the sun outside his house when Ridlington approached. His wife woke him, saying that a sahib was coming. Lalbir got to his feet and rubbed the sleep from his eyes as he went to greet the visitor. He grinned broadly when he recognized Ridlington; they had served together in the 2/6th in 1952.

News of Kosbahadur's death had not yet reached him, and Ridlington told him in 'a brutal statement, quick and to the point'. He saw Lalbir's hand tighten. 'It is God's will,' he said. Then he called for his wife to make tea and told her. It was not until he began to speak of his hopes and expectations for his son that he broke down and wept.

When Ridlington rose to leave, Lalbir also stood up, saluted and said: 'Sahib, I served the Queen and achieved officer rank. My son has done his duty and given her his life. My second son is not yet old enough to serve her, but when he is, I will send him.'

The military history of some Gurkha families extends back for well over a hundred years, members often serving in the same regiment. In 1790 Jabbar Sing Thapa enlisted as a soldier in the Indian Army and fought at the siege of Bhurtpore. His son, Ballea Thapa, enlisted in the Nasiri Battalion in 1837, became a havildar in 1851, and in 1857 was promoted to subadar for saving the lives of two British officers. He was transferred to the 4th Gurkhas and served in that battalion through six campaigns, becoming subadar-major in 1861. He was Orderly Officer to King Edward VII when, as Prince of Wales, he visited India in 1875. The Prince presented Ballea Thapa with a specially made hunting knife; in the officers' mess of the 4th Gurkhas is a statuette of him with the knife, as well as his portrait by W. Simpson of the *Illustrated London News*.

Ballea's son, Nathu Thapa, also served in the 4th Gurkhas and rose to be a subadar. He died in 1885 after serving in five campaigns, leaving three sons, two of whom served in the 4th Gurkhas while the youngest, Partiman, served in the 10th. The second son, Sheru, died of cholera shortly after his return from the Manipur Campaign of 1891. The eldest son, Rannu, served in the Miranzai Campaign of 1891, the Waziristan Campaign of 1894 and the China Expedition of 1900. His portrait, painted by Major C.G. Borrowman, hangs in the officers' mess.

Rannu's eldest son, Lachman Thapa, enlisted in 1905, became a jemadar in 1913 and was killed in France in 1914 while leading a brave counter-attack at Givenchy. Rannu's second son was captured at Kut-el-Amara in World War I and spent the rest of the war in a Turkish prison, but in 1919 he was commissioned in the 1/4th Gurkhas and served in Waziristan in 1920, 1923 and 1934. He became subadar-major – the third generation of his family to hold that distinguished rank in the same battalion. At the beginning of World War II, eight grandsons of Rannu Thapa were serving in the two battalions of the 4th Gurkhas. Members of this family are still serving.

In 1978, in a single battalion, the 6th Queen Elizabeth's Own Gurkha Rifles, forty-six sets of brothers were serving at the same time. In 1979, in the 7th Duke of Edinburgh's Own Gurkha Rifles, Gurkha Major Danbahadur Rai was succeeded when he retired by his younger brother, Deokumar Rai.

The problems of recruitment were not those met by recruiters in other armies. They had no trouble finding enough men; their difficulty lay in selecting the best from the over-supply available – a situation that still prevails. Before a young man left home to enlist, parties were often given by his friends and kinsmen, though the final parting was solemn. Major A.M. Langlands of the 2nd Gurkhas watched a Gurung would-be recruit leave home in 1963. His father had consulted a priest on the best day for his son to leave. The young man said his farewells to everyone, those to senior members of his family being solemn and graceful. His mother presented him with a handful of small coins which he distributed among his girl-friends, who were waiting along the path. 'I can now understand,' said Langlands, 'why many failed recruits do not wish to return home. After such a ceremonial farewell it is rather an anti-climax to return in less than a month.'

Every young man who set off for the depot was confident of acceptance. (one British officer said that he never knew a Gurkha with an inferiority complex), but few realized the high physical standards required. Often they were ignorant of the germs living within them. Even as late as 1970 there were only 220 civilian doctors in Nepal, which had an estimated population of twelve million. Almost none of those seeking to be recruits had ever seen a doctor, and the army doctors, particularly after they acquired X-ray machines, discovered diseases the young men had never known they harboured.

All too prevalent were smallpox, diphtheria, cholera, leprosy and, most common of all, tuberculosis. They frequently had worms or skin diseases, but most of these the army could easily cure and they were not handicaps. Thus those selected were not typical Nepalese hillmen; they were the best, or at least the fittest. Most had extremely strong legs; some had abnormally developed thighs and calves from carrying heavy loads up and down mountains almost from the time they could walk. For the most part, however, they were scrawny, but the doctors and recruiting officers understood the effects of milk and good food: they would quickly fill out. In fact it was the delight of their officers to turn these ill-nourished youngsters into healthy, fit young men through plenty of food and proper exercise. In the days before 1970 the Brigade of Gurkhas had a Boys' Company composed of youths too young to be soldiers, but with good potential, who were educated, exercised and fed. In 1950 the commander of the Boys' Company boasted: 'The boys have gained 3,054½ lbs in the last year and have grown 18 yds, 1 ft, 1 in. Quite a jump that! Eighteen yards of Gurkha, weighing well over a ton, is no mean asset in our continual fight against communism.'

All recruits were supposed to be at least seventeen years old, but many tried to enlist when they were younger. Most did not know their exact date of birth. The ages of Gurungs could be assessed more accurately than those of members of other tribes, for the Gurungs had adopted a Tibetan time-cycle of twelve years in which each year has a *barkha*, a name of a bird or animal. A Gurung usually knew his *barkha* and since it is rare to over- or under-estimate the age of a young man by twelve years, a fairly accurate age could be determined.

The potential recruit arrived at the depot after having walked a considerable distance. When the depots were in India, those nearest travelled only a few days; others spent more than three weeks walking down from their remote villages and valleys. When they arrived they were instantly rewarded with a generous army meal. For some, it was the largest meal they had ever eaten. They were also given what was generally considered to be the necessities for eating and sleeping – knives, forks, army cots and sheets: all were strange and new.

Rejection was usually for a physical defect or simply failure to come up to the minimum physical standards, but such rejection was often felt to be a disgrace. Major G. Somerville, an army doctor, described the process:

> They knew of the perils of the doctor's examination and of his dreaded decision to fail for a reason they could not under-stand. The ordeal was beginning to tell on nerves and they stood naked and frail before the doctor, anxiously trying to say the right things and do things correctly. About 10 per cent would

fail, half of these from an abnormal X-ray, the remainder with perforated ears, colour blindness, enlarged thyroids, heart murmurs, etc. It was heartbreaking to fail them. Some broke down and cried and pleaded for a second chance; others accepted their fate enigmatically, but I wondered what thoughts lay behind their impassive faces.

Lieutenant (later Brigadier) E.D. ('Birdie') Smith was in charge of a recruiting depot in January 1948 when a young man was rejected because he was twenty pounds underweight. He burst into tears, and that night he found Smith's quarters and begged for a second chance. He offered to work without pay in the cookhouse if he were given his meals and could be considered again when he had gained weight. Smith consented: 'I agreed and he worked like a Trojan. He also ate like a horse and was soon over the minimum weight. We enlisted him and he eventually became a first-class N.C.O. in a battalion in Malaya.'

Very few were ever given a second chance. The selection process involved marking the men's chests and backs with indelible ink. Some who had been rejected got friends to rub off the ink with an abrasive stone and then reappeared in the line-up the next day, a futile attempt rewarded only by painful sores.

Most British officers with the Gurkhas had a prejudice against 'line boys', sons and grandsons of soldiers who had been born in the family lines of a Gurkha battalion in India or Malaya, who had gone to school and learned foreign (that is, non-Nepalese) ways. It was felt that such young men lacked the hardy virtues of those from the hills and had grown too clever by half. In 1973 Lieutenant-Colonel A.M. Langlands, M.B.E. (who, when still a major, had watched the family leave-taking of a recruit in 1963), said:

> I know some Gurkhas who have reached high rank without having lived in the hills: they were exceptional men who would reach the top no matter where they had been brought up.
>
> But for the average Gurkha soldier, the backbone of the Brigade of Gurkhas, give me a man who has been moulded in the hills.

His village school may not teach English as well as a British Army School, but the hills will have taught him far more useful lessons: self-reliance and toughness.

These were sentiments with which 'Birdie' Smith as recruiting officer fully agreed. From time to time distinguished-looking pensioners, wearing their medals, would arrive at his recruiting depot with a son or grandson in tow, the young boy having been educated at considerable parental expense and sacrifice at Darjeeling. 'In some cases,' said Smith, 'the boys were more Indian than Gurkha in habits and we didn't want to enlist many Indian domiciled Gurkhas. But to have said so would have upset the old soldiers with years of loyal service behind them . . .' At such times, Smith would mark on the doctor's list of men due for medical examinations: 'Doc, fail this chap. We cannot take him.' The doctor was shocked, as well he might be, but he complied. 'Thus,' said Smith, 'honour was satisfied and no one's feelings were hurt.'

Many of those who were rejected, for whatever reason, could not face returning to their homes with their disappointed hopes and dreams, so they stayed in India or perhaps found work in the Katmandu Valley.

It has been said that the Gurkhas, being mercenaries, enlisted only for the pay. Indeed the pay, low though it was, seemed attractive to those from a land where there is little hard cash. But it was the sole reason for only very few. Paraschandra Rai, a driver in the Gurkha Transport Regiment in 1970, said: 'Every man in this world wants to be brave and would like other people to call him brave. The Army is the easiest way by which one can demonstrate one's braveness to the world. It is this that makes men enlist in the Army.'

Captain Maniprasad Rai of the 7th Gurkha Rifles admitted that money was an inducement and that soldiering was a 'manly thing to do', but he thought that there were other, more compelling reasons for a young man to enlist. They wanted to leave the 'confined and restrictive life of the village' and to see the world beyond the mountains. Writing in 1965, he spoke of 'the lure of the South':

There is the glittering life of trains, cars, boats, studded by brilliant electric lights; of buildings taller than the forest trees, teeming with busy men, women and children all wishing to get somewhere; of bazaars and markets which never shut, hotels and women of doubtful virtue, thieves, murderers and Lord Sahibs in sprawling palaces veiled by succulent fruit trees . . .

A boy left the village a few years ago feeling nervous, shy and full of trepidation, now he is a man in all respects: with money in his pocket, confidence in his heart, wonderfully enlightened by rich experiences and clothes of exotic material on self. There lies the way to the South, to adventure and riches . . .

The lucky young man accepted as a recruit was at once exposed to a world of new experiences; one of the first was to have his head shaved except for a scalplock, and this style was retained throughout his army career, regardless of his rank. After World War II, however, at the personal request of the King of Nepal, Gurkhas were permitted to grow their hair. Old soldiers were horrified by the change, but Gurkhas remained Gurkhas and were as good soldiers as ever.

More strange than the shaved head for the recruit were all the other novelties he encountered and all the new skills he was required to master – the use of toilets, for example. In Nepalese villages there were not only no toilets, but no particular space set aside as a latrine. The very idea of a particular place in which to defecate, and the use of a special piece of equipment, was a curious notion to him. Most had never sat on a chair or a bench. They did not always understand what was required of them. One recruit in the 4th Gurkhas, when told to take more milk, was found rubbing it on his legs.

To the recruit, brought up in privation in a hard and hungry land, the army's bounty seemed munificent, but its ways were strange and its customs sometimes caused pain. Most recruits had gone barefoot all their lives; none had worn heavy boots before. One English officer described a Gurkha in his first pair of boots as resembling a newly shod New Forest pony. For his first month, the recruit's every step was agony.

At the recruiting depot the recruit was issued with his uniform, documentation was completed, there was an attestation ceremony and then he was sent off to his regiment or to a training depot. Time, previously a meaningless abstraction except in the most general terms, suddenly became something to be remembered and reckoned with. And an unfamiliar world of new sights, sounds, and activities assailed him: noise, wheeled vehicles, traffic, flat land, eating at tables, riding in trains and, at a later date, the sensations of being transported in ships and aircraft.

Disciplinary problems with Gurkha recruits were almost non-existent, a situation quite different from that prevailing in the training camps and depots of other armies. There was a difference, too, in the way the recruits were treated. The bullying and intimidation common in European and American armies were absent. There is no record of a Gurkha ever having been flogged. The Gurkha recruit was gently handled. Toughness was not equated with harshness. The non-commissioned officers in charge of recruits used humour, example, persuasion and great patience.

Gurkhas possessed an easy self-confidence. Punctilious as trained soldiers, they were never servile. As recruits they were overawed neither by the wonders of civilization nor by the ranks and ceremonies of the army. John Masters in the 4th Gurkhas had this brought home to him one day when a recruit, called in for questioning, entered his office as he was in the act of lighting a cigarette, a pause the young man filled by perching on the edge of his desk and pulling out his own pack. Asked sternly to give his name, he replied affably, 'Puranbahadur. What's yours?'

At the beginning of World War I, when the British first began to add more than two battalions to their Gurkha regiments, the quality of the recruits was high, but as the demand intensified and more and more men were needed, the recruiting system felt the strain. The supply of men in the favourite recruiting areas, from tribes the British preferred, began to dry up and orders were given to recruit from all Nepalese classes. Physical standards were lowered and any man with a physical defect the army thought it could cure was taken in, so Newars, Sherpas, Bhatias, Lepchas and some Tibetans were gathered into the great war machine. At one time the 2/10th Gurkhas even had two Chinese. No one could understand them and they could understand no one else. They were a 'source of great merriment', according to the regimental history; they were, however, considered 'apt pupils and would probably have made excellent soldiers, but authorities decided that they must be sent home again'.

In all, Nepal's despotic ruler permitted 200,000 male subjects of his medieval kingdom to join and fight in a war in which the world was to be made safe for democracy. Of these, 55,000 served in the ten regular Gurkha infantry regiments of Britain's Indian Army. Others served in labour battalions, bearer corps and other types of units. Nepal was nearly denuded of its able young men.

There were 20,000 Gurkha casualties.

CHAPTER
8

World War I: France

A former officer in the 5th Gurkha Rifles wrote: 'Of those years before the Great War it can truly be said that there was an attractiveness about them not so easily associated with the less settled period which followed it. Rifle green has made way for khaki on all occasions; the three arms . . . have been supplemented by aeroplanes, tanks, and gas; that which was simple has become complicated.' Indeed, the First World War upset the world and nothing has ever been quite the same since. The internal combustion engine and the increased destructive power of new weapons accelerated the tempo of combat and added to the physical and psychological pressures upon the combatants. Everything was indeed more complicated.

The war seemed to have arrived at an unexpected and inconvenient moment for most Englishmen. Even soldiers, who perhaps ought to have had more foresight in view of the alarming series of events leading up to its outbreak, were taken by surprise and were unprepared. When news of the war's beginning arrived in the orderly room of the 1/5th Gurkhas at Abbottabad on 5 August 1914, there was a scramble to get ready for it. The battalion had a marching-out strength of twelve British officers, seventeen Gurkha officers and 808 other ranks, but many of its British officers were in England on leave; some 150 Gurkha ranks were on

leave in the distant Nepal mountains. Not until November
was the battalion ready to go to war. The situation was
much the same in the other Gurkha battalions.

The fact that hardly anyone was prepared for war did
not diminish everyone's immense enthusiasm for the Great
Adventure. In India, all Britons were eager to 'do their bit'.
When on 17 November 1914 the 1/5th prepared to embark
on the SS *Barpeta*, the Ladies Patriotic League of Karachi
distributed tea, dried fruits, chillies and cigarettes to the
men, and books to the officers. Later the Ladies of Lahore
and the Comforts Committee of Abbottabad sent bundles
of clothing, cigarettes, writing paper and small necessities.

The 1/4th Gurkhas were ready – or almost ready (the
battalion was short of nearly half of its British officers) –
earlier than the 1/5th and sailed in the SS *Baroda* for Suez
on 24 August 1914. The ship's engine broke down several
times en route, each time leaving the ship to wallow help-
lessly in the monsoon. The Gurkhas, always poor sailors,
were dreadfully seasick. The sea was a foreign element; they
never felt at ease on shipboard. Indeed, some were known
to have been sick before their ship left the quay. They often
asked where all the water came from and where it went.
One man, hanging over the rail, explained that he was
trying to see the ship's legs. A Gurkha on the *Baroda* asked
the battalion adjutant if the ship ran on rails at the bottom
of the sea, for he could not understand how otherwise it
found its way. It all seemed inexplicable: there was an
obvious, well-defined trail behind, but why was there none
in front?

The Gurkhas were delighted to be going to war, though
they had little notion of exactly where they were going. They
had scant knowledge of geography and the men in one battalion started sharpening their *kukris* when the train neared
Calcutta. They also had no idea of the causes of the war.
Coming from an oriental kingdom governed by an absolute
ruler, a land where elections were unknown, they certainly
were not consciously fighting to preserve Western civilization or to make the world safe for democracy. They fought
for the honour of their battalion and regiment, for their

comrades, for pay and pension, for the excitement of battle, and, quite simply, because their officers told them to.

Special arrangements were necessary before they were permitted to embark on their journey to fight the Germans and Turks. Hindus were forbidden to cross the sea on pain of loss of caste unless given special dispensation. In any case a special purification ceremony, the *pani patiya*, was required when a Hindu returned from overseas. The Maharajah of Nepal, Sir Chandra Shumshere Jang Bahadur, was appealed to and, thanks to his influence, the Raj Guru, Nepal's supreme religious authority, gave his approval for the mercenary troops to cross the *kala pani* ('black water').

Nepal proved a valuable ally. In addition to its young men it contributed more than a million rupees to the war effort, and on the occasion of King George's birthday in 1915 presented him with thirty-one machine guns.

All regiments except the 4th and 10th raised third battalions during the war and for two years the 1/10th served as a training battalion, training recruits for their second battalion and for other regiments as well. In the officers' mess there came to be a nightly toast: 'To the second battalion and our comrades at the front.' The 3rd Gurkhas raised a fourth battalion and a completely new regiment was formed, the 11th, which raised four battalions. Before the war, each battalion had in Nepal about a hundred men designated as reserves. In the event, this number was pitiably inadequate; moreover, many who came back were found to be unfit and had to be sent home. From the very beginning there was a need for more men. The Burma Rifles and Burma Military Police, both units composed largely of Gurkhas, volunteered *en masse* and were soon used as replacements in regular Gurkha battalions.

The Indian Army sent off to France a corps consisting of two divisions: the 7th, or Meerut, Division and the 3rd, or Lahore, Division; both contained Gurkha battalions. Each division had three infantry brigades, but the Lahore Division left one, called the Sirhind Brigade, to guard the Suez Canal.

On 29 October 1914 the first Gurkhas, the 2/8th, arrived

at the Western Front and went into trenches near Festubert. It was a miserable, grim introduction to a miserable,
grim war. Cold, hungry and wet, they found themselves in
mud-filled trenches too deep for them to see over the par-
apet. Trenches of the wrong depth were to be a perennial
problem: if Gurkhas dug them, they were too shallow for
the next unit occupying them; if Gurkhas took over existing trenches, they had an immediate, pressing and dangerous problem in trying to construct higher fire steps that
would enable them to see and shoot at the enemy. The 2/8th
were taught this lesson quickly, for no sooner had they
arrived in their trenches than the Germans gave them a
heavy shelling and then attacked. The Gurkhas beat them
back and survived – but barely. Within twenty-four hours,
six out of ten British officers were killed and three were
wounded; of other ranks, thirty-seven were killed and sixty-
one wounded; in addition, more than a hundred were missing and believed dead, probably blown to bits by artillery
fire.

Lieutenant-Colonel J.W.B. Merewether and Sir Frederick Smith, in a history of the Indian Corps in France, wrote:
'The 2/8th Gurkhas were fortunate in embarking on this
war in possession of a particularly fine body of officers, and
it was the cruelest of bad luck that the regiment at the very
outset suffered the loss of no less than nine of their small
number.' An English officer writing home from the front
spoke of the 'splendid dash' of the 2/8th Gurkhas: 'The Regiment has acquired a magnificent reputation amongst those
who know – at the expense of its existence.'

Other Gurkha units were soon similarly heavily engaged –
the first battalions of the 1st, 4th and 9th, and the second
battalions of the 2nd and 3rd Gurkhas. Within a few days
in early November 1914 the 2/2nd Gurkhas lost all its British officers. The 1/4th left its home at Bakloh, India, with a
strength of 736 officers and men. There were 650 when on
17 November 1914 the battalion went into trenches at Givenchy. One week later only 423 were left.

The winter of 1914 – 15 in northern France and Belgium
was severe, with frequent snowstorms and biting wind. The

Gurkhas felt the cold intensely; it was damp, not the dry cold to which they were accustomed. Frostbite was a major problem among troops of all nations. Men wore sandbags filled with straw over their shoes; whale oil was issued to rub on their feet.

In spite of the strange climate and the fearful casualties, the Gurkhas were not long in distinguishing themselves. At Givenchy in December 1914 the scouts of the 1/4th Gurkhas, under the command of the battalion's adjutant, Captain D. Inglis, were, according to the regimental history, 'given the honour of cutting the enemy's wire and guiding the attacking companies to the gaps'. Captain Inglis also had the honour of having his brains shot out. Two of the riflemen with him were also killed while crawling toward the German wire; two others made it to the wire but were killed while cutting it; and still another pair were shot dead still gripping the guiding telephone wire. Only four survived this débâcle and two of these were awarded the Indian Order of Merit.

In March 1915 the British had an initial success in a well-planned attack at Neuve Chapelle, but poor staff work and mismanagement prevented a proper follow-through and the Germans quickly re-established a line. The Indian Corps alone suffered 4,000 casualties in ten days. Heavy rains had saturated the low-lying ground around Neuve Chapelle and there was much flooding. Artillery had shredded the trees. When men tried to seek shelter in the earth, water was struck almost at the touch of the spade; existing trenches were muddy streams. On 2 November the Germans launched a vigorous attack with overwhelming numbers. For the 2/2nd Gurkhas the results were catastrophic. Out of a fighting strength of 529, 147 fell, including all eight British officers, of whom seven were killed and the only survivor seriously wounded.

There were some small successes. And there was heroism. Rifleman Gane Gurung of the 2/3rd Gurkhas, seeing heavy small arms fire coming from a battered house in Neuve Chapelle, made a one-man attack on it and emerged with eight prisoners. The 2nd Rifle Brigade, moving up into

Rifleman Panchbir Mall of the 1/9th Gurkha Rifles wearing a greatcoat, 1915. He was recommended for the Victoria Cross but was only awarded the Indian Order of Merit for his gallantry. Sketch by Lt. Col. B. Granville Baker (*National Army Museum*)

position, were so taken by the sight of the grinning little Gurkha herding the tall Germans that they spontaneously gave him three cheers. He was awarded the Indian Order of Merit.

Having created a muddle at Neuve Chapelle, the British generals and their staffs prepared for another co-ordinated offensive, but their plans were spoiled by clouds of chlorine gas spewing from 5,000 cylinders and moving in dense clouds toward the Allied lines near Ypres. Behind the gas came two full German corps, which drove through two demoralized French divisions and bit deep into the British lines. It was, however, a peculiarity of high command on both sides in this war that they so quickly became accustomed to failures or limited successes that they never made adequate plans to exploit gains. So it was that the Germans found themselves incapable of marching through the great hole they had created in the Allied lines; because of the build-up of German forces on the Eastern Front, there were no reserves available to exploit the advantage obtained. After some bitter fighting, principally by the British Second Army, the German advance was brought to a halt. German losses exceeded 35,000: the French lost 10,000 and the British 60,000.

Naturally, gas masks were unknown when gas was introduced to the battlefield. Men were told to urinate on their handkerchieves and hold these over their noses in case of another gas attack. Then tins of water containing bicarbonate of soda were placed in trenches and soldiers were ordered to wear scarves around their necks so that these could be quickly dipped in the tins and used to cover their faces. When the first real gas masks did arrive, the Gurkha ranks thought they were a huge joke. It was difficult to hold practice drills, for each time a man donned his mask, his colleagues collapsed in gales of laughter.

After stopping the German offensive, the British counterattacked in an attempt to gain a feature known as Aubers Ridge, but they were brought to a halt at Festubert in mid May. It was a bitter time for the participants. The 2/2nd lost five British officers within five minutes. The 1/4th lost

243 men out of 603 engaged. One of these was No. 4817 Rifleman Motilal Thapa.

Captain J.R. Hartwell, wounded, crawled into a ditch and found Motilal Thapa lying on the lip, his shattered arm hanging by a thread of flesh. Both had been in the first line of an advance. When the second line came up, Hartwell had Motilal dragged into the ditch with him and saw that his arm was bandaged. The attack passed on, no stretcher-bearers arrived, and an exhausted Hartwell fell asleep. He awoke to find that Motilal had managed to prop himself against the side of the ditch and with his one good arm was holding his field service cap over the captain's face to keep the sun from his eyes. He was softly muttering: 'I must not cry out. I am a Gurkha.' He died before reaching an aid station.

Both the Allies and the Germans were exhausted after their costly winter and spring offensives. The summer of 1915 was spent in reorganizing, reinforcing and building up stocks of ammunition and supplies. Then in September came the battle of Loos.

The British exploded a huge mine under the German trenches and then laid down a heavy bombardment. Field guns were brought forward to knock out machine gun nests. Gas, too, was to have been used, but German shells blew off the cylinder heads and the British suffered casualties from their own gas. However, smoke shells were fired and behind the smoke came the Meerut Division, which included the 2/8th and the 2/3rd Gurkhas. The Germans had not been beaten into the ground by all the sound and fury, and when the Indians and Gurkhas emerged through the smoke, they shot them down.

A party of thirty-eight Gurkhas attacking near Fauquissart managed to crawl through the German wire and rush the Germans they found. Rifleman Kulbir Thapa of the 2/3rd suddenly found himself alone and wounded. Then he stumbled upon a severely wounded soldier of the Leicestershire Regiment. Thapa made him as comfortable as possible and lay beside him through the rest of the day and night. In the early morning when a heavy mist over the battlefield provided some cover, he decided to move out. Hoisting the wounded man on his back, he set off for his own lines. In places the way lay within a few feet of the Germans and it was often necessary to ease the wounded man to the ground and drag him through barbed wire. More than once he came close to being discovered. At one spot he came upon two badly wounded Gurkhas whom he was at the moment powerless to help. Farther on, he found a shell hole in which he could shelter the Leicestershire soldier while he went back for the Gurkhas. He brought them both safely into the Allied lines, then turned back to the shell hole. The mist had now lifted and his last trip, with the Leicestershire soldier on his back, was accomplished under heavy fire.

Kulbir received the Victoria Cross he richly deserved. It was the first to be won by a Gurkha. Unlike most of the valorous acts that merit the award, his was not an act performed in the hot-blooded excitement of battle but was heroism sustained over a forty-eight-hour period. Philip Mason thought that as a single act of valour 'it must surely rank with the highest of all'. Perhaps so.

After thirteen months in France the Indian Corps was withdrawn and the battered battalions were sent to fight elsewhere. The Indian Corps had done well in France and had sustained 21,000 casualties: eight of its members won the Victoria Cross. Indian and Gurkha troops had also behaved well off-duty and there were no complaints from French civilians or officials. General Sir James Willcocks, who commanded the Indian Corps, later said of the Gurkhas: 'I have now come to the conclusion that the best of my troops in France were the Gurkhas.'

In spite of the Indian Corps' good record in France, military historians have doubted the wisdom of sending it. There should be no debate. It was a mistake. Indian troops were to perform better on the hot sands of Mesopotamia than in the wet cold of France. They were neither trained nor equipped for war on the Western Front. They were inadequately clothed and carried a mere two machine guns per battalion; they had no mortars and only jam-tin grenades; they required special food and the thousands of tons of rice and curry powder shipped to France took up shipping space which could have been better employed. Replacements were also difficult and had to be transported long distances. British officers who spoke Hindustani and Gurkhali, and who understood the ways of the Indian Army, were difficult to replace. The plan to send two divisions of the Indian Army to France was ill-conceived; the decision to withdraw them for use elsewhere was wise.

CHAPTER
9

World War I: Gallipoli

Early in 1915 plans were afoot to knock Turkey out of the war and open a clear line of communication with Russia, beginning with an attack upon the Gallipoli peninsula, key to the Dardanelles. Ian Hamilton, the experienced soldier who was to lead the land forces, wrote on 25 March 1915 to Lord Kitchener, Secretary of State for War:

> I am very anxious, if possible, to get a brigade of Gurkhas, so as to complete the New Zealand Divisional Organization with a type of man who will, I am most certain, be most valuable on the Gallipoli Peninsula. The scrubby hillsides on the south-west faces of the plateau are just the sort of terrain where these little fellows are their brilliant best . . . each little 'Gurk' might be worth his full weight in gold at Gallipoli.

With the planned invasion less than a month away, Hamilton's request for an as yet unformed brigade must have been an afterthought, yet it was typical of the slap-dash way in which this ill-fated expedition was prepared. Kitchener did not give Hamilton all the men and arms he requested, but he did give him a hastily whipped together brigade. Named 29 Brigade, it consisted of the 1/5th, 1/6th and 2/10th Gurkhas.

From the beginning, everything that could go wrong did.

In February 1915 the Royal Navy, with some help from the French, bombarded the forts guarding the narrow straits of the Dardanelles. Victory was at hand and the Turks had almost exhausted their resources when three old battleships blundered into an undetected minefield and sank. This so discouraged the British admiral that he scurried away lest he should lose more ships. As a result of this sad effort the Turks were now alerted to the vulnerability and importance of the Gallipoli peninsula.

Meanwhile General Hamilton, who had no control over the naval operations, was preparing to launch 78,000 men onto the Gallipoli beaches. Unfortunately the ships from England had not been combat loaded (men with their weapons, ammunition and equipment all on the same ship and packed so that the first needed came off first) and there was delay while ships were unloaded in Greece and reloaded. By the time the British, with one French division, set forth at last, 60,000 Turks commanded by German General Liman von Sanders were waiting for them in an elastic defence.

On 25 April 1915 the expeditionary force landed in five places on Cape Hellas at the tip of the peninsula, and at Ari Burnu, about fifteen miles north on the western side. The key to the Cape Hellas position was a dominant hill mass called Achi Baba. It probably could have been captured, but the division commander remained on shipboard and out of touch with his forward troops, who had stopped to brew tea. It proved to be expensive tea: expensive in the lives of British, New Zealand, Australian and Gurkha soldiers. At Ari Burnu the dominant height was Chunuk Bair and the Australian and New Zealand Army Corps (A.N.Z.A.C.) tried to take it. They were beaten back, with a loss of 5,000 men, by the particularly able commander of a Turkish reserve division: Mustafa Kemal, later to win fame as Ataturk, the creator of modern Turkey.

It was not until five days after these initial landings that the first Gurkhas, the 1/6th, commanded by the Honourable Charles Bruce, arrived at Gallipoli, landing in the Cape Hellas sector. They were placed in immediate reserve and

within a few hours suffered their first casualties. On 12 May
they took part in their first major operation. To the west of
the beachhead was a bluff some 300 feet high which the
Turks had converted into a strongpoint bristling with
machine guns. Two attempts to capture it by the Royal
Dublin Fusiliers and the Royal Marines had failed before
the 1/6th Gurkhas were given the task. With speed and daring the bluff was taken – at a cost of eighteen killed and
forty-two wounded. Thereafter, by Army Order, this feature of the landscape was known as Gurkha Bluff.

Only under the protection of overhanging cliffs were the
men safe from Turkish guns. But in addition to the ferocity
of the Turks, the crowded beachheads at Gallipoli were
uncomfortable and unhealthy. The heat was intense, the
smell of decomposing corpses in no-man's-land permeated
the air, and millions of flies flew from the dead to the
rations. The Cape Hellas bridgehead area below Achi Baba
was said to have 'looked like a midden and smelt like a
cemetery'. Thousands were felled by dysentery; lice made
life miserable for all.

In early June the 2/10th and the 1/5th Gurkhas arrived to
complete 29 Brigade in Gallipoli, and almost immediately
the 1/5th was thrown into the Third Battle of Krithia, in
which the 1/6th had just suffered a setback. In spite of
repeated attacks by the Gurkhas, this battle proved no more
successful than had others in the area. Achi Baba, the 700-
foot dominant height, remained in Turkish hands. The effort
cost the British 7,000 casualties. Within a few hours the
1/6th lost ninety-five men and the 1/5th lost 129, including
seven British officers.

It seems remarkable that romantic notions of war and
martial behaviour could survive even a few hours at Gallipoli, but Captain W.K. Brown of the 1/5th Gurkhas had
brought along his sword which he flourished in the classic
manner as he called on his men to charge. He was quickly
shot down.

It was in the course of this battle that Naik Dhan Sing
Gurung was captured by the Turks. He was being marched
away into captivity when he bolted and threw himself over

a cliff. He survived his fall but was again captured, this
time on the beach. Again he escaped, on this occasion by
diving into the sea. Few Gurkhas could swim but Dhan Sing
was an exception; in spite of the hail of bullets that pursued him he managed to make his way, still in all his clothes
(even his boots), out to sea and then to swim parallel to the
shore until at last he could land safely behind the Allied
lines.

The Turks, not content to remain on the defensive and
determined to throw the invaders into the sea, launched a
series of counter-attacks. They were bloody affairs, local
battles often being decided by hand-to-hand fighting. All
three Gurkha battalions were engaged and they often used
their *kukris* to good effect. The Turks are said to have lost
10,000 men a week, but British casualties were also enormous. In the first five weeks at Gallipoli the 2/10th Gurkhas
lost seventy per cent of its British officers and nearly forty
per cent of its other ranks.

The Gurkha brigade needed to rest, refit and refill the
depleted ranks of its rifle companies. Wisely, it was withdrawn from Gallipoli and sent to the Isle of Imbros for a
month. Meanwhile General Hamilton was belatedly given
more divisions and plans were made for an assault on Sari
Bair, a ridge whose principal peaks (called Battleship Hill,
Chunuk Bair and Hill Q) were obviously keys to the entire
Gallipoli peninsula. The main attack was to be made from
the A.N.Z.A.C. beaches at Ari Burnu, with supporting operations in the Cape Hellas area and a landing at Suvla Bay,
just north of Ari Burun.

Some 20,000 additional troops disembarked at A.N.Z.A.C.
beaches, including 29 Brigade which was assigned the task
of leading the assault on Hill Q, located in the middle of
the Sari Bair feature. The terrain over which the advancing
force would have to move was rugged in the extreme, with
steep spurs and gullies covered with dense prickly scrub.
The few maps available were all inaccurate; the guides had
little knowledge of the ground, having had too little time
for a thorough reconnaissance. This would have been considered formidable country to pass through in peacetime

during daylight hours. The Gurkhas and those who were to follow them were expected to make their way through it in the dark in the face of a determined, well-equipped enemy.

On the night of 6–7 August the 2/10th and the 1/5th (plus one company of the 2/5th, newly arrived from France) set off on the nightmare march to capture Hill Q. The 1/6th reinforced the Australians, who were attacking an adjacent peak. The first task – essential to ensure success – was the capture of the Chunuk Bair peak before daylight, but guides lost their way and, inexplicably, orders halting the Gurkhas arrived when they were only a thousand yards short of the summit, just before first light. The delay was fatal to the enterprise. The attack which ought to have gone in with at least four battalions was launched by five companies – and seven and a half hours too late. The Turks were ready for them. It was the end of a great opportunity, although not, of course, the end of the slaughter.

Early on the morning of the following day the 1/6th Gurkhas advanced under fire up the slopes of Hill Q. After five hours' work they reached a point only two hundred yards below the crest; here the attack seemed to die. The Gurkhas clung to the slope, and some even managed in the course of the day to inch forward another fifty yards, but then had to fight desperately to hold what had been gained. Some reinforcements arrived from the South Lancashires and the Warwickshires. (In the Warwickshire Regiment was Lieutenant William J. Slim, who was so impressed by the 1/6th that he later joined the regiment; later still, in his rise to a peerage and a field-marshal's baton, he commanded the famous Fourteenth Army in Burma during World War II.)

The Gurkhas and British soldiers plastered against the hot rocks of Hill Q were burned by the sun, parched for water, very hungry and short of ammunition. They were in a most unenviable position under the Turkish guns. The wounded suffered most, for they could not be evacuated until after dark.

At dawn on 9 August Chunuk Bair, Hill Q and the neck between them were shelled by every available gun on land

and on the warships off-shore. A brigade of four battalions
under Brigadier-General A.H. Baldwin started up to reinforce the attackers, but again the guides lost their way.
When the barrage lifted at 5.20 a.m. only the survivors of
the first advance were on hand to charge: the 1/6th Gurkhas, the Warwicks, the South Lancs, the 1/5th, which had
drifted over to join the others, and a Maori battalion from
New Zealand – all much reduced in strength. Major C.J.L.
Allanson of the 1/6th Gurkhas described the drama of the
British attack:

> Then off we dashed, all hand in hand, most perfect and a
> wonderful sight. At the top we met the Turks; Le Marchant was
> down, a bayonet through the heart. I got one through the leg,
> and then for about what appeared to be ten minutes we fought
> hand to hand, we hit and fisted, and used rifles and pistols as
> clubs and then the Turks turned and fled, and I felt a very proud
> man: the key of the whole peninsula was ours, and our losses
> had not been so very great for such a result. Below I saw the
> strait, motors and wheeled transport on the road leading to
> Achi Baba. As I looked round I saw that we were not going to
> be supported and thought I could help best by going after those
> who had retreated in front of us. We dashed down toward Mai-
> dos but only about two hundred feet when suddenly our Navy
> put six twelve-inch monitor shells into us and all was terrible
> confusion. It was a deplorable disaster; we were obviously
> mistaken for Turks and we had to go back . . . We all flew back
> to the summit and took our old positions just below. I remained
> on the crest with about fifteen men; it was a wonderful sight . . .

The way had been prepared for Baldwin's fresh battalions, but they never arrived. For about fifteen minutes the
Gurkhas occupied the all-important crest, but the Turks
had seen the bombardment by the Royal Navy and the confusion it created. They rallied and counter-attacked. The
position so hardly won after three nights and two days of
bitter fighting passed out of Allied hands and was never
regained.

Although General Hamilton wrote in his diary: 'Next time
we'll get them,' there was no next time. The chance to capture the Sari Bair ridge was gone for ever and with it the

last chance of a successful British conclusion to the campaign in Gallipoli. By the time Baldwin's men arrived in the right position, the reinforced Turks were manning positions on the crest in unassailable strength.

Although the foothold on Hill Q no longer had any significance, the troops remained on its slopes through 10 August, clinging precariously to their fraction of hillside. As no combatant British officers were left in the 1/6th, the remnants were commanded by Subadar-Major Gambirsing Pun. He was an able soldier, but he spoke no English and all communications to and from higher headquarters had to be translated by the battalion's medical officer. At last a withdrawal was ordered. The fiasco had cost the British, Australian, New Zealand and Gurkha troops 12,000 casualties.

The heat, stench, filth and flies of summer were replaced in time by winter, which brought fierce winds, freezing rains and flooded trenches. On 26 November 1915 a wild southwesterly gale veered to the north and turned into a blizzard. For three days the storm raged over the Gallipoli peninsula and no boat could reach the beaches; all supplies of food and ammunition were cut off. Two hundred men drowned in the trenches; more died of exposure and many froze to death. Fifty Gurkhas lost one or both feet from frostbite. In all, the Allies lost ten per cent of their strength.

Captain Watson Smith, who commanded B Company, 1/6th Gurkhas, spoke feelingly of the horrors of this terrible time:

> The 29th was the first time since the 26th evening that I was able to get off the men's boots, and the state of their feet appalled me. In nearly every case they had lumps of ice between their toes; their feet were white as far as the ankle and insensible to touch.
>
> Throughout all this time I never heard a single complaint. The men were cheerful and ready to laugh at a joke. No praise could be too high for them.
>
> To give one instance, my field orderly, Hastabir Pun, had accompanied me everywhere during the three days; always he was at my heels, and never had been anything but cheerful and

keen. Yet on the 30th, when I made him show me his feet, to my horror I found them black with gangrene from neglected frostbite. He had never said a word to me and never would have. His case is not an exceptional one, but merely a typical example of the courage these Gurkhas displayed.

The 2/10th had 477 cases of frostbite; ten men died, others were invalided out of the service, some were maimed for life. When the blizzard ended, the battalion was reduced to slightly more than a hundred men. When the 2/10th left Egypt to come to Gallipoli in May 1915, it had carried thirteen British officers, seventeen Gurkha officers, 734 other ranks and fifty-three followers. When the battalion left the peninsula to lick its wounds on Murdos some six months later, it numbered one British officer and seventy-nine Gurkha other ranks out of the original battalion. In the twenty-one months since this battalion had left India, it had suffered casualties of more than double its original strength. Of the forty-two British officers, fifty-two Gurkha officers and 2,310 other ranks who had served in the battalion, 1,450 became casualties.

Although reinforcements arrived for the forces on the peninsula, there was little hope of success; the campaign was really over. Kitchener paid a personal visit and then ordered an evacuation. Ian Hamilton was relieved of his command and replaced by General Sir Charles Monro, who then became responsible for the delicate and dangerous task of disengaging from the enemy, who in places was only a hundred yards away. This feat was, in contrast with the rest of the campaign, brilliantly handled.

It appealed to the Gurkhas that they were permitted – ordered, even – to destroy all government property which could not be carried away, and they went about it with great glee. The very last unit to leave Gallipoli was C Company of the 2/5th Gurkhas on the night of 19–20 November 1915. With boots wrapped in pieces of blanket to muffle the noise, they faded back to the beaches and stole away in the navy's boats. The only casualty in the entire withdrawal of tens of thousands of men was a naik from the 1/6th Gur-

khas who became lost, wandered into the Turkish lines and
was captured. So ended this disastrous campaign.

General Hamilton had his secretary write to the colonel
of the 6th Gurkha Rifles: 'It is Sir Ian Hamilton's most
cherished conviction that had he been given more Gurkhas
in the Dardanelles then he would never have been held up
by the Turks.'

CHAPTER
10

World War I: Suez and Mesopotamia

The Indian Corps reached France with despatch, passing through the Suez Canal. The shortest way to France for the Australian and New Zealander Army Corps was also through that narrow waterway, and it was vulnerable. Had the Turks been more energetic when they entered the war on the side of the Central Powers, they might well have choked off Britain's route to its eastern dominions and possessions, but Djemal Pasha, commanding the Turkish army in the Sinai, was sluggish and scornful of the hastily raised A.N.Z.A.C. and the troops of the Indian Army. When the Sirhind Brigade of the Lahore Division, originally destined for France, was held back to guard Suez, Turkey's fine opportunity vanished.

It was a great disappointment to the officers and men of the Sirhind Brigade that they were left behind at Suez. 'Everyone feared that the war would be over in a few months. It was hard to watch the ships carrying our more fortunate comrades of our own Division, and then of the Meerut Division and the Indian Cavalry Corps, passing through the Canal daily.' So wrote one officer, and doubtless these were widely shared sentiments. J.N. Mackay of the 1/7th, who remained in India for the first three years of the war, wrote: 'It was galling to be left behind when others went whose claim to go was certainly no stronger than ours.'

Suez was not France, but it was here that the 1/6th, 2/7th and 2/10th, among others, received their baptism of fire. For the 1/6th it was the first time it had come under fire since 1891. The first major attack by the Turks was near the Great Bitter Lake. It was beaten back by a mixed force of Indian Army troops with help from the guns of Allied men-of-war. There were smaller battles at Quantara and El Kabri, in both of which the Turks were soundly trounced.

In February 1915 a raid was launched on an Arab village on the Gulf of Suez where Arabs friendly to the Turks had been mischievous. Gurkhas were carried by night in HMS *Minerva* to within nine miles of their objective. The water was choppy and the Gurkhas were seasick, but the landing was made without mishap and the village successfully attacked at daybreak. By noon the fight was over: about sixty Arabs were dead and a hundred more were prisoners. One rifleman from the 2/6th was killed in the fight.

In France, men by the tens of thousands were quickly shovelled into hastily dug graves with little ceremony, but this lone Gurkha rifleman, the first of his regiment to fall in battle (for the 7th Gurkha Rifles was the junior Gurkha regiment), was buried with full military honours; the Royal Marines provided a firing party and all His Majesty's ships in the area lowered their flags to half-mast. Generals have been interred with less pomp. A comment in the regimental history says: 'It is improbable that any Gurkha rifleman has ever been, or will ever be again, attended to his grave with so much honour.' Unfortunately, no one thought to record his name.

By World War I the reputation of the Gurkha sentry for literal and faithful obedience to his orders was well established. No wise man ever questioned a Gurkha's challenge. At Suez a sentry of the 1/6th challenged a British man-of-war proceeding at a stately pace through the canal. When he levelled his rifle at the bridge, the captain halted his vessel and explanations were attempted while the Gurkha, who spoke no English, steadily held his rifle on his target. Not until one of his officers arrived was His Majesty's man-of-war allowed to proceed.

It was the practice to send out camel patrols on the east side of the canal and some of the Gurkhas became reasonably proficient camel-riders. Later in the war, a havildar with sixteen men of the 2/3rd Gurkhas and thirteen men of the 3/3rd Gurkhas served under the famed Lawrence of Arabia when they volunteered for a secret mission on camelback into the Hejaz with Bimbashi (Major) F.G. Peake of the Egyptian Army.

The fate of the world was decided in Europe, but for the Muslims in Asia, Africa and the Middle East, the war in Mesopotamia, where Christian Britain fought Muslim Turkey, created a painful confusion of religious and political values. This became particularly acute when on 14 November 1914 Turkey proclaimed a holy war. For Europeans and Americans, the war in Mesopotamia was a sideshow; for most Asians, Arabs and North Africans, it was the main event.

All ten Gurkha regiments had one or more battalions in Mesopotamia at some time during the war. The fighting took place in a land which had once, long ago, been fertile, but was now barren and inhospitable. There is an Arab saying that when Allah made hell he found it was not bad enough, so he made Iraq – and added flies. British Tommies described it as 'miles and miles of fuck-all'. A transport camp on the banks of the Tigris was named Gomorrah by the troops. In June 1917 the 2/5th Gurkhas recorded a temperature of 128° in the shade.

Operations in this theatre were under the control of the Government of India and their first concern was the protection of the oilfields in the Persian Gulf. As soon as Turkey entered the war on the side of Germany and Austria (29 October 1914), Britain moved into southern Mesopotamia, capturing Basra on 23 November. General Sir John E. Nixon assumed command with orders to control lower Mesopotamia 'and such portions of neighbouring territories as may affect your operations.' It was a broad directive. Under Nixon's command were two infantry divisions and a cavalry brigade.

In April, after beating off two Turkish attacks, Major-

General C.V.F. Townshend, commanding the 9th Indian Division, was ordered to advance up the Tigris. Using a flotilla of boats to help move men and supplies, he captured the Turkish outpost at Qurna on 31 May. To protect Townshend's flank and his lines of communication, Major-General George F. Gorringe was sent up the Euphrates. His passage was not easy.

In the summer heat, made worse by the humidity of the marshes, boats were pulled through swamps and the men fell in scores from heat exhaustion, dysentery and malaria. The 2/7th Gurkhas, part of Gorringe's force, was soon reduced from 800 to 350 men.

In spite of the weakened condition of the troops, Gorringe's force pressed forward, reducing several Turkish outposts. On 24 July, after a hard-fought battle, Nasiriya was captured. At one point in this battle, the Gurkha attack faltered. At the crucial moment young Naik Harkarat Rai of the 2/7th leapt to his feet swinging his naked *kukri* and, calling on his comrades to follow, dashed toward the Turkish trenches. He was followed by his section, all crying 'Ayo Gurkhali!' Thirteen Turks fell under their *kukris*. 'They looked conquerors every inch, ready for anything,' said an officer who saw them after the battle. The anniversary of this battle, 24 July, has become Nasiriya Day in the 7th Gurkhas and is celebrated as their regimental day.

A few days after the capture of Nasiriya, the 2/5th Gurkhas were put aboard steamers and transported to the village of Abu Hussein, where the chief had been recalcitrant. They found the village deserted and they gleefully set about blowing up its three towers and leveling its houses. As the anonymous regimental historian wrote: 'Creating a desert and calling it peace is a pursuit not entirely unacceptable to the Gurkha.'

British officers in Gurkha battalions in Mesopotamia voiced a complaint that was repeated in World War II. When their men were sent away to hospital or on special duties elsewhere, they were often retained long after their recovery was complete or their duties were over. Gurkhas were so handy at making things and they so cheerfully turned their hand to any sort of work assigned to them that units were reluctant to give them up. Gurkha battalions were also fearful of losing good officers who spoke Gurkhali and understood Gurkhas. When they were sent away to attend courses they were often warned before they left to do well, but not too well – in fact, not to be so good that they might be retained as instructors.

Operations in Mesopotamia progressed so steadily that there seemed no reason to bring them to a halt. General Nixon and doubtless others in high places began to think it would be a glorious thing to capture Baghdad. Townshend, with 11,000 men and thirty-eight guns, was given permission to advance to Kut-el-Amara at the confluence of the Tigris and the Shatt-el-Hai rivers, near which a Turkish force of 10,000 men under Nur-ud-Din Pasha was entrenched astride the Tigris. Townshend feinted on the south bank, then crossed the river and drove the Turks from their positions, capturing 1,300 prisoners and all their guns. The Turks then retreated to prepared positions near Ctesiphon and on 6 October 1915 the British entered Kut-el-Amara.

There was some disagreement as to the wisdom of attempting to push on and capture Baghdad. Lord Kitchener, Secretary of State for War in London, opposed it; General Townshend feared that he did not have enough troops and that not enough reinforcements were available. But General Nixon was keen to push on, and so was the Viceroy of India. Permission was granted and in November Townshend was ordered to advance to Ctesiphon. Townshend could muster only 10,000 infantry, 1,000 cavalry and thirty guns, but he also had a squadron of seven aeroplanes. Nur-ud-Din had forty-five guns and 18,000 regulars, plus some Arab auxiliaries.

Ctesiphon was once a great city, but most of its stones had long since been carried off to help build Baghdad. What remains is the historic Arch of Ctesiphon, which is, in fact, all that is left of what must have been a huge fourth-century palace. Near this arch is a slightly elevated piece of land, which during Townshend's unsuccessful attacks

became known as Gurkha Mound. Here some 300 men of
the 2/7th Gurkhas and about 100 men of the 21st Punjab
Regiment withstood the determined assaults of an entire
Turkish division. A Turkish officer could not conceal his
admiration for what he regarded as one of the outstanding
feats of arms in the campaign: 'The 35th Division strove
for hours in front of that brave, determined little force, alone
on the little hill top, and though it lost many men, did not
gain its end. They did not succeed in even drawing near.'
Later he added: 'I must confess to a deep hidden feeling of
appreciation for that brave and self-sacrificing enemy
detachment which, though only 400 strong, for hours
opposed the thousands of riflemen of the 35th Division.'

After several days of fighting and the loss of 4,600 men,
Townshend was forced to withdraw his force into Kut-el-
Amara. The Turks, reinforced, invested the town and the
long siege began; it extended from 3 December 1915 until
29 April 1916. In spite of the shortage of food and the generally insanitary conditions that prevailed, the Gurkhas
were described as "happy and keen and busy as ferrets".

Determined efforts by a relief force of two newly arrived
Indian divisions under Major-General Fenton J. Aylmer,
V.C., were unable to break through the strong Turkish con-
travallation.

Aylmer was succeeded by General Gorringe, who
attempted a surprise attack on the south bank of the Tigris,
but he was repulsed by a Turkish army commanded by
German General Kilmer von der Goltz. All in all, the
unsuccessful relief force suffered 21,000 casualties before
Townsend, his garrison facing starvation, 'shook the
Empire' by surrendering 2,680 British and 10,486 Indian
and Gurkha troops to the tender mercies of the Turk, in
whose hands more than 4,000 died.

Townshend himself was well treated. In fact, he became
so friendly and was so trusted by his captors that later,
when it appeared that Turkey would lose the war, they
released him to be their emissary to England, a task he
undertook with an enthusiasm many considered inappropriate. Townshend appears to have lost interest in his men

and their sufferings as prisoners of war under treatment vastly different from his own.

Shortages of food and medical supplies during the siege had resulted in all the troops being in very poor condition. Many Indians had refused to eat horse meat and so were even weaker and less resistant to disease than others. Gurkhas, on whom religious taboos rested more lightly than on most Hindus, had eaten it without question, as had the British.

When the Kut-el-Amara garrison laid down its arms, British officers were separated from their men. Such actions tend to convert military units into mobs, but in the 2/7th Gurkhas, Colour Havildar Fatehbahadur Limbu, the senior N.C.O., assumed command of the battalion and Colour Havildar Bhotri Khattri took over the duties of adjutant. Standing orders were observed and discipline was maintained. A whistle brought other N.C.O.s forward to receive orders, and section leaders called their rolls and reported as if on peacetime parade. It was said that a word of disapproval was the severest punishment ever required or ever used. After the armistice, when the battalion disembarked in Egypt, it carried itself as smartly as it had in 1914.

Of the British troops, more than half died in captivity or remained untraced. Of the Indian and Gurkha troops, about a third died or disappeared without a trace. Most of the losses occurred shortly after their capture when, in the middle of a Mesopotamian summer, they were forced to make a 500-mile death march across the desert from Samarrah to Aleppo.

The fall of Kut-el-Amara was not the end of the war and did not even end the campaign in Mesopotamia, but there was a lull in the fighting as both sides fell back exhausted. For the troops there was time to relax, time for recreation and time to become bored. Officers and other ranks had to fight ennui, for there were no wireless sets, no travelling troupes of performers, few amusements. 'We argued a lot,' said one officer later. Officers played bridge and poker and in the 1/7th they invented a game certain to engender arguments among the Englishmen. They called it 'London'. On a large sheet of paper one officer would begin a map by drawing and naming two connecting roads and pinpointing one well-known place. Each player added his bit, and as the map grew, so did the arguments, each addition the subject of fierce debate.

It was at this time that many soldiers were introduced to the cinema. The Y.M.C.A. possessed a travelling cinematograph and the Gurkhas had no need for subtitles in order to enjoy Charlie Chaplin, who quickly became their favourite. It was in Mesopotamia that they first heard and enjoyed jazz. They liked to fish in the Tigris, too; not for the sport (Gurkhas never understood hunting and fishing as sports), but for the fish. They were often able to catch quite large fish that had been killed or stunned by explosives upstream. Sometimes, if there seemed little danger of being caught, they used their favourite fishing technique: throwing a grenade into the water and then scooping up the dead or stunned fish that floated to the surface.

When the 2/7th Gurkhas were captured at Kut-el-Amara, a completely new 2/7th was formed and sent to Mesopotamia. Men of this reconstituted battalion were fishing in the Tigris one day when they came upon a large copper cylinder floating in the water. They dragged it out, slung it between poles and carried it into camp, proudly depositing it before the dugout of their company commander, Captain S.S. Whitaker. He saw at once that it was a mine fused to explode if jarred. It was carefully defused by experts and eventually adorned the officers' mess in India.

In December 1916 the British under a new commander, Major-General Frederick S. Maude, resumed an offensive role in Mesopotamia. Until he died of cholera a year later, Maude proved himself an efficient and able general who reorganized the forces under his command and then advanced up both sides of the Tigris with 166,000 men, two thirds of them Indian and Gurkha, including the 1/2nd, 4/4th, 1/7th, 2/9th and 1/10th.

The march to Baghdad was not an easy one and there was hard fighting along the way. In one battle the 1/2nd suffered 100 killed and its total casualties halved its strength. Soon after, on 23 February 1916, the same battalion lost eighty killed and forty-three wounded during a crossing of the Tigris. This crossing of a treacherous river in the face of a determined enemy was a brave feat of arms and Tigris Day is still celebrated yearly in the 7th Gurkhas.

On 9 March 1917, near Baghdad, young Second-Lieutenant A.M.L. Harrison of the 2/4th was leading his men in an attack on an Arab village when one fell with a bullet through his thigh. A comrade stopped to attend him, but Harrison called him away: 'Don't worry about him -- he's the supporting line's job now.'

A few minutes later Harrison 'felt the devil's own bang on the middle of my back, and turned two somersaults'. Then he heard Havildar Narbir Thapa shout cheerily: 'Come on! The sahib's the supporting line's job now!

When the supporting line arrived, a Gurkha stopped to cut away his coat and shirt and hastily applied a field dressing – 'about six inches below the wound'. Harrison told his bumbling good Samaritan to stay, but with a 'No, Sahib, there's a battle ahead', he scampered off, 'as chirpy as a chicken, rolling me into a nullah [ravine] before he departed,' as Harrison said.

On 11 March 1917 the British entered Baghdad, then a city of about 170,000, dirty and unlovely. The Gurkhas were disappointed, regarding it as 'a place not worth fighting for'. Its name held no romantic connotations for them. The entire campaign in Mesopotamia had cost the British the loss of 4,335 officers and 93,244 other ranks; of these, 29,700 were killed. It is hard to justify such heavy casualties in a campaign which would appear to have been unnecessary. Seven months later the Turks capitulated.

The end of the war was not the end of active service for some Gurkha battalions. The 1/10th, for example, did not leave its depot at Maymyo until 14 August 1915, a year after war was declared; it did not return for four and a half years, after having fought Turks, Arabs and Kurds. Fighting was not ended on the North-West Frontier either, and in 1919 Britain engaged in its third war with Afghanistan.

The small wars and revolutions in a world weary of fighting excited little attention in the West; even historians have largely failed to make them known, but men died in them. J.D. Crowdy of the 2/5th left his battalion in November 1914 to become brigade major at Poona. He spent the entire war outside his regiment, mostly in Mesopotamia, and was promoted to the rank of major. After having been away for more than five years he rejoined his battalion at Abbottabad on Christmas Day, 1919. Instead of a warm welcome back and a joyous day of conviviality at the mess, he found that he was the battalion's senior officer and was due to take it to Waziristan the next day. He assumed command and less than three weeks later – on 14 January 1920 – he was killed while gallantly leading a charge against Mahsud tribesmen at the Ahnai Tangi.

The Gurkhas had greatly distinguished themselves in all theatres of the Great War and were now considered a *corps d'élite*, a reputation which ensured that there would be competition among serious officers to join their battalions. From this point on, only those considered the brightest and best would be selected to serve with the Gurkhas.

CHAPTER
11

Officers

When Adrian Hayter, a New Zealander, was about to graduate from the Royal Military Academy, Sandhurst, he was asked to list three choices of regiments he would like to join. He wrote:

1. A Gurkha regiment
2. A Gurkha regiment
3. A Gurkha regiment

But it was not so easy to be accepted into the Brigade of Gurkhas. No Gurkha regiment accepted officers fresh out of Sandhurst until 1950, and since then the Gurkhas have been highly selective. (In 1977 – 78 no cadet was accepted, for it was believed that none came up to the desired standard.) An officer tentatively scheduled for Gurkhas was first posted to a British regiment stationed in India, where he was listed as Unattached List Indian Army (U.L.I.A.). In that year he was expected to learn something about soldiering in India and to study for the elementary examination in Urdu or Hindustani, which he had to pass at the end of the year. Then, if he was fortunate enough to be accepted by a Gurkha battalion after being vetted, he had at once to begin to study Gurkhali, for he had to pass examinations in that language within three years and before he could be given home leave.

There were many reasons why young officers from Britain and the dominions wanted to join Gurkha regiments. Many were the sons and grandsons of former British Gurkha officers and the Brigade of Gurkhas was to a considerable degree a family affair. The first two Sandhurst graduates to go directly to the Brigade of Gurkhas were both sons of former officers of Gurkhas. They were posted to the 1/6th. When Robert Bristow wanted to become a soldier, his father, an old soldier who retired as a major after World War I, advised him to join a British regiment, not an Indian Army regiment, for he prophesied (correctly) that India would be independent before he had finished his career. When he insisted on joining the Indian Army, his father advised him to try to join a Gurkha regiment, as Gurkhas were 'the nearest approach to British soldiers'. In spite of the strong competition, Bristow was accepted into the 9th Gurkhas and was posted to its second battalion. He was particularly delighted as he was a keen polo player: then, as now, the 9th had a reputation as a polo-playing regiment.

All the officers in Gurkha regiments held the King's (or Queen's) commission. They were all British or Dominion (Commonwealth) officers (although in World War II there were a small number of Americans). The only Indian officers with Gurkhas were a few doctors of the Indian Medical Service who were attached to Gurkha battalions. Indian officers were told that this was because Britain's treaty with Nepal demanded that all officers be British. They were surprised and bitter in 1948 when they discovered that this was not, in fact, true.

In the nineteenth century the commanders-in-chief in India jealously guarded their patronage of appointments to Gurkhas and both Lord Roberts and Lord Kitchener made all such appointments personally. For a long time it was an unwritten law that officers assigned to Gurkhas should not be tall. Kitchener, himself an exceptionally tall man, laid down that the maximum height was to be five feet nine inches. His successor, O'Moore Creagh, annulled the order.

In the post-war years of the 1920s and 1930s it was the battalion commander who made the selection from among the many who wished to serve with Gurkhas. In the 2/4th it was the custom to invite the most likely candidate to spend ten days' leave with the battalion. The junior subaltern took him in hand and saw that he appeared at all military, sporting and social occasions, and (according to John Masters, who was vetted by the battalion in 1935) there was a deliberate effort to get the aspirant drunk. All observed him, but it was the opinion of the subalterns, who would be living and working closest with the new officer, whose opinions carried the greatest weight with the commandant.

In most battalions junior subalterns were expected to remain silent in the mess for the first few months and if they entertained any opinions they were encouraged to keep them to themselves. In the mess of the 5th Gurkhas at Abbottabad one day a particularly lively discussion so engrossed the junior subaltern present that he was about to forget himself and inject a word. His hawk-eyed battalion commander, noting the eager look of a young man about to speak, effectively extinguished him with, 'Now then, no more of your stories, Mr Brown.'

The life of a young officer in India in peacetime was active and gentlemanly. There were servants; he dined off fine china and drank from crystal. It was easy to believe that one had reached a loftier financial plane than was generally reflected in government pay cheques. It was easy to fall into debt and not unusual for officers to find themselves in this sad situation. Probably few fell as miserably into debt as did Lieutenant Adrian Hayter of the 2/2nd Gurkhas in the inter-war years, but his story illustrates how such matters were handled.

Hayter, while away from his battalion taking a course in physical training at Kasauli (a hill station 7,000 feet up in the Himalayas), fell in love, or perhaps almost fell in love, with a beautiful Frenchwoman, the wife of a civilian friend. She moved in a dashing social circle, which Hayter joined. There were champagne parties and dances – and soon a debt of Rs. 3,000. Young Hayter saw no way in which he could make up such a sum on his salary of Rs. 350 a month. However, he gulped hard and, as he was required to do, reported his indebtedness and its extent to his battalion commander.

Hayter was required to bring a complete list of all his debts to his colonel, who arranged for them to be paid off immediately out of the regimental polo fund. He was cautioned to sign no more chits and told to bring his pay to the adjutant every month. Each month the adjutant paid his mess bill (allowing him Rs. 20 for wine); he was allotted enough cash to pay his servants and given Rs. 30 for incidental expenses; the rest went towards repaying the regimental polo fund. In other words, he was required to continue to live as a gentleman, but could spend no money that was not absolutely necessary to maintain his station in life. The colonel reckoned it would take about five years for young Hayter to repay his debt to the regiment.

Before an officer could be of much use to his unit, he had to learn the language. His acceptance by his men, and their trust, could only be earned after he learned to speak to them and to understand what they said. The Gurkha officers gave what help they could to a new British officer, but the working language of the regiments was, until the 1970s, what in the army was called Gurkhali, and the sooner a new officer mastered it the better. During World War II competence in Gurkhali was made a condition for holding active rank, and some emergency commissioned officers (serving only for the duration of the war plus one year) were deprived of their rank when they failed to pass a competency test. One such officer, in civil life a senior executive of one of the world's largest chain stores, was stunned to learn that he had lost his rank by his failure in the language examination.

Gurkhali (known outside the army as Nepali, Nepalese or Parbatiya) is one among many related dialects known generically as *khas kura;* it is derived from Sanskrit and related to Hindustani, Hindi and Urdu. It has a full, comprehensive vocabulary and is the *lingua franca* of Nepal, but prior to World War II many recruits could not speak it and spoke only their own tribal tongue. (Some of these tribal languages are spoken by fewer than a thousand people, and it is not uncommon for the speech of adjoining villages to be mutually unintelligible.) The tribal languages are spoken but never written. Gurkhali, however, is both a spoken and a written language and uses either Roman or Deva Nagari characters.

Patrick Davis, a former officer of Gurkhas, noted an unforeseen consequence of the requirement that British officers learn the language of their men. Although there are cultured forms of Gurkhali, the language the officers learned was no different from that of hill peasants. The accents, inflexions and vocabulary of the officers did not, as in British regiments, carry overtones of a higher social class. It was the rough and ready, simple, sometimes coarse speech of soldiers. Any variations were caused by mistakes in usage and were readily corrected by the Gurkha ranks.

It is said (by the Ministry of Defence) that Gurkhali is easily learned. It has frequently been noted that Englishmen who could never master a European language learn it easily. John Morris, a former officer in the 2/3rd Gurkhas and later controller of the B.B.C.'s Third Programme, claimed that he was always at the bottom of his class in French and German, but he learned to speak Gurkhali fluently within a year.

Of course there was a natural tendency to mix common English military terms with Gurkhali. Thus Gurkha Captain Bhaktabahadur Rai said of an operation in Malaya in 1949: 'Pakka training ko demonstration jasto thyo.' ('It was just a training demonstration.') And a paratrooper captain was heard to congratulate his men with 'Ramro jump!' ('Good jump!'). Bits and pieces of Hindustani and other tongues also wandered in. In the Nepalese Army a naik was called an *amaldar* and in Gurkha battalions of the Indian Army a naik was sometimes referred to as an *amaldar*.

The routine of a company officer in the inter-war years was not arduous. His day began with early morning tea at about 6 a.m. This was followed by physical training in which all junior officers were encouraged to participate, then drill or musketry before breakfast, which was usually at 8.30 or 9 a.m. Breakfasts in Gurkha regiments were legendary and were considered one of the two major meals of the day. Some regiments ate them in silence. Major Duncan Forbes remembers with a shudder one breakfast that included fried rice at 9.15 a.m. in the mess of the 1/2nd Gurkhas in Singapore in 1960. Among the substantial dishes served nearly every day in every Gurkha battalion was that great Indian dish, mulligatawny soup, sometimes followed by kippers or kedgeree, bacon and eggs, toast and, naturally, marmalade. The traditional Gurkha breakfast, and the mulligatawny soup in particular, was reputed to be a wondrous restorer for those with hangovers.

After breakfast the company commanders held orderly room, where they listened to complaints and requests and dealt with minor breaches of discipline. At about 11.30 a.m. the battalion commander held court and he and the adjutant were busy while the other officers wrote reports or studied. By the time the colonel's work was finished, the other officers were usually free for the day and they changed clothes to play tennis, squash, football or other games. In the late afternoon the servants scurried to prepare baths and lay out clean mess dress, polished boots and starched white shirts. Mess was more of a ritual than a meal. So much was this a part of the way of life that when World War II, began, some reserve officers who had spent their careers in this kind of atmosphere reported for duty bringing with them formal clothes, white flannels and cricket gear.

An officer's life in the British Army, probably more than in any other army in the world, was a life of sport and games of every description: polo, tennis, football, basketball, cricket, fishing, hunting, shooting, mountain climbing, racing, sailing, golf, swimming and, where there was nothing else to do, walking. What officers in other units did, British officers with the Gurkhas always seem to have done more often and more energetically. Among the attractions of life

The officers' mess of 4th Gurkha Rifles, *c.* 1938. Sketch by G.G. Borrowman (*National Army Museum*)

in the 5th Gurkhas were the invitations to the Wali of Swat's annual duck and chikor shoots, 'where a day's bag sometimes ran into four figures'. Battalion messes were lined with the heads of animals shot, and replete with the trophies, shields and bowls won in competitions ranging from the Nepal Cup (soccer) to the Muree Brewery Tournament (polo).

Nothing, it seems, could daunt the British Gurkha officers' athleticism. Captain F.F. Babcock, D.S.O., was sitting at dinner in the Khanki Valley during the Tirah Campaign when a sniper's large-bore bullet shattered his left elbow; his arm had to be amputated near the shoulder. Loss of an arm was no reason to give up a military career or abandon an enthusiasm for games. He continued to be a formidable

opponent at tennis and it was said that at racquets he could
'hold his own against the best players to be found in Northern India'. He lived to command his battalion, the 2/6th, in
the Chitral Campaign and he served in Mesopotamia until
he was invalided out. He was twice mentioned in despatches and retired as an honorary brigadier-general in
1919.

Gurkhas and their British officers have accompanied
every British Himalayan expedition by land since 1892
when Martin Conway, with the backing of the Royal Geographical Society, set off to survey the passes of the Kara-
koram, the great glaciers and their tributaries, and to collect
biological, botanical and geological data. With him went
Lieutenant the Honourable C.G. Bruce and four Gurkhas of
the 1/5th. In 1895 two riflemen of the 5th Gurkhas were
killed with Albert Mummery, political economist and
mountain climber, on the north face of Nanga Parbat.

C.G. Bruce was a large man (his men in the 5th Gurkhas
called him *Bhalu*, the bear) and an enthusiastic climber.
He commanded the 1/6th in World War I and rose to become
a brigadier-general. In 1924 he organized an Everest expedition that attracted worldwide attention when he attained
an altitude of 27,000 feet, then a record. With him were his
cousin, Captain J. Geoffrey Bruce of the 1/6th, his Gurkha
orderly and three young Gurkha N.C.O.s from the 6th. Captain Bruce and Naik Tejbir Bura were presented with
Olympic gold medals by the president of France.

There were Gurkhas on Hugh Rutledge's expedition of
1933, which had three N.C.O.s from the 1/3rd; John Morris
of the 3rd Gurkhas was part of the 1936 expedition; and
the successful British Everest expedition of 1953, of which
Major Charles Wylie of the 1/10th was organizing secretary, had two corporals of the 2/6th as 'escorts to porters'.
It was usually easy for officers to obtain permission to take
part in these expeditions and generous leave was given.

In addition to local leave for hunting or exploring, every
officer received two months' 'privilege leave' per year and
at the end of three years a six-month 'long leave'. Not all of
this generous leave was taken. If the battalion was short-

handed, officers would sometimes elect to stay and help out. Commanding officers and adjutants could rarely afford to take their full share of leave, for it was these two, with the aid of the Gurkha officers, who made the unit function and were responsible for its efficiency.

The qualities considered most-desirable in officers of Gurkhas can be inferred from their comments about each other. Lieutenant-Colonel J.K. Jones, D.S.O., of the 2/6th and later the 1/1st, was lauded as 'an ideal regimental officer, cheerful, debonair and a pattern of smartness'. Of Major K.M. ('Dod') Govan, killed at Gallipoli in July 1915, it was said that he was 'a fine soldier. Always fit and hard, he never spared himself . . . Essentially an outdoor man, he was a good rider and could hold his own with a shotgun in any company.' And of Lieutenant G.W. Thomas of the 3/3rd, his regimental history records: 'He went to his death heroically and steadfastly, without any fuss.' Never mentioned in any list of admirable or desirable qualities were knowledge of tactics, compassionate understanding of other ranks, or interest in the arts and sciences.

In spite of the increasingly elite character of the Brigade of Gurkhas and the custom of taking in sons and grandsons of former Brigade officers by preference, regiments were not completely xenophobic – at least not in wartime – and men from Commonwealth countries, and even a few Americans, became officers. All quickly subscribed to the prevailing notion that officers in Gurkha battalions were markedly superior to all others and that Gurkha troops were unquestionably the best. At the War College and other institutions of higher education within the defence structure, there was a tendency to propose as the solution to a complex military problem the employment of a battalion or two of Gurkhas. Tim Carew, a former Gurkha officer, confessed to some difficulty in being objective. Hearing a British Gurkha officer discuss his profession was something like hearing a priest discuss his vocation. All would have agreed with Colonel B.R. Mullaly of the 10th Princess Mary's Own Gurkha Rifles that 'to serve with a Gurkha soldier under the British Crown was, and is, a rare privilege which nobody who has shared it can ever forget'

After World War II officers serving with Gurkhas received about £30 a month extra as Gurkha Service Money, for it was felt that career opportunities in the Gurkha regiments were not as bright as were those in the regular service. Yet many officers who served with Gurkhas rose to become generals and at least four in this century – Birdwood, Harding, Slim, and Templer – became field-marshals. At one point in World War II British Gurkha officers seemed to predominate on the Burma front. When William Slim was a corps commander, both of his divisions were commanded by men who, like Slim, had served in the 1/6th.*

Retirement often came too early for these people, British and Gurkha, who had led active physical lives. John Masters wrote a moving description of the day he relinquished command of the 3/4th: the bagpipes playing, the men lining the dusty path out of camp, the havildars, jemadars and subadars putting garlands round his neck and pressing his hand in theirs.

Many retired British officers found other occupations, some of them interesting. Masters became a successful novelist. When Lieutenant-Colonel James Owen Marion Roberts left the 2nd Gurkhas he moved to Katmandu and in the 1960s ran a service for trekkers, supplying camping equipment, servants and porters (his slogan: 'Pack a suitcase and take off for Mount Everest'). Charles Bruce was invalided out of the service, but four years later he led a famous Everest expedition. He became governor of a girls' school, and was employed by the Brewers Association to advise brewers on how to improve the amenities of the public houses. In the last few months of his life General Bruce's memory would sometimes fail him. At such times he would burst out with, 'Well, anyway I've had a damned good life', sentiments which many former British Gurkha officers would echo.

---

* Major-General Bruce Scott commanded the 1st Burma Division and Major-General D.T. ('Punch') Cowan commanded the 17th Indian Division.

CHAPTER

12

Relationships

There were fewer British officers in a Gurkha battalio
than in a British infantry battalion, for Gurkha offi
cers –jemadars, subadars and the subadar-major – di
much of the work that King's (or Queen's) commissioned
officers performed in other regiments. Officers and thei
men were foreigners in every land in which they served.
British officers felt themselves set apart even from their
fellow officers in the Indian Army. Perhaps, as John Morris
of the 1/2nd explained, they knew 'true contentment only
when surrounded by people of an alien culture', but even
so, they needed each other and they took great care in their
selection of junior officers for they would be living together
intimately, often without other companionship. Their home,
their refuge, the place where they could be themselves by
themselves, speak their own language and abide by their
own customs, was the officers' mess. Morris spoke of it as
'a sort of holy place'. It could also be a place where a man
unhappy with his wife could escape from his marital difficulties and responsibilities.

This home around which an officer's life revolved was
also his unit's attic and museum. Its walls were hung with
spears, rifles, daggers, shields, animals' heads (some badly
moth-eaten), prints and pictures of former commanding
officers. The mess of the 2/3rd at Lansdowne took pride in

two large brass Buddhas, their features blurred from daily polishing, which had been brought back from Younghusband's expedition to Tibet. In the mess of the 2nd Gurkhas there was, and still is, a black polished table top from the house of Hindu Rao, an ornately carved mantelpiece presented to the regiment by the Maharajah of Nepal in 1904, a state umbrella from Manipur, and stone carvings from the Swat Valley. Among the souvenirs of the 4th Gurkhas at Bakloh were three Afghan helmets, seven iron shells from the Second Afghan War of 1878–80, a Chinese gun, a bayonet with a bullet mark on its socket, an elephant tusk presented by Lord Woiseley, an iron cannon presented by the Mektar of Chitral, a stone from the Great Wall of China, a German howitzer, nine German *pickelhaube* helmets from World War I, seven Turkish shells from Gallipoli and three Mahsud copper pots.

All British regiments are proud of their silver, which includes trophies, cups, statuettes and official gifts. The 4th Gurkhas displayed a silver bugle, a silver bell and a hunting knife presented to Subadar-Major Ballea by Edward VII when, as Prince of Wales, he visited India. Officers sometimes gave a piece when they retired or were promoted. In 1884 the silver of the 4th was stolen; it was never recovered. Only a silver claret jug escaped, having been left in the mess by mistake and not put away in the storeroom.

Perhaps the most curious piece of silver found in any Gurkha regiment is the Queen's Truncheon of the 2nd Gurkhas. It was presented to them in 1863 by Queen Victoria when it was decided that it was inappropriate for the regiment to carry colours (rifle regiments do not carry colours), and it has become their sacred icon. Recruits are attested while touching it. Before January 1948 it was carried by a jemadar for whom special provision was made in the Indian Army establishment. When the regiment was transferred to the British Army, this provision was continued by the War Office and a Gurkha officer (still called the 'Truncheon Jemadar') has the Truncheon as his special charge today. George VI, after reading an account of its origin and history, gave his personal approval for the continuation of the ritual that has grown up around it.

On the two regimental days – the anniversary of the assault on the Kashmir Gate at Delhi on 14 September 1857 and the crossing of the Tigris at Shumran on 23 February 1917 – the Truncheon (always capitalized in regimental correspondence) is positioned outside the quarter-guard. All who pass salute it. It was carried in the procession for the coronation of Queen Elizabeth II and afterward a representative party of the regiment took the Truncheon to Buckingham Palace for the Queen's inspection. To commemorate this event two silver collars were affixed to the staff, inscribed: 'The Queen's Truncheon was carried in procession at Her Majesty's Coronation, 2nd June, 1953. Inscribed by order of Her Majesty Queen Elizabeth II.'

The furnishings of a mess, once put in place, were almost never rearranged. John Morris told how he and other young officers in the 3rd Gurkhas once tried to change things:

> The chairs in the ante-room, where we foregathered before dinner, were ranged uncomfortably against the walls. Some of the younger among us, whose spirit had not yet been completely broken, thought it would be a good idea to rearrange them and so make the room look less formal. The Colonel, when he saw what we had done, was horrified; not, as he was careful to tell us, because the new arrangement was less pleasing, but because he felt that our predecessors (most of them long since dead) would not have approved. We replaced the furniture in its original position, and having learnt our lesson refrained from suggesting further innovations. During the whole of my service in Lansdowne nothing was ever changed in the mess; it remained, a museum piece, exactly as it had been when it was built and furnished thirty years before.

The old order held even after the British left India. When Major M.G.D. Henderson of the 7th Gurkhas visited the mess of the 9th Gurkhas in December 1966 – the 9th had then been part of India's army for nearly twenty years – he found that 'its furnishings and fittings appear to have changed little from a 1909 photograph which I discovered in one of the Mess Albums'.

The cooks and wine waiters were usually not from the

recruited Gurkha tribes. In the 6th they were generally
Tamangs or Sherpas, 'cheerful rascals with few morals',
according to H.R.K. Gibbs, a former officer with that regiment. The customs of the mess were the usual customs of
British officers' messes, though every regiment had its own
peculiarities. In the 4th Gurkhas, for example, only field
officers added 'God bless her!' after the royal toast; captains and ranks below merely toasted and drank.

Until 1938 full mess kit* was worn in every officers' mess
throughout the Indian Army, but this rule was relaxed in
an army order which permitted the wearing of dinner jackets except on guest nights. Thereafter on ordinary nights
officers appeared for dinner in 'penguin order – white shirt,
black bow tie, dinner jacket and trousers, with a cummerbund of rifle green. In fact, a civilian uniform. On guest
night mess kit was still worn, and Gurkha pipers with
plaids, following the traditions of Highland regiments,
entered the mess after dinner and marched round the table
playing, after which the pipe-major took his tot of whisky
with the colonel and called 'Slanthe!' It is still the custom.

Bagpipes in a confined space produce a fearful amount
of noise. It was the opinion of Patrick Davis, a former officer with the Gurkhas during World War II, that only Scots-
men and old men whose ears had been bludgeoned by
'tradition or shell-fire' could enjoy the sound in an officers'
mess. Many a guest would have agreed.

In the closeness of life in the mess, men learned each other's values, weaknesses and strengths. It was a purely mas-
culine society and most of the officers were bachelors. In
the 1st Gurkhas there was a 'bachelor's *kukri*' for the oldest
unmarried man in the regiment. Without a private income,
an officer could not afford to marry before he was thirty
and at least a captain. In some battalions marriage was
frowned upon, for it was thought to create divided loyalties

---

* Mess kit or mess dress is the formal uniform for dining in the officers'
mess. While somewhat different for each regiment, all mess kits generally conform to a similar design: a short jacket that cannot be but-
toned, a waistcoat of a regimental pattern or a cummerbund, and full
dress trousers with a stripe down the side. Sometimes the waistcoat
extends to the neck; if not, then a black bow tie is worn.

and to distract an officer from his duties and his care for his men.

Life was made smooth for the young officer by a full complement of servants, some soldiers and some civilians. Chief of these was the officer's Gurkha orderly. Every officer, however young or lowly in rank, had at least one. Domestic arrangements were entirely under the orderly's control. Lieutenant Patrick Davis, twenty years old, only once dug his own foxhole in Burma during World War II; this task was normally performed for him by Rifleman No. 85002 Nandalal Thapa, whose sole occupation was to care for the needs of the young officer. Davis accepted this: 'Of course my job was not to burrow. At the end of a day in the field or march, a bath would be ready, cot up, mosquito net slung and a clean change of clothes laid out. After dawn stand-to the orderly would be ready with a hot cup of tea and hot water for shaving.' Newly retired British Gurkha officers, unaccustomed to doing anything for themselves, often found life complicated.

An orderly belonged to his officer almost as if he were a slave. But the officer also belonged to his orderly, as the wife of every newly married officer discovered. The orderly knew all the little habits and quirks of his officer better than did the bride; he knew the other servants and ordered them about; he and his officer spoke in a language which excluded the bride; however much English the orderly might have learned or whatever Gurkhali the bride might have acquired, the orderly made it a point never to understand her. Any new wife who tried to order household affairs in her own way or who tried to alter domestic arrangements had a task which was nearly impossible.

Adrian Hayter spoke of how closely the officers lived to their men, how they were together with them on parade, on manoeuvres, in sport and, in wartime, in battle. He spoke too, as have all officers who served with Gurkhas, of the tremendous affection the officers developed for their men. Hayter spoke of the 'spiritual companionship' which evolved.

Sometimes all this affection, companionship and physi-

cal proximity combined with an absence of female company to produce sexual relationships. One officer applied
for leave, paid all his debts, handed over his military
responsibilities to another officer in an orderly manner, then
shot himself. He had been twice warned against making
homosexual advances to his men. If there was a third time,
his colonel had warned, he would face a court martial.
There had been a third time.

The extent of homosexuality in Gurkha regiments was
unknown; only one officer ever spoke openly on the subject.
John Morris had an interesting career – several, actually.
When he was young he had wanted to be a pianist, but at
the age of twenty he was a subaltern in the 2/3rd Gurkhas
and he made the Brigade of Gurkhas his first career, serving in Palestine and France in World War I, and later on
the North-West Frontier. After he retired from the army, he
was a university lecturer in Japan until World War II put
an end to that career. He then became controller of the
B.B.C.'s Third Programme. He did not, as a youth, understand his own sexual nature, and was still a virgin when he
joined the Brigade of Gurkhas. Although many muscular
puritans became good regimental officers, Morris came to
believe that their uneasy sublimation was achieved at the
expense of their mental stability and that some became
sadistic as a result of their unnatural continence.

As his first orderly, Morris chose a handsome teenaged
boy in his company whose easy 'animal way of moving'
attracted him, but it was another, somewhat more daring,
orderly who, sensing the sexual proclivity of his officer,
slipped into Morris's bed one night after liquor had loos-
ened inhibitions and Morris at last succumbed.

One afternoon in 1921 on the North-West Frontier, Morris, now a captain in the 2/3rd, was in charge of a picket
that was carelessly withdrawn. The waiting Pathans
pounced and attacked the party. Morris stood frozen until
his orderly and a signaller pulled him away. Only about
thirty out of one hundred escaped. The wounded were left
on the ground. When they reached the safety of the battalion lines, Morris pleaded with his colonel to go to the res-

cue of the helpless wounded, for all knew the sickening fate
in store for them, but the colonel, knowing that the Pathans
were waiting for just such an opportunity, refused.

One captured man of Morris's picket escaped – or was
allowed to escape. He came staggering naked down the
dusty road. A knife had roughly punctured his belly. His
penis had been hacked off and his testicles had been slashed
and now hung in ribbons of bloody sinew. As men rushed
towards him, he collapsed in the dust.

That night Morris lay in his bivouac trying to digest the
horror of the day, tortured by thoughts of what he ought to
have done, his nerves, conscience and imagination a tangle. Then Umar Sing, his orderly, came quietly into his tent,
shrugged off his clothes and snuggled down beside him. In
silence he began gently to massage his officer's taut, aching
body. Morris, who had been trying desperately to control
his wildly fluttering emotions, burst into tears.

Sex complicated the lives of many young Englishmen in
India. In the early nineteenth century many officers 'kept a
delightful Gurkhali mistress in the *bibi-khana* [lady's
house] behind the bungalow', but the arrival of British
women put a stop to this practice, and John Morris wrote:
'It is not, I think, an exaggeration to say that the decline of
human relations between Indians and British dates from
the arrival of the Englishwoman in the country.'

From the post-Mutiny period, when India was again safe
for British women, there were no more Gurkha mistresses,
but there were temptations. John Masters as a young lieutenant in charge of the regimental depot while his battalion was on the North-West Frontier was inspecting the
married quarters when he encountered a beautiful, sexually hungry young Nepalese woman who turned his stomach to water as she looked longingly at him. He felt that he
had only to say the word and she would be in his bed, but
after wrestling with his conscience for several nights he
remained unsullied – and saved his career.

During the hot weather, young British women, eager to
meet eligible bachelors, flocked to the hill stations from
Calcutta, from the plains, and even from England. They

were welcomed but warily watched. Collectively they were
unkindly known as 'The Fishing Fleet'. Young officers were
not all immune. Many fell in love and had to be dissuaded
by their families and commanding officers from making
what were generally regarded as premature marriages.

Even married officers struggled with sexual frustrations;
the frontiers were usually unsettled and separation of husband and wife was frequent. When a battalion was sent to
the North-West Frontier, often for years, officers' wives were
not permitted to travel past Bannu, and even here only a
limited number could be accommodated in the starkly
named Abandoned Wives Hostel. Even so, in the years
before World War II there appears to have been remarkably little scandal, and, in spite of the usual number of
unfortunate matings, very few divorces. John Morris
believed that the prevailing puritanical standards contributed 'in some indefinable way' to his battalion's efficiency.

British officers felt very close to their men, but their real
link was through the Gurkha officers. These were men of at
least fifteen years' experience, selected from the cream of
the havildars, whose intelligence, experience and accumu-
lated wisdom more than made up for their lack of formal
education. Some of them inspired awe in Gurkha ranks and
British officers alike. When Adrian Hayter joined the 2/2nd
Gurkhas in the 1930s, his company's second-in-command
was a wrinkled-faced subadar about twice his age. He had
rows of medals for service and gallantry in World War I
and on the North-West Frontier, and he was always
impeccably turned out to Sandhurst standard. The men
regarded him as a father and Hayter said: 'I secretly wor-
shipped him. If only I could be so that such as he accepted
me.'

Gurkha officers had no equivalent outside the Indian
Army or, later, the Brigade of Gurkhas in the British Army
(see Appendix A). In the old Indian Army of the British raj
these officers were known as Viceroy's Commissioned Officers (V.C.O.s). They ranked just below the most junior officer holding the sovereign's commission and they could not

command British troops. Today in the Indian Army they are called Junior Commissioned Officers (J.C.O.s), and in the British Army, Queen's Gurkha Officers (Q.G.O.s). In the British Army, exceptional Q.G.O.s are made honorary lieutenants or captains when close to retirement. Today, too, a very small number graduate from the Royal Military Academy, Sandhurst (R.M.A.S.) or from the Indian Military Academy, and receive regular commissions. There are still few of these and almost all have been line boys, sons of Gurkha officers or senior N.C.O.s who have been educated in India, Malaya or Hong Kong. (There is a British-run high school in Hong Kong.) The scheme to admit Gurkhas to military institutions of higher learning began in the 1950s. Henry Stanhope, writing in 1979, said: 'British officers . . . argue that R.M.A.S. Gurkhas tend always to be inferior to their British counterparts and are likely to remain second-class citizens in the officers' mess.' Just two years later, on 6 August 1981, Officer Cadet Bijay Kumar Rawat gave the lie to the inferiority of Gurkhas as officers, and perhaps gave the death blow to the prejudice against line boys, when on 6 August 1981 he was presented with the Sword of Honour as the best overall officer cadet at Sandhurst.

Bijay was the son and grandson of Gurkha soldiers. He was born in Malaya where his father was Gurkha Major of the Gurkha Signals Regiment. He was educated in Singapore and at St George's Military School in Hong Kong. Although the headquarters of the Brigade of Gurkhas was in Hong Kong he had to go to Dharan, Nepal, to enlist, which he did in January 1973 as soon as he turned seventeen, for, as he later said, 'My sole intention in life was to be a soldier.' He served in the 1/2nd Gurkhas for seven years in Hong Kong, Brunei, Australia, Belize and England, reaching the rank of corporal before being accepted, on his third application, at Sandhurst. Although receiving the Queen's commission as a second lieutenant on graduation, he was at once promoted to lieutenant, with antedated seniority to 11 August 1979 for his service in the ranks, and posted to the newly formed 2/7th in Hong Kong.

Bijay Kumar Rawat was easily accepted in the officers'

mess and was certainly not considered an inferior. Like his
British comrades in arms, he now has older Gurkha Commissioned Officers under him and his future success as a
company officer will depend upon them. Gurkha officers
have always handled most of the petty problems that plague
officers in other armies, and often enough they nip incipi-
ent problems in the bud. Morale and discipline have largely
been in their hands. They have their own mess, which used
to be called a club, where they eat their hot, spicy food and
unleavened bread. On special occasions British officers are
invited to their mess, and British officers usually recipro-
cate at Christmas, although in the 8th Gurkhas this was a
monthly social event.

Gurkha officers were skilful in tactfully correcting the
faults of junior British officers without destroying their
confidence; young officers learned to respect their knowledge and experience without feeling any loss of authority.
In May 1944 in Burma, Lieutenant-Colonel J.G. Marindin
of the 3/5th had a battalion filled with inexperienced officers. Faced with a delicate and dangerous operation not
unlike the withdrawal of pickets on the North-West Frontier, he instructed them: 'When in doubt, listen to your
Gurkha officers.' Writing about it later, Marindin said, 'I
and the Gurkha officers felt we had had a good day in the
country. The British officers were, however, a little dazed.'

On 28 October 1817 the rank of subadar-major was created. It was the most senior rank for a 'native' officer of the
Indian Army and only one man in each battalion held it.
The subadar-major (called Gurkha major after 1947) commanded nothing and everything; his duties were vague and
large, permitting him such scope as he desired. He was the
second most influential person in the battalion and,
although in theory below the rank of the most junior second lieutenant, he held the respect of everyone. No mere
lieutenant would consider ordering him about. On the con-
trary, as Patrick Davis pointed out, junior officers 'were
careful not to cross him.'

Colonel B.R. Mullaly described the first subadar-major
of the newly formed second battalion of the 10th Gurkhas

in 1908. His name was Chittahang Limbu and he had been
senior subadar in the 2/4th. He was 'even more thickset
and round-faced than average . . . A strong and determined character, he had an authoritative, indeed a pontif-
ical manner which secured him instant attention and he
had a steely quality which inspired the Gurkha ranks with
a wholesome awe. There was never any doubt who ruled
the battalion and when the Subadar-Major spoke the world
was hushed.'

Unlike British officers the Gurkha officers were not usually transferred, or limited in the number of years they
could command. Chittahang Limbu remained subadar-
major of the 2/10th for eleven years. He won the Indian
Order of Merit at Gallipoli and was twice mentioned in dis-
patches. In 1911, with Lance-Naik Nandaram Limbu as his
orderly, he went to London for the coronation of King
George V and received the Coronation Medal from his
hands. He retired as an honorary captain and Sirdar
Bahadur.

Subadar-majors did not hesitate to reprimand British
officers as well as Gurkha ranks. Colonel Mullaly knew of
one occasion when a young officer, exasperated, swore in
an unbecoming manner at a soldier on parade, using a particularly offensive Gurkhali expletive. After the parade, the
subadar-major took the officer aside and said: 'Sahib, you
are young. You might say that to a *desi* [Indian], but you
will never say it to one of our men while I am subadar-
major.'

Although it was literally true that the subadar-major had
no fixed duties, other than to advise the commandant on
strictly Gurkha matters, there was one function which, by
custom, was and is solely his responsibility to direct: the
events connected with *Dashera*.

CHAPTER
13

Festivals

Gurkhas are nominally Hindu but as in much of Nepal there is a considerable mixture of Buddhism and animism, a mixture varying from tribe to tribe and among different clans. In Nepal itself one can see statues of Buddha in Hindu temples, and in the cloisters of Swayambhunath, the most sacred Buddhist shrine in the country, there is a Hindu temple dedicated to Devi Sitla (whose assistance is necessary for recovery from smallpox). In general, people are more Hindu in the south; there are more lamaistic Buddhists in the north, and more are dedicated to the cult of the mountain gods and the deities of rocks and streams in the higher reaches of Nepal. However, it is interesting that in all the long series of bloody wars and feuds that mark Nepal's history, there has never been a religious war. The people in general are tolerant of the religious beliefs of others, and Gurkha soldiers understand – and their children enjoy – the pagan customs involving Father Christmas.

There was one religious celebration that was a favourite of all soldiers, Gurkha and British. Although Hindu it was never much observed in India, but was always a grand affair in the army and may properly be deemed a soldier's festival. Called *Dashera* (there are at least seven different spellings) or sometimes the *Durga-puja*, it commemorated the heroic battle in which the goddess Durga conquered Ma-hishashura, a demon with the head of a buffalo. British officers liked to think that the festival celebrated the triumph of good over evil, right over wrong, but Durga is hardly an attractive heroine. She is a hideous goddess of destruction in the Hindu pantheon, a terrifying and fierce form of the wife of the god Siva and also a manifestation of Kali. Death, bloodshed and devastation are associated with the goddess's name. *Dashera* was a ten-day festival, but only three or four of these days were kept as real holidays in the army. The first day, perhaps the most significant from a religious standpoint, was the day the regiment's resident priest (known as the *pandit* or *bahun*) began his prayers and sowed maize, barley and rice in a darkened room.

On the seventh day the *bahun* led a procession of soldiers out of the barracks carrying an effigy of Durga, called the *devi*. (In the 1/10th Gurkhas the *devi* was for many years made by a certain family in Chittagong, regardless of where the battalion happened to be stationed. It was modelled in coloured clay and was destroyed after *Dashera*. In 1939, however, a permanent *devi* was cast in bronze.) Guards with rifles loaded with blanks escorted the procession as it moved slowly across the countryside, the men chanting prayers and picking flowers; from time to time the guards fired their rifles to call the god's attention to their devotion.

On the day called *Kalratri* the battalion was given over to singing, dancing and drinking, and it was in the organization of this entertainment that the subadar-major was judged, for all the arrangements were in his charge. Most of the men took part in the singing and dancing, but young men dressed as women (called *marunis*) were usually the stars. Tables were laid out and the subadar-major and the other Gurkha officers entertained the British officers and usually some dignitaries as their guests. There was always curried rice and plenty of rum to wash it down. If there were women guests they were usually taken away before midnight, when a black goat was sacrificed. The celebrations lasted through the night and the British officers, at least the younger ones, were persuaded to learn the dances

and join the *marunis* on the stage. Sometimes there were
skits in which the foibles, mannerisms and quirks of Gurkha
and British officers were mocked; wives, too, were often
mimicked. Calypso-type songs with improvised words could
go on for hours. (In recent years, folk songs and folk customs have given way to Indian popular songs from the
music-hall.)

Young officers attending their first *Dashera* were sometimes taken aback by the *marunis*. When Lieutenant N.F.
Fisher of the Queen's Gurkha Signals saw his first *marunis*
in 1978, he was a bit disturbed. They were, he found, 'totally
different from the pantomime figures I had imagined. In
fact, perhaps just a little too much like the genuine article!'
In 1967, during *Kalratri* in the 3/3rd Gurkhas, the Indian
officers noticed that their shy wives would not dance with
the young male dancers who were dressed as men (*por-
senges*), but cheerfully put their arms around the *marunis*,
'much to the amusement and embarrassment of the
"girls" '. So realistic was the make-up of *marunis* that many
guests found it hard to believe that Gurkha battalions did
not have girls on the strength.

There was never any difficulty in obtaining *marunis*, for
the young men took pride in appearing as women. Considerable time was spent in selecting the most promising and
training them in what was regarded as a social accomplishment. Although older Gurkha officers frequently managed to grow moustaches, young Gurkhas have little or no
facial hair; what they have they pluck out with tweezers
which they sometimes carry on a string round the neck.

The sexual implications of soldiers dressing as female
dancers and performing before their colleagues and officers has never been explored. The *marunis* obviously excited
the concupiscence of some and among the Gurkha ranks
there were ribald comments, but sex, whether heterosex-
ual or homosexual, seems to have been more casually
accepted among them. Unlike their officers, they usually
married young; the separations caused by their military
service led them to take sex where they could find it. Their
sexually constrained officers often considered them 'wom-
anizers'.

British officers looked forward to *Dashera*, and particularly to *Kalratri*, as eagerly as did their men. It was considered particularly dastardly of the communist terrorists in Malaya in 1951, when most of the Gurkha battalions in the British Army were on operations there, to murder Sir Henry Gurney, the British High Commissioner in Malaya, just before the festival, thus putting British officers in mourning.

The climax of *Dashera* came on *Mar*, the day following *Kalratri*, when a male buffalo was beheaded – if one could be found that was not too expensive and if the battalion was not stationed in a country such as the United Kingdom, where animals may be sacrificed for the sake of the stomach but not for the gods. The buffalo, duly anointed, was led or dragged into a square of soldiers, wives and guests and its head tied securely to a post (*maula*) decorated with flowers. The man selected to do the deed was armed with a razor-sharp, outsized *kukri* called a *khanra*. It was a tense moment when he raised his knife. The luck of the battalion depended on his skill. If he severed the head with one blow and, ideally, if the buffalo sank to its knees and did not fall on its side, good luck in the coming year was assured and he was rewarded by the cheers of all ranks, a purse of money from the commandant, and a white scarf of honour tied around his head by the subadar-major. If he failed, he ran for shelter, pursued by a shouting mob of irate soldiers, throwing blood at him. But the executioner rarely failed. When the beast's body sank to the ground, leaving the bloody head still tied to the *maula*, a *feu de joie* was fired. A number of sacrifices of smaller male animals were then made while the buffalo's carcass was dragged about for all to see. The stench of blood permeated the area.

Dashera was regarded as a test of an officer's drinking stamina, a time when the Gurkha officers did their best to make the British officers drunk. Patrick Davis described the beginning of a *Dashera* in October 1945 when he was a young officer:

I raised my glass to Jemadar Manbahadur and took a brave sip and shuddered. Manbahadur was made in a sterner mould.

He lowered his neat rum by an inch and stroked his moustache sensuously.

Dashera could be expensive. Gurkhas – and the British officers as well – liked their dancers, particularly the *marunis*, to be beautifully dressed. There was also the expense of the stage and its settings; buffaloes and other sacrificial animals were costly; and, of course, rum had to be bought, in spite of the extra allowance of army rum issued. Officers contributed money and sometimes wealthy planters and businessmen in the area contributed as well.

On the festival's last day the *bahun* placed the holy mark of the *tika* on each man's forehead and *Dashera* ended. On the following day all returned to duty, and it was customary (as it was in British infantry regiments the day after Christmas) to sweat out all the dissipation on a long route march.

The regimental *bahun* was an important member of the battalion and had many of the duties performed by chaplains in British battalions, though he did not eat with the officers, had no rank and wore no uniform. He was responsible for advising the commandant on religious matters affecting the men and their families and, before the day of army schools, for educating the children. He could be an influence for good in Gurkha units and he usually was. The *bahun* himself identified closely with his regiment, often more than British officers realized. In 1948 the officers of the 7th Gurkhas gave a party to honour their *pandit*, who had served the regiment since 1907. The subadar-major read an address to which the *bahun* replied; speaking without notes, he mentioned the name of every commanding officer and every subadar-major who had served in either battalion in the previous fifty years.

British officers learned not to scoff at the *bahun*'s advice: he was too often right. At the Regimental Centre at Abbottabad in December 1943 Gaje Ghale of the 2/5th was honoured by his battalion for having won the Victoria Cross. He had not yet been presented with his medal, however, and it was thought that this would be done at a special parade in the Assam–Burma area. A date was fixed and preparations made for his departure, but at this point there was a strong protest from the regimental *pandit*, who stoutly declared that the proposed departure date was inauspicious. In deference to his wishes the departure was set back by a day. The *bahun*'s reputation was enhanced among all ranks when, a few hours after Gaje Ghale was originally scheduled to leave, a signal arrived changing both the date and place of the ceremony.

Dashera usually takes place some time in October but the exact day of the month varies, for the year follows the Samvat calendar which dates from 57 B.C. and starts in February. In 1967 Dashera fell at the end of the monsoons and the 3/3rd Gurkhas (by then part of the Republic of India's army) were afraid there would be rain on the all-important *Kalratri*. The *pandit* was consulted – and also the nearby air force meteorological station. The air force predicted a thunderstorm that evening; *panditji* consulted his scriptures and predicted a fair evening. The scriptures were right. It was a splendid evening.

It was almost impossible for officers of the Indian Army not to become involved in the religious customs and beliefs of their men. In 1913 Subadar-Major Santbir Gurung, a distinguished officer, spent a year in England as one of the King's Orderly Officers. When he returned he went through a brief *pani patiya* ceremony in his battalion to regain caste after crossing the 'black water'. Soon after, he retired and returned home, where he discovered that Nepal's religious authorities had taken exception to the skimpy *pani patiya* procedure used in his regiment and that the Nepal Durbar had proclaimed him an outcast. This created a flurry of correspondence. It was finally agreed that the Nepal Durbar would maintain a special *pandit* at Dehra Dun and that the army would maintain special facilities there for the full three-day *pani patiya* rite. The agreement coincided with the beginning of World War I and the special *pandit* had much to do for the next few years, for all Gurkhas returning from overseas were sent there. A soldier who entered Nepal without having been ritually purified was liable to arrest and punishment.

Diwali, the festival of illumination and the second most

important religious festival celebrated in Gurkha regiments, takes place about three weeks after *Dashera*. Hundreds of candles are placed in doorways and windows, and unrestrained gambling is the order of the day. When Vishnu killed Marakasur, a hitherto invincible giant, he returned to find his city illuminated in his honour: thus the candles. But *Diwali* was also sacred to Lakshmi, consort of Vishnu and goddess of wealth and prosperity, and it is in her honour that men gamble.

Gurkhas were generally considered born gamblers, and gambling was considered their worst vice. It was forbidden both in Nepal and in the army except for the days of *Diwali*, when the entire population of Nepal and all the Gurkha ranks in the British Army indulged this mad, all-absorbing passion for gambling. *Diwali* was a five-day festival, but the army reduced the festivities to three days.

Holi, the festival in honour of Krishna, is perhaps the most popular Hindu festival in India, but it was not much observed in the Gurkha regiments. Although only officers – and not all of them, perhaps – were Christians, Christmas was always celebrated. Often parties were organized for the Gurkha children, with an officer playing Father Christmas. It was a time to drink more than usual. Of a cricket match held two days after Christmas in Calcutta in 1952 in which the British Gurkha officers lost fifty to eighty-eight, one officer said, 'there is no doubt that if one or two of our batsmen could only have seen the ball we would have done a lot better'.

Traditionally the British officers entertained the Gurkha officers in the mess at Christmas, as the Gurkha officers entertained the British officers at *Dashera*. In 1939 the 1/8th was on the North-West Frontier, but the British officers, dressed in their best tweed jackets and suede shoes, still welcomed the Gurkha officers in their Western civilian uniforms: rifle green regimental blazers, pressed grey flannels, regimental ties and pillbox hats.

In addition to religious holidays each battalion had its own special holiday, called its regimental day, which commemorated a battle or notable feat of arms. If the battalion was newly formed and had not yet fought, it celebrated its 'raising day'. In the 4th Gurkhas, by a curious coincidence, not only the two regular battalions but also its two war-time battalions celebrated their regimental day on the same date, 11 March: each battalion commemorated a different event. In the First Battalion it was called Neuve Chapelle Day for the day in 1915 when it entered that bloody battle; in the Second Battalion it was Baghdad Day for the date the first elements of the battalion entered Baghdad in 1917 after an arduous three-month campaign; in the Third Battalion it was Irrawaddy Day; and in the Fourth Battalion it was Mandalay Day. The 2/8th celebrated Gyantse Day on 6 July; the 1/3rd had Ahmed Khel Day on 19 April; the 2/10th had Gallipoli Day and the 1/9th Malakand Day, and so it goes on.

On regimental days there was a ceremonial parade, usually with a display of the regimental icons, the souvenirs that had become sacred. Sometimes the subadar major would read an account of the event being commemorated. Usually there were sports in the afternoon. Always it was a time when old comrades, the 'old and bold', were welcomed back; some pensioners travelled for days to be with their battalion on its regimental day. In 1924, when the 2/10th celebrated its first Gallipoli Day at Fort Sandeman in Baluchistan, there were no fewer than thirty-eight veterans, eight of them Gurkha officers, who had made the long journey from Nepal to be with their battalion.

CHAPTER
14

Home and
Family

Other types of units, both in the British and the Indian armies, had home bases of a sort, but none had homes in quite the same sense as the Gurkhas. As early as 1856 the men of the Sirmoor Battalion petitioned Lieutenant-Colonel F.R. Evans, their commanding officer, for permission to convert some disused barracks at Dehra Dun into homes for soldiers' families. Evans approved, for he saw the desirability of having the men's wives and children nearby rather than in the distant Nepal highlands. However, the government of India could see no reason why Gurkhas should be treated any differently from other 'native' battalions. The request was refused.

The 2nd Goorkhas (as they became) persisted, and finally on 18 March 1864, Letter No. 692, signed by Lieutenant-Colonel H.W. Norman, Secretary to the Government of India, Military Department, was sent to the Quartermaster-General of India:

I am directed to acquaint you that the Right Honourable Governor-General in Council sanctions the retention of the lines at Dehra by the families of the 2nd Goorkha Regiment during the absence of the corps as His Excellency in Council considers it very desirable – looking to the different circumstances in which recruits from Nepal find themselves as compared with men of other races   that each of the four Gurkha Regiments should have a station peculiarly its own, at which it should usually be stationed; though liable of course to removal anywhere and at any time for active service, or for a tour of regular duties at Peshawar or at any other station, where it might be considered desirable to have a regiment composed of men of that class.

This letter was followed by another in which the commander-in-chief gave permission for these homes to be granted 'in perpetuity'. This became known in the first four regiments as 'The Charter', and it was frequently produced in subsequent years to fight off attempts to abandon or shift the regimental homes.

Thus were established the first Gurkha regimental homes in India: the 1st were at Dharmsala, the 2nd at Dehra Dun, the 3rd at Almora in the Kumaon hills (later, in 1894, the 2/3rd established its home at Lansdowne), and the 4th at Bakloh. The 5th and 6th later made their homes in Abbottabad, the 1/8th at Shillong, the 2/8th at Lansdowne, the 9th near that of the 2nd at Dehra Dun, and the 10th at Maymyo.

Unfortunately, there were never enough quarters for the families of all the married men. Until recent years, government supplied only about a quarter of the living facilities needed. Some men had to wait as long as ten years before their families could join them. Bureaucratic logic justified this by claiming that Gurkhas preferred to keep their families in Nepal because it was cheaper, a demonstrably unjustified charge and a clumsy attempt to shift the blame from a parsimonious government.

Although the families' travel from Nepal was paid by the army, home stations were largely developed by the enterprise of the units themselves and eventually included clubs, institutes, sports facilities and even permanent museums. Around the regimental homes there sprang up communities of Gurkha civilians, some of whom were Gurkhas who had retired and chose to stay near their old regiments instead of returning to Nepal.

The regimental home was also a place where the dead could be buried or commemorated. A fountain once in the lines of the 1/2nd still stands at Dehra Dun, donated by a grieving mother. Its inscription, in English and Gurkhali, records the death of young Captain John Graham Robinson, mortally wounded at Dargai on 20 October 1897. At Abbottabad in 1905 two bath-houses were constructed with Rs. 896 given by the mother of Bugler Chuni Damai of the 5th Gurkhas to perpetuate the memory of her son, killed on the North-West Frontier.

The troops found it good to have a home in India, a familiar place to come back to where a welcome awaited them after arduous campaigns. When the 1/2nd returned to Dehra Dun after the Tirah Campaign, in which they had been engaged thirty-two times in battles with tribesmen and had fought nineteen rearguard actions, it was welcomed not only by the families of the regiment, but by the entire civilian population as well. A considerable sum had been collected from Europeans and Indians for a celebration, and the battalion was treated to a banquet and fireworks; a handsome piece of plate was presented to the officers' mess and a generous donation made to the Widows' Fund.

Regimental homes did not mean an undisturbed family life, even for those fortunate enough to have their wives and children with them. Active service kept men away for months, even years. The 2/5th left its home in Abbottabad in December 1915 and did not return until June 1919. Captain G.A. Maconcky and his company had only one night at home. The morning after arrival the company marched out to take part in the Third Afghan War. Captain Maconcky never returned. He was killed at a place called Ahni Tangi on 14 January 1920.

Families grieved when the men marched away to fight, but grieving was a private affair. Any public expression was so unusual that when the 5th Royal Gurkha Rifles (Frontier Force) moved out at short notice to quell rioting at Peshawar in April 1930, men were startled and a little shaken on hearing a 'high-pitched keening from the married lines as the march began, which, though quickly suppressed, was a weird and unique experience'.

Polygamy (now forbidden) was once permitted and a man could have as many wives as he could afford, but most young Gurkhas could afford only one. Those who had two usually left the oldest wife (*beahita*) in Nepal and took the youngest (*leahita*) to the regiment with them. There was no wedding ceremony when a man took a second wife and the position of the *leahita* was insecure because he could cast her aside at any time. When a man took a *leahita* he usually stopped having sexual intercourse with his *beahita*. However, marriage usually did not put an end to casual sexual encounters.

The soldier who wanted to marry had to obtain the permission of his commanding officer and such permission was routinely refused if the girl was a local Indian. This was at the request of the Nepal Durbar; marriages in western and central Nepal were often arranged by families, and such families did not take kindly to a young man who returned home with a strange wife. First marriages frequently took place at an early age – about sixteen for boys and fourteen for girls – and many of the seventeen-year-old recruits were married men. Sometimes a Magar or Gurung soldier would return home from leave to find that in his absence his parents had arranged a marriage for him. He rarely rebelled, but shrugged and said 'Hunchcha!' – 'So be it!' There was a strong desire to preserve the family structure.

Gurkha men were generally considered to be kind and affectionate husbands, and their wives were by no means subservient to them. Men and women were more companionable, more on an equal footing, than were couples in Islamic or in most other Hindu societies, and men often helped with the cooking, child care and other domestic tasks. Gurkha women were generally regarded as bright and intelligent, possessing the same fine sense of humour and gift of repartee as the men. Like their men, they enjoyed smoking and drinking. They were also said (by men) to be prone to intrigue.

When their men were away the women were naturally lonely and bored. They were alone in a strange land; they usually spoke little Urdu or Hindi. Sometimes, when bach-

elor lines were too close to the married lines of a battalion
on active service, there was trouble. This appears to have
been the case at the end of World War I when all men
returning from active service abroad were sent to Dehra
Dun to regain their caste by the *pani patiya* ceremony, and
some were quartered close to the married lines of a battalion still on active service. Some wives found solace with
lovers from among the soldiers soon to be discharged, and
a few left with them for Nepal. The commandant of the
2/2nd Gurkhas protested to the brigade major of the 17th
Indian Division at 'much interference and annoyance by
men of the stranger battalions'.

Divorce was possible among Gurkhas, but it was uncommon. It was not unusual, however, for a woman simply to
leave her husband and live with another man. In a formal
divorce a wife guilty of adultery had to repay her husband
for his original expense: the cost of the wedding, the presents to the family, and so on. Indeed, recovery of property
taken by the wife was often the primary concern of the
wronged husband.

A rifleman once came to Captain John Morris of the 2/3rd
with a complaint. Standing rigidly at attention he delivered a long speech which began with his childhood in Nepal,
worked its way through his marriage, and culminated with
a summation of his own unblemished character and the
misdeeds of his wife, who had run off with a soldier from
another regiment. What was the sahib going to do about
it? Morris assured him that he would at once write to the
adjutant of the other battalion and demand the return of
the erring wife, but it was obvious from the soldier's stolid
expression and firm stance that Morris had somehow
missed the point. 'It's not my wife I am worried about, the
rifleman explained. 'When she left she went off with my
umbrella and I'd be glad if you could get it back for me.'

The care of families while soldiers were away became,
with the establishment of regimental homes, the responsibility of the battalion, and a depot commander was always
left behind to care for them. Among the civilians who
became attached to units was the regimental midwife, who,

like the *pandit*, often became as much a part of the regimental home as the buildings themselves. When Khemkala,
the midwife of the 1/6th Gurkhas, died in 1967 she had
served the battalion for twenty-six years. Sobhackumari
Chhetri served as a midwife for the 10th Gurkhas for thirty-
four years, from 1938 until 1972. Her son was Gurkha major
of the Gurkha Transport Regiment and her son-in-law was
a Gurkha captain.

Today there are military hospitals and welfare centres
for Gurkhas in Nepal and Hong Kong, but in the years prior
to World War II each battalion took care of its own as best
it could. Gurkha Major Rakansing Rai of the 1/10th, remin-
iscing about his childhood in the married lines at Maymyo,
said:

> Before 1935 family arrangements only existed for the barest
> essentials. There was a room and a kitchen for each family.
> There was no family hospital, family welfare room, W.V.S.
> [Woman's Voluntary Service] lady or *dhai* [nurse]. So if the
> women and children were dying, or babies were being born, it
> all took place in the one room. As there were no *dhai*, the women
> had to get together and help one another. No advice about not
> doing this or not doing that was given by the government.

> In order to make the fires in the cooking place, husband and
> wife had to go out into the forest and cut firewood. The women
> sat at home all day long knitting stockings or scarves. Their
> chief responsibility was cleaning the house, caring for the chil-
> dren and helping their husbands prepare the curry and rice.

Gurkha family life grew increasingly westernized as time
passed, particularly after the Indians threw the British and
all their institutions, civil and military, out of India and
Gurkhas joined the order of battle of the British Army. One
manifestation of Western influence was the formation of
Boy Scout, Girl Scout, Cub Scout and Brownie troops. For
those unfamiliar with Gurkhas, it was perhaps startling to
see charming, giggling Nepalese Brownies in uniform with
representations of the murderous crossed *kukris* as their cap
badge.

When the young men joined the army they were exposed
to a world of new experiences, but to adapt they had only
to do as they were told; the army took care of them. Life
was more uncertain and held more difficulties for the young
brides coming down from the hills of Nepal to be part of
their husbands' lives. How did they feel and how did they
react? We don't know. No Nepalese woman has ever written about her life as an army bride. This is not surprising,
perhaps, but it is curious that no Englishman or Englishwoman ever tried to discover and record the thoughts and
feelings of these young women.

Occasionally the women came, not as young brides to be
with their husbands, but to take part in the sahibs' ceremonies. In World War II Subadar Netrabahadur Thapa of
the 2/5th Royal Gurkha Rifles won the Victoria Cross, but
at the cost of his life. His wife, Namasara Thapini, had never
been more than a few miles from her mountain village when
she was brought down and taken to Nowshera, India, to be
given her husband's medal. The ceremony was held on the
old polo ground on the banks of the Kabul River, a rectan-
gle of green turf surrounded by trees. The troops were
formed up on three sides of a hollow square; on the fourth
side was the saluting base and an enclosure for spectators.
Field-Marshal Viscount Wavell, the Viceroy of India, had
come to present the Victoria Cross to Naik Agansing Rai of
the 2/5th, who had won the medal and survived, and to
Namasara Thapini. The pipes and the band played. The
Viceroy inspected the troops and then presented the medals. Brigadier N. Eustace, D.S.O., formerly of the 6th Gurkhas, stood beside the widow as her escort and translator.
Then the troops marched past, vigorous young men from
the hills such as her husband had commanded, and it was
over.

Agansing Rai was besieged by reporters. What had been
his feelings during the battle? What had been his thoughts?
He shrugged and grinned. 'I'm sorry. I forget,' he said. No
one asked Namasara what she felt as she stood in this alien
place with her dead husband's medal in her hand.

The long trip to and from Nowshera must have been

alarming, perhaps frightening. The grand personages whom she met must have meant little to her. And what did she make of the medal on its dark red ribbon? In pictures taken of her holding it, still in its little box, her face is impassive. The medal itself is neither gold nor silver, but bronze from Russian guns captured at Sevastopol in a war she had never heard of. And what became of her? No one ever thought it worthwhile to climb into the mountains north-west of Katmandu where the Magars live to find out.

CHAPTER
15

Catastrophes

From the moment of his birth a Nepalese hillman was in danger and his entire life was lived amid varying degrees of peril. Disabling and killing diseases and maiming injuries were a normal feature of life. Perhaps the greatest scourge of the mountains was tuberculosis. It is still rampant and an estimated ten per cent of the population suffer from it. Gurkhas seem particularly susceptible to chills and lung diseases. Curiously, X-ray was not used in recruit selection until after World War II, and so tuberculosis found its way into the army. Communicable diseases could, of course, be passed on to officers, and they were. James Morris contracted tuberculosis, probably from his Gurkhas, while on active duty in India in the 1920s and was sent back to England. His mother met him at Victoria Station: 'Its your own fault,' she said, 'going to live among all those dirty people.' Today the army has special tuberculosis hospitals, and some Gurkhas are sent to England for operations or special treatment. It is at least arguable that the army has saved more Nepalese lives than it has sacrificed in its wars.

Leprosy was also common and greatly feared. Lepers were driven away from villages with the greatest cruelty. Gurkhas still contract the disease and in the British Army lepers are sent to special hospitals. Diseases which have almost disappeared elsewhere are still found in Nepal, where before 1955 health services were practically non-existent. Unfortunately the British Army's medical services have never been the best. When the 7th Gurkhas were inoculated for typhoid fever (enteric) in 1909 they were among the first units in the Indian Army to receive injections though the procedure had been known for more than a decade. Both the German and the French Armies were vaccinated against smallpox before World War I, but – incredibly – the British Army did not insist on vaccination even as late as World War II, and in January 1943 Captain H.D.N. ffinch, M.C., an exceptionally excellent and gallant officer in the 1/3rd Gurkhas, died of smallpox at Imphal.

Most units suffered epidemics of malaria. In 1915 the hospitals at Abbottabad were overflowing with malaria patients from the 5th and 6th Gurkhas. The 2/5th had fifty-two deaths. During World War II at Imphal the 1/4th was reduced to only 400 men, and of these only seventy-five were able to enjoy *Dashera*, the rest being laid low by malaria. In Burma in 1943, for every man with wounds there were 120 too sick for duty.

Colonel Nigel Woodyatt wrote that 'when sick, the Gurkha is *very* sick, and in hospital he looks the very picture of woe; but about going there or reporting himself ill, he is very whimsical'. Indeed, the problem was not to ensure that men did not malinger, but that they be made to report themselves ill and so prevented from carrying on to breaking-point. Sickness was often thought to be a visitation of evil spirits, better combated by old medicines and old ways. Sometimes, too, men took a dislike to the doctor or his assistant and refused to report sick.

Medical officers were not integral to a Gurkha battalion and were not required to speak Gurkhali; they were British or Indian officers of the Indian Army Medical Service who were merely attached. Although no Indian was allowed to be a combatant officer in a Gurkha regiment, Indian medical officers were readily accepted and regimental histories and personal memoirs are often full of praise for their work. These doctors must often have felt like foreigners in their own country. In the 2/5th in 1942 Captain R.S. Tata of the Indian Army Medical Service earned the respect and affection of all ranks: he was a 'very large, voluble and cheerful man' who was indefatigable in his work. He took the trouble to learn Gurkhali, but he sometimes stumbled over English idioms – thus 'fast awake' or 'wide asleep' – but he was remembered as 'a tonic in himself'.

Prior to World War I – and, indeed, in some units for some time after the war – Gurkhas preferred to consult *damais* rather than doctors. These were tailors who, like medieval barbers in Europe, were believed to have medical knowledge and served as medical practitioners. Many Gurkhas had 'greater faith in drums beaten at midnight than in modern science'. The stoicism of wounded Gurkhas impressed all who witnessed their sufferings. Often enough their first question on reaching the field dressing station was, 'How soon can I get back?'

Peacetime held its own dangers. Even going home on leave could be hazardous. After 1885 the army gave soldiers proceeding on leave a free pass on the railway, but from the Nepal frontier their way was all on foot up the mountain trails, carrying on their backs the presents they had bought and their personal belongings. It was often a two-week trek from railhead to village. Because the soldier on leave carried new clothes, ornaments and cash, he was sometimes waylaid by dacoits.

And bandits were not the only danger. Gorges were spanned by ramshackle rope bridges; many mountain ledges were so narrow that men had to inch along them; rockfalls and landslides were a constant threat. So too were wild beasts. Ajamlal Rai was returning to Darjeeling from leave when he was set upon and mauled by a leopard, which mangled his left hand. Asked how he escaped, he said simply that he had killed the leopard with his *kukri*. Pressed to explain how he had managed to get his *kukri* unsheathed, he said that he had not drawn it but had hit the beast with his *kukri* in its scabbard and the blow had split the scabbard apart. The rest was easy, he said. In spite of his wounds, he had skinned the leopard and taken the head to

Gurkha officer and villagers in the hills above Pokhara (*J. Allan Cash*)

Village near Naudhanra, north-west of Pokhara (*Major Robin Adshead*)

1824

1827
1ˢᵀ BATTⁿ 8ᵀᴴ GURKHA RIFLES
1824 – 1914

1857

1914
(SYLHET LIGHT INFANTRY)

Officers' uniform of the 1/8th Gurkha Rifles (*National Army Museum*)

Above, left: 3rd Goorkha Rifles, skirmishing, *c.*1890 (*National Army Museum*)

Opposite: An outpost of the British position at Delhi during the Indian Mutiny was called 'Sammy's House' and it was frequently manned by Gurkhas. The picture illustrates an episode that occurred when a mutineer, perhaps a member of a patrol, stuck his head through a window: a Gurkha of the Sirmoor Battalion (later 2nd Goorkhas) grabbed him by the hair and sliced off his head with his *kukri* (*Gurkha Museum*)

Gurkhas clearing the remaining Germans out of the trenches by
hand grenades during First World War (*British Library*)

Opposite: The 2/1st Gurkha Rifles in an operation against the
Mahsuds on the North-West Frontier in 1917 (*Imperial War
Museum*)

Blessing the animals before their sacrifice at a *Dashera* ceremony. The post on the left is the *maula*, to which the buffalo's head will be lashed before being severed by a single stroke of a large *kukri* (*Major Robin Adshead*)

Children watch soldiers of the Gurkha Engineers performing as 'Maruni' dancers in Kluang, Malaya (*Major Robin Adshead*)

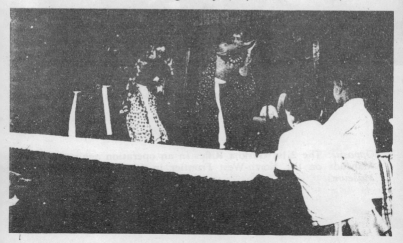

Quinine parade of the 1st Gurkha Rifles (*Gurkha Museum*)

Marking a recruit for the 2nd Gurkha Rifles during a medical inspection at recruiting depot (*Major John Mackinlay*)

Gurkha paratrooper, 1944 (*National Army Museum*)

A platoon of the 2/4th Prince of Wales's Own Gurkha Rifles going through Sogiliano al Rubicone, Italy, October 1944 (*Imperial War Museum*)

On the road to Mandalay, Burma, March 1945 (*Imperial War Museum*)

Opposite: The liberation of Prome, 3 May 1945. The 4/10th Gurkha Rifles march past grotesque *chinthe*, guardians of the temple (*Imperial War Museum*)

Below, left: Training for jungle warfare with three-inch mortars, October 1941 (*Imperial War Museum*)

Men of the 10th Gurkha Rifles after winning the battle for 'Scraggy', on the Palel–Tamu Road, Burma (*Imperial War Museum*)

Above: Lance-Corporal Rambahadur Limbu shows the Victoria Cross which he has just received from Queen Elizabeth II at Buckingham Palace. Field-Marshal William Slim holds his son's hand. Rambahadur won his medal on 21 November 1965 for action against Indonesians in Borneo. Rambahadur, now a Lieutenant (QCO), is the only serving VC in the British Army (*Keystone Press Agency*)

Above, right: Gurkha line boys, so called because they were born and bred in the lines of a regiment in India (*Royal Geographical Society*)

Opposite: A Gurkha husband and wife coming down to a depot to claim their son's estate. He had been killed in action. Such people often walked as far as 150 miles over mountain trails to reach the depot (*Royal Geographical Society*)

Dining room of the officers' mess of the 2nd Goorkhas, Dehra Dun, 1873 (*National Army Museum*)

The officers' mess of the 6th Queen Elizabeth's Own Gurkha Rifles, Hong Kong (*Major John Mackinlay*)

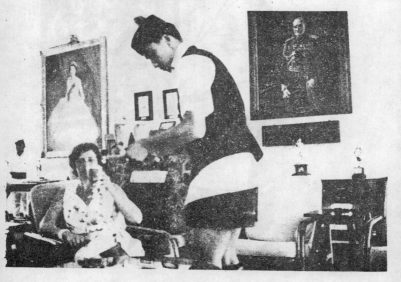

Officers paying pensions to ex-servicemen (*Major John Mackinlay*)

Evening meal of *bhat* (rice) being served to men of the 6th Queen Elizabeth's Own Gurkha Rifles in Kluang, Malaya (*Major Robin Adshead*)

1/7th Duke of Edinburgh's Own Gurkha Rifles serving in Hong Kong, 1969 (*Courtesy 1/7th Gurkha Regiment*)

Gurkhas cleaning weapons in Belize, where they help the new nation (formerly British Honduras) to protect itself from Guatemala (*Lt. Tim Morris*)

1/7th Duke of Edinburgh's Own Gurkha Rifles saw action and suffered casualties as part of 5 Brigade in the Falklands. One Gurkha lost his life clearing Argentine mines after the fighting (*Lt. D.G. Macaulay*)

Gurkhas of the 1/7th Duke of Edinburgh's Own Gurkha Rifles applying camouflage before setting out on a patrol in the Falklands (*Press Association*)

The 2/2nd King Edward's Own Gurkha Rifles mount guard outside Buckingham Palace in November 1975 displaying the Queen's Truncheon granted to the regiment in 1863 in place of colours for service at the Siege of Delhi in 1857 (*Keystone Press Agency*)

When the *QE II* docked in New York on her maiden voyage after refitting following the Falklands War, passengers were greeted by some who succumbed to the popular Argentine myth of Gurkha ferocity (*Ken Kelley*)

the office of the administrative district for the reward of Rs. 5.

Among the natural disasters – torrential monsoon rains that washed away terraced fields and bridges, droughts that killed crops on which life depended, and avalanches that swept away entire villages – Nepal seemed to experience a severe earthquake in every generation. Added to these were those the Gurkhas encountered abroad. Gurkhas took part in rescue and relief operations when a violent earthquake struck the North-East Frontier near Shillong on 12 June 1897. More disastrous for the Gurkhas was the severe earthquake that hit Dharmsala in the Kangra hills, home of the 1st Gurkhas, that began on 4 April 1905. Less than a month before, on 12 March, the 2/8th had arrived at Dharmsala – in time to suffer the loss of 139 dead and fifty-four severely injured; many wives and children were also killed or injured; the band was wiped out and all its instruments lost.

It was said that the buildings did not sway or topple over, but just 'sat down'. Many of the barracks were levelled. The shocks went on intermittently for a fortnight, fraying nerves, for no one knew when the next would come or how severe it would be. The first shock proved to be the worst, however. On that first day, Major C.H. Clay, commanding the 2/8th, managed to extricate himself from his ruined bungalow and, mounting his horse, rode to the quarter-guard. The guard-room was in ruins but the guard turned out as the major rode up and stood stiffly at attention. The N.C.O. in charge reported: 'There has been an earthquake. What are your orders?'

One rifleman, 'not considered ordinarily a good soldier', jumped from an upper-storey window of his barracks at the first shock and injured himself. Nevertheless, he carried a message to Major H. St Anthony Wake, who was in another camp below the barracks, returned with a party of men and worked all that day and the next. When the urgent work was done, he said, 'I think I'll go to hospital.' He had a broken pelvis.

Lord Kitchener started a relief fund for injured men and

their families to which other Gurkha regiments, the King's Royal Rifle Corps and the Rifle Brigade gave generously. So many had behaved bravely during the crisis that it was difficult to determine who should be rewarded, so one man from each company was selected to receive the Order of St John of Jerusalam. It was the first time these medals had been awarded to troops other than British.

In January 1934 there occurred in eastern Nepal and northern Bihar what has been called the 'most devastating earthquake of modern time'. Certainly it was the most devastating in the modern history of Nepal. In a disastrous series of tremors, mountains heaved and monstrous landslides carried away trees, rocks and the laboriously terraced fields. Entire villages, with their men, women and children as well as their cattle, barns and houses, were swept down mountainsides, often into rivers that ran in newly formed channels. Even temples, pagodas and houses in Katmandu were damaged. An estimated 7,000 buildings were destroyed. The Gurkha regiments, ignorant of the fate of families and farms, were in great anxiety, particularly in the 7th and 10th regiments, which recruited Limbus, Rais and Sunwars from eastern Nepal. In the absence of reliable news, rumours were rife; each man feared the worst. British officers did their best to get away furlough parties and to send relief.

The 10th Gurkhas sent a reconnaissance party to Nepal to assess the damage to serving soldiers' and pensioners' homes and the needs of their families, and to make lists of those items most urgently required. Gurkha officers and men immediately began to raise money and offer what help they could. It was a splendid effort, but it was not enough. Colonel J.N. Mackay, formerly of the 7th Gurkhas, wrote of this tragedy that 'the loss suffered by most of them was irreparable and many years afterwards men were still serving to save enough to rebuild homes that they ought long since to have been enjoying in retirement'.

Such tragedies do not just happen. The mountain gods were angry and the Nepalese were sure they knew why. The person responsible was Dame Fanny Lucy Houston

(1857–1936), a philanthropist and eccentric who had caused more than one upheaval in London society. Dame Fanny, the delightfully gay, charming and perhaps talented daughter of a warehouseman, was an actress before the first of her three marriages, each of which increased her wealth enormously. Her freewheeling spending, together with her militant stand on women's rights before such attitudes were popular, brought her fame – or, as some unkindly said, notoriety. In any case, in 1933 Dame Fanny financed an expedition led by the Marquess of Clydesdale which flew an aeroplane over Mount Everest for the first time, an event which generated considerable excitement in the Western world and considerable apprehension in Nepal. A few months later the gods of the Himalayan peaks expressed their rage over the violation of their sacred lands. The earthquake was so clearly a punishment for the sacrilege that the Maharajah issued an edict forbidding any aircraft from flying over any part of Nepal, an edict which remained in force until World War II.

More than a thousand miles away in Quetta, there had been frequent earth tremors. In 1931 these were sufficiently violent to tumble some of the least stable buildings and terrify the populace: 'A fearful moan rose from the bazaar like the cry of a thousand jackals.' But this was only a prologue. At three minutes past three on the morning of 31 May 1935 a devastating earthquake shrugged its way down the valley. It lasted less than a minute, but it left 20,000 dead. The 8th Gurkhas were at Quetta, but fortunately their lines were outside the main area of destruction and they lost only a few riflemen who had been on guard duty in the town. However, of the 656 soldiers and airmen at the nearby Royal Air Force station, 148 were killed and 200 injured. The men of the 8th Gurkhas worked heroically for days, digging out people trapped beneath rubble and clearing away debris. Two Gurkhas were awarded the Order of the British Empire for Gallantry (a medal instituted in 1922 and commonly known as the Empire Gallantry Medal).

CHAPTER
16

World War II: Preparing for Battle

War came slowly to India. Why this was so remains one of the mysteries of World War II. While Whitehall whined about a shortage of men, one of the world's greatest sources of military manpower was at hand, ready to be enrolled. Yet it remained untapped for many months. In the first two years of the war the Indian Army was called on to provide a mere two divisions for service outside India. Not until nearly a year after the war began on 3 September 1939 was any real expansion of the Indian Army begun. Eventually Britain's Indian Army numbered two million men, the largest all-volunteer army in the history of the world, but it was certainly slow off the mark.

It seems particularly bizarre that no consideration was given to expanding the Brigade of Gurkhas. As soon as war became a threat to Britain – at the time of the Munich crisis, in fact – the Maharajah of Nepal offered his aid. It was refused. When war was actually declared, the Maharajah again put forward his offer, which was, incomprehensibly, once more refused. It was not until 1940 that the British minister to Nepal was ordered to request permission to raise ten additional battalions and permission for Gurkhas to serve overseas. The Maharajah, in granting the request, reminded the British minister of the 'perpetual friendship' clause in the Treaty of Segauli and asked rather sharply why the British had waited so long before making their request. Why indeed? Later there were further requests and eventually some fifty battalions were raised. Furthermore, the Maharajah sent two brigades of the Royal Nepalese Army, commanded by two of his sons, to India, freeing Indian troops for overseas service.

Within the Gurkha regiments there appears to have been no intimation that war would be declared, and the outbreak of war found them with large numbers of men on leave. Someone suggested that aircraft might be used to drop recall notices over the mountains and valleys of the Gurungs, Magars, Rais, Limbus and Sunwars, forgetting that flights over Nepal were forbidden after Dame Fanny's aerial expedition. However, word slowly penetrated the Himalayas and men trickled back to their units. In practice, the outbreak of war had little effect on the way of life in the Gurkha battalions: men carried on much as before. Officers donned mess kit or evening clothes, swords and medals were worn, the bands played retreat and foxtrots for dances at the mess. There was no general mobilization, no sense of urgency; the reserves, inadequate as they were, remained uncalled, while regimental training centres, provided for in the war plans, remained merely plans. Recruiting went on at the normal speed and there were the usual discharges and transfers.

Life in Landi Kotal on the North-West Frontier went on at its usual pace, except that the commanding officer of the 2/5th thought there might be a bit more mechanization in this war; so the battalion bought an old Austin 7 and a cadre of one Gurkha officer and six N.C.O.s was turned loose with it on the polo field. Amid shouts of alarm and the crashing of gears considerable progress was made, and it was thought remarkable that both the Austin and the fledgling drivers survived.

When at last in July 1940 orders were received for the regiments to raise third battalions, fresh young Gurkhas came down from their hills and walked with their casual friendliness into the regimental depots to learn the art of soldiering and to practise that art in war. Their manners, as Duncan Forbes has described them, were like those of 'guests coming to a party'.

They were to see a good deal of war, these casual, light-hearted young men from the Himalayan hills, for they served in what General Sir Claude Auchinleck euphemistically described as 'high wastage roles' in places where young men in uniform were quickly killed in quantity. The 1st and 2nd Gurkhas served in Burma; the 2nd Gurkhas raised five battalions, some of which also served in Persia, Italy, Greece, Malaya, and in the Western Desert of North Africa. The 3rd, 4th and 5th regiments had battalions in Burma and Italy, the 5th Royal Gurkha Rifles winning four of the ten Victoria Crosses awarded to Gurkhas in the war. The 1/7th fought in Burma; the 2/7th was captured in North Africa and, as in World War I, was reconstituted, the new one serving in Syria, Lebanon, Palestine and at Monte Cassino in Italy. The 8th and 9th had battalions in Italy and Burma. The 9th also had men serving with Wingate's Chindits. The 10th expanded to four battalions, which served in Syria, Iraq, Italy, Palestine and Burma. Two new regiments, numbered the 25th and 26th, were raised for the duration of the war and disbanded soon after. They were composed of ex-soldiers and pensioners who had re-enlisted but could not stand the strain of modern war. They were used mostly for garrison duties. Many of the third and fourth battalions were not raised until 1941.

There was a Gurkha Reserve, but not much thought had been given to it. Men joined voluntarily or were urged to do so as a convenient alternative to discharge. It never mustered more than 2,000, of whom perhaps half were effective. As for officers, the war was more than a year old before the Brigade of Gurkhas received its first consignment of 'Emergency Commissioned Officers' (E.C.O.s).

None of the battalions had all the weapons and equipment it was supposed to have. The strength of each battalion varied somewhat, but perhaps that of the 2/5th when it left Secunderabad for war might be taken as typical. There were fourteen British officers: a lieutenant-colonel, a major, five captains, two lieutenants and five second lieutenants,

Rifleman of 4th Gurkha Rifles in bush shirt and beret, 1945. Sketch
by G.G. Borrowman (*National Army Museum*)

plus an Indian Army Medical Service lieutenant who was attached. There were twenty-three Gurkha officers, including one subadar-major, six subadars and sixteen jemadars, 762 other ranks and sixty-two followers.

The 2/4th and the 2/7th discovered where some of their missing weapons were when they arrived in Iraq in April 1941, particularly the 3-inch mortars that had been authorized but never received. They had been told that none were available, an excuse they were inclined to believe until they were shelled by these selfsame mortars in the hands of Iraqi soldiers. They had gone to arm Britain's 'allies', and unfortunately for the Gurkhas, friendly nations can quickly become enemies in the Middle East.

War with Germany and Italy, and later with Japan, did not mean that old quarrels with the Pathans were ended. Traditional antagonists, such as the Faqir of Ipi, the Wazirs and the Masuds, had no desire for peace in their time, so battalions were still needed on the North-West Frontier. Robert Bristow recorded his 'bitter disappointment' when his unit was sent to the Frontier, for this 'greatly reduced the chances of going to the war'.

Before World War II each battalion had its own training company and each battalion commander was responsible for the training of his own recruits. The adjutant was usually charged with this responsibility and one Gurkha officer and eight N.C.O.s were assigned to the company. The recruits usually came in once a year in a single intake. The malaria season in the low-lying Terai in the summer and the snows in the hills in winter dictated that recruits would arrive at their battalions in October and November. They then completed their training in September of the following year.

Although plans had been made before the war to establish regimental centres for recruit training and to handle many of the administrative chores of the service battalions, not until 15 November 1940 were orders issued for their formation. To prepare Gurkha riflemen for modern warfare required more than the usual physical training, drill, fieldcraft and knowledge of minor tactics necessary to deal with Pathans on the North-West Frontier and mobs in India's city streets. There was a need for mechanics, truck drivers, men who could use 2-inch and 3-inch mortars, anti-tank guns, new machine guns, and all the other equipment of a modern army. Even if these weapons and this equipment were not readily available to all battalions on active service, men had to be ready to use them when and if they did arrive. The length of the training period varied throughout the war but was never less than five months, and when this reduced period was adopted the hours of training each day were increased.

Before the war young men of twenty were considered too old. During the war men over twenty were accepted, but it was believed that it took too long to train and toughen them. Old notions died hard in the regular battalions and far too much attention was devoted to drill, turnout, ceremonial parades and military frills. The war had been in progress for some time before it was decided that the pipers, drummers and bandsmen should be drawn from the ranks of the old stagers and under-age recruits.

The Emergency Service Officers in particular found it difficult to see the relationship between military punctil-iousness and the campaigns being fought. Yet the emphasis was still on smart turnout, military discipline and all the military courtesies. The aim of the regimental centre was 'to create a happy and well-run regimental home from which those who set out would do so as well equipped and prepared as it was possible to make them, and in which those who returned would find comfort and a warm welcome'. Young Patrick Davis, an E.C.O. who joined the regimental centre at Dehra Dun, found the atmosphere 'unwelcoming'. He was greatly embarrassed as well by the mandatory day he spent with a recruit squad trying to learn the peculiarities of regimental drill without being able to speak Gurkhali. Language was, of course, a major hurdle for E.C.O.s assigned to Gurkha units during the war.

As the war went on, the regimental centres took on responsibility for more and more functions: the welfare of the families left behind; after-care for the wounded, sick and returned prisoners of war (a conscious effort was made to keep the maimed and ill away from the fresh recruits); maintenance of the records of every man; and all battalion accounts and funds; the forwarding of monthly allowances; and language classes for E.C.O.s. When the government ran out of *kukris* the regimental centre of the 8th set up its own *kukri* factory and, using scrap metal and imported artisans, produced quite satisfactory weapons. At the end of the war the regimental centres shifted their roles and became demobilization, pre-release or rehabilitation centres for the sick and wounded.

A shortage of instructors remained a problem throughout the war. Sometimes the centres were fortunate in receiving E.C.O.s who had been teachers in civilian life; these were retained and not sent on to active service battalions. The regimental centre of the 3rd Gurkhas had the good fortune to be assigned Second Lieutenant H.R. Hornsby, a distinguished headmaster of an English public school. He soon became the major in charge of training. Many bright officers on their way to war never got past the regimental centres. Keeping these officers out of the shooting war was described as 'perhaps the most heart-breaking task of the commandant'.

Obtaining clerical help for the regimental centres, literate men who spoke Gurkhali, was also a major problem. Clerk recruiters were sent to the Gurkha colonies which had grown up around the regimental homes. However, local units vigorously opposed this siphoning-off of educated Gurkhas and some had actually to be smuggled out under the seats of railway carriages. Not all these clerks were good – some were quite bad – but all tried hard. In some centres clerks' clubs were established to mark their superior status.

In spite of all difficulties, the regimental centres did their job as well as could be expected, considering that so little thought had been given to them before the war. The centres provided the basic training and physical fitness programmes that were needed, but it was difficult for them also to provide tactical training, particularly training in jungle warfare. In 1943 special formations were brought into being: training battalions where men could acquire a bit more military polish. These training battalions also acted as holding organizations, human warehouses from which battalions on active service could requisition men as they were needed. Soldiers normally remained for two or three months in a training battalion. There were five of these battalions, each serving two regiments and forming its title from the two regimental numbers. Thus, the men from the 1st and 4th Gurkhas joined the 14th Gurkha Rifles Training Battalion, men from the 2nd and 9th joined the 29th, those from the 3rd and 8th the 38th, from the 5th and 6th the 56th and from the 7th and 10th the 710th. The concept of these Siamese-twin training battalions was greeted with considerable opposition and it was difficult to persuade commandants of regimental centres or of active battalions of their benefits. There was a strong feeling that their tenderly raised recruits would absorb alien, un-regimental ideas. The training battalions ended with the war.

One of the instructors in jungle training was Jim Corbett, author of *Man-Eaters of Kumaon*. He was more than sixty years old but he possessed greater stamina than most of the young men. His knowledge of jungle lore was 'unique and invaluable'. He taught the men how to recognize edible fruits and roots, showed them trees that could provide dyes for camouflage, taught them to light fires without matches, and even demonstrated how certain leaves could be used to make soap. Most of those he trained would soon be able to put his teaching to practical use.

CHAPTER
17

World War II:
North Africa

The Iraqi Army provided a minor obstacle to the 10th Indian Division under the command of the newly promoted former British Gurkha officer, Major General William J. Slim. He also quickly disposed of the Vichy French in Syria. There were still German elements in Persia and the Shah exhibited pro-German sentiments, so an invasion by British forces under Slim from the south and by Russians from the north in July 1941 resulted in a brisk campaign that culminated in a giant party organized by the Red Army. Gurkhas and Cossacks, British and Russians drank and sang and danced until a late hour. To the officers it appeared an international drinking contest and it was noted that the British Gurkha officers, educated in the severe schooling of the *Dashera* ceremonies, were conspicuous among the survivors.

In January and February 1941 General Richard N. O'Connor conducted a brilliant campaign in Cyrenaica, advancing 500 miles and capturing 130,000 prisoners (mostly Italians), 400 tanks, 1,290 guns, and the important port of Tobruk; British casualties were 500 killed and 1,373 wounded. But in March Hitler sent General Erwin Rommel and his Panzer Afrika Korps to Tripolitania and he at once began an attack that drove the British back on Tobruk.

Unfortunately, at this critical moment in the Western Desert, on 17 April 1941, Britain lost one of her most brilliant generals. In the realm of might-have-been, General O'Connor was perhaps the man to beat Rommel, but while reconnoitering on the Barce–Derna road he was captured by a German patrol.

The British decided to hold Tobruk and reinforce it by sea, thus denying the port to Rommel. The garrison made a gallant defence and Rommel was finally forced by a determined offensive back to his starting line. This was only temporary, however, and in a second offensive, attacking on a narrow front, he crashed through the British line and rolled back the Eighth Army beyond Benghazi, capturing immense quantities of stores.

General Sir Claude Auchinleck, who took personal command of the Eighth Army, was finally able to stop Rommel at El Alamein and the German steamroller came to a halt. For four months both sides rested and replenished their supplies of men, ammunition and stores. In June 1942 Rommel again attacked, taking his panzers on a wide sweep south into the desert and then swinging north inside the British lines. There he created a desert fortress in an area called 'the cauldron'. During the fighting here the 2/4th Gurkhas were overrun at a place called Bir Harmat on 6 June; only one British officer and 158 Gurkha ranks escaped. It was at about this time that back at the battalion's home in Bakloh the regiment's memorial bell cracked. No one could be exactly sure of times and dates, but it became an article of faith in the battalion that the bell cracked when the 2/4th was scuppered at Bir Harmat.

The British Eighth Army retreated and Tobruk was again isolated. Churchill demanded another stubborn defence, but conditions had changed and Tobruk fell on 21 June. Captured in the débâcle was 11 Indian Brigade, which included the 2/5th and 2/7th Gurkhas who had not received word of the surrender and who fought on for thirty-six hours longer, until their water and ammunition were finished and they could fight no more. A British Gurkha officer tried to describe the end for the 2/7th:

The men were fairly bursting with confidence. Things were a bit chaotic but this really was war and it was fun. They had knocked everything for six that had come up against them and had received almost perfect battle inoculation. Their sense of superiority did not leave them until the end. After they had fought it out against overwhelming odds and had lost, the stunned expression on their faces was a sight that few who saw it will forget.

It was the second time in its history that this battalion had been captured through no fault of its own – and in quite similar circumstances. It was the 2/7th that had been captured with the fall of Kut-el-Amara in the First World War; now again at Tobruk. In both instances a reconstructed battalion was formed.

A disaster of a different kind struck the 1/2nd Gurkhas who, after the fall of Tobruk, were transferred from Cyprus to Egypt, where 28 August became the blackest day in the regiment's history. A sapper instructor giving a demonstration inadvertently inserted a detonator into a live mine and pressed the plunger. The blast killed sixty-eight officers and men, and another eighty-five were severely wounded. Nearly all were hard to replace – Gurkha officers and specialists such as signallers, mortarmen and drivers. The 2nd Gurkhas had never in its long history lost so many men in a single day as it lost in that one terrible second.

Many of the captured 2/4th managed to escape. Although escaped prisoners were entitled to leave, none of the men of the 2/4th would take it – 'they were afraid to miss the war'. Those who had not been able to escape in Africa were sent to prisoner-of-war camps in Italy, but even here some escaped and made their way back to their units.

Havildar Kharkabahadur Rai of the 2/7th was among those captured at Tobruk. He soon escaped, but was recaptured and sent to Italy. In fifteen months he again escaped and lived in the mountains for three months before he was captured once more. This time he was sent first to Germany and then to southern France. Here for the third time he escaped. He joined a band of maquis led by an American colonel and took part in several ambushes on German posts near the Swiss frontier. When American troops reached the area, he was sent first to Paris, then to London, and from there, at the end of the war, he returned at last to his regiment.

Havildar Singbahadur Rai of the 2/7th escaped from a prisoner-of-war camp about ten miles from Tobruk by worming his way through the wire and dodging the sentries. He travelled only by night, following the coastline until he came to the railway at Salum. Keeping to the rails, he managed to avoid enemy patrols, occasionally obtaining food from Arab villages, and finally he arrived at El Daba, an Arab town where he bought a camel for fifty piastres – all the money he had. Then, disguised as an Arab, he travelled for four more days until he reached the British lines at El Alamein. His trip to freedom took him five weeks.

By April 1943 the military situation in North Africa was much changed. Allied forces had landed in Morocco and Algeria; in the Western Desert Rommel had been beaten back, but his Afrika Korps was far from finished and occupied strong, almost ideal natural defensive positions just north of Gabes. The German and British armies seemed deadlocked along a series of hills, cliffs and gullies running 120 miles inland from the sea. The key to the position was a rugged geographical feature called Wadi Akarit, with high ground which ran for ten miles through a salt marsh and culminated in an escarpment of extravagant contours. The 4th Indian Division, commanded by General Francis ('Gertie') Tuker (a former officer in the 1/2nd Gurkhas) was ordered to push through this position. Tuker's division included the 1/9th and the 1/2nd Gurkhas and these he planned to use as his spearhead, with 1/2nd in the van.

Unlike fiction or films, individual gallant deeds rarely have an effect upon the final outcome of a battle and almost never change the course of an entire campaign. Yet such a feat was performed by Subadar Lalbahadur Thapa of the 1/2nd Gurkhas at the battle of Akarit.

General Tuker, when he issued the necessary orders for the 1/2nd, worried: 'Perhaps I have asked too much of them and have set them a task beyond human accomplishment.'

It was indeed a difficult assignment: a night attack over mountainous terrain. Doubtless Tuker remembered the experience of the Gurkhas at Gallipoli.

On the night of 5 April 1943 the 1/2nd Gurkhas began a six-mile approach march before fanning out by companies for a climb into the hills. The men moved slowly, their scouts reconnoitering ahead of them. A new moon had risen and a slight mist hung over the ground. There was an occasional clang as mortarmen or machine-gunners shifted their weapons, a cough, the roll of turned stones, but otherwise the march was made in silence. Several low ridges were crossed. Then, shortly after midnight, the first of the main escarpments could dimly be made out in the darkness ahead.

C Company encountered the first enemy sentry. He was asleep and never knew of the *kukri* that slit his throat. There were others in the sangar and these were quickly dispatched, but not before the alarm was given. A stream of machine-gun bullets swept over the heads of the Gurkhas. Then there came a sound described as 'an excited whimper not unlike hounds finding the scent'. It was the remainder of C Company, chattering as they pushed up over the escarpment and moved along the crest, killing all they encountered. B and A companies moved up to attack points on the right and left.

By now the enemy was fully alert to his danger and a barrage of high explosive artillery and mortar shells rained down on the approaches to his sensitive positions. One salvo of mortar shells hit the headquarters of the 1/2nd, wounding several officers and destroying the battalion's wireless set as well as that of the artillery observation group. This came at a critical moment, for D Company had entered the hills and was in the chimney between the two escarpments; there was furious fighting, which Lieutenant-Colonel L.J. Showers could hear but could no longer control.

But at the very point of this spearhead attack, moving up a steep gully on a winding path guarded by well-placed machine guns, was Subadar Lalbahadur Thapa with two sections of D Company. Across a canyon at the top of a 200-

foot cliff there were more machine guns, mortars and, by this time, wide-awake enemy riflemen. Nevertheless, they were able to reach the first enemy sangar without being challenged. The picket was rushed and every man in it was killed with *kukris*. Lalbahadur did not pause. Although a perfect sheet of bullets swept down the ravine, he raced to a second sangar and killed its four machine-gunners single-handed: two with his pistol and two with his *kukri*.

Under the rain of fire only Lalbahadur and two of his men survived. Undaunted, he charged up the twisting, corkscrew path to the sangar at the top and leapt among its garrison, killing two. The rest fled. The passage through the hills was open two hours before dawn, and up the trail soon came the 1/9th Gurkhas and then all of 5 Brigade. The Axis line was split and, according to General Tuker, Rommel should have been whipped there and then, but the British Eighth Army was unprepared for such a brilliant breakthrough and no adequate *corps de chasse* was available. Nevertheless, Montgomery was credited with another splendid victory and from Wadi Akarit the road now lay open to Enfideville in the mountains below Tunis, where Rommel again made a stand.

On a warm day in June 1943 the men of the 4th Division lined the streets of Tripoli while His Majesty King George VI rode slowly through their ranks and then pinned the Victoria Cross on the breast of Lalbahadur Thapa.

Lalbahadur was carried off to England and was the first of several brave Gurkhas put on exhibit there. Field-Marshal Lord Birdwood once introduced him to a large audience in London: 'I made Lalbahadur come out and stand at the front of the platform, and then told him to draw his *kukri* and show the audience exactly how he used it to destroy his enemies. His exposition, accompanied by bloodcurdling shouts, was most realistic, and if it at first alarmed the audience, it afterwards delighted them.'

CHAPTER
18

World War II: South-East Asia

The first major disaster to strike Gurkha troops in the war occurred when Singapore surrendered in February 1942. Among the 138,700 British casualties there (mostly taken prisoner) were the entire second battalions of the 2nd and 9th Gurkhas. Singapore did not fall because its guns were pointing out to sea and could not be turned landward (the popular myth); all but one of the big guns had a 360-degree traverse and in fact they did fire at the invading Japanese attacking from the north, but unfortunately most of their shells were armour-piercing rather than high explosive and firing tables were inadequate. Singapore fell because there was not enough well-equipped infantry, not enough aircraft, not enough warships, and because leadership proved inadequate for the required role. Even the meagre resources available were badly handled. One result was that the remains of two battalions of Gurkha infantry found themselves in the hands of the Imperial Japanese Army.

Two days after the capture of Singapore the Japanese separated the Indian and Gurkha soldiers from the British and Australians. 'Asians here, Europeans there' was the order. Thus the Gurkhas were cut off from their officers. British and Australian prisoners were marched to Changri Barracks at the east end of Singapore Island.

Initially at least, the soldiers of Singapore's garrison were not brutally treated. Not so those captured in Malaya, who were sent to Kuala Lumpur and subjected to intensive interrogation. British officers who claimed to possess conveniently poor memories were tied to trees, flogged with steel-cored dog whips, and left hanging through the night in their bloody bonds. One of these was Major R.A.N. ('David') Davidson of the 4th Gurkhas, who had been serving with 22 Indian Infantry Brigade near Johore Bahru when he was captured on 1 February 1942.

For eight months Davidson and others subsisted on broken rice, small quantities of *kong kang*, a chopped weed, and little else. At the end of October, all fit men were ordered to Thailand to work on the infamous railway that was to link Burma and Siam. Major Davidson was scarcely fit, for he was suffering recurring bouts of malaria, but he had made a *kongsi* with three cell mates – a pact to stay together regardless of consequences – when he was included in a group sent to Nong Pladuk, base camp for the railway.

Korean guards under Japanese officers and N.C.O.s made life unpleasant from the start, but in the spring of 1943, when the railway reached the Burma hills and engineering problems developed, the situation became appalling. The authorities in Tokyo had ordered the railway to be completed by November; those in charge found themselves behind schedule, so the prisoner-coolies were pushed to exhaustion. There were no medical facilities, and through the summer heat and the rains the prisoners, staggering from malnutrition and tropical diseases, sometimes worked for sixty hours at a stretch, followed by only a four-hour break, in which the men slept in their sodden clothes under leaking thatch lean-tos.

In the three and a half years that Davidson was a prisoner of war, only one consignment of Red Cross parcels was allowed to reach them. It was distributed on the basis of one package per ten men.

In his camp, Davidson acted as adjutant. Added to the normal duties of an adjutant was responsibility for the clandestine activities necessary to conceal and maintain the radio receivers they built to gain news of the outside world. (Discovery of such sets meant torture, often death from beating, the corpses being thrown into latrines.)

Sad to relate, many prisoners were killed when camps were attacked by Allied aircraft whose pilots mistook them for enemy installations. Others were killed by Allied bombs when in 1944 the Japanese began to evacuate prisoners to Japan, Korea, Manchuria and Indo-China. Of the 45,000 prisoners of war employed on the 'railway of death', some 17,500 died; many others suffered for the rest of their lives from the effects of the ill-treatment they received and the diseases they contracted. David Davidson was one of the lucky ones. He survived and retired as a colonel.

The Indians and Gurkhas captured at Singapore – about 45,000 in all – were put into a separate camp at Farrar Park, where they were pressed by Indian deserters to join the Indian National Army (I.N.A.) – a force at this time about the size of an understrength division. Chandra Bose, an Indian revolutionary, had convinced the Japanese that it would be an easy matter to persuade prisoners of war to desert by telling them they would be patriots fighting to free India from Britain's yoke.

Many Indian prisoners did succumb and join the I.N.A., becoming what the British called 'jifs'. No Gurkha joined. In fact in the entire course of the war, although some 20,000 Indians changed sides, only one Gurkha, Durga Sing Lama – a former line boy, it was pointed out – did so. When captured by the British later in the war, he was hanged. When none of the Singapore prisoners of the 2/2nd or the 2/9th Gurkhas signed up for the I.N.A., their Gurkha officers and N.C.O.s were taken away to Skeleton Camp for intensive coercion. It began with talks, which lasted late into the night. Emphasis was placed upon the similarity between the Nepalese and Japanese people and how alien were the British to the Asians. Still none changed sides. Many refused to send cards home or to sign for Japanese working pay, fearing that they would unwittingly be enrolled in the I.N.A. Twenty-six were selected for brutal treatment, then returned to camp 'to think again'. Five were put in solitary confinement for forty-eight hours and then badly beaten. Still none joined.

The Japanese then decided to concentrate their efforts on Gurkha officers. They were made to work at heavy tasks, clubbed with rifle butts, brutally beaten with poles, and sand was mixed with their food; they were given no shelter at night and no blankets. Subadar Jitbahadur Gurung and Dilbahadur Gurung were repeatedly knocked senseless, brought round and then beaten senseless again. Dilbahadur's wrist was broken when he shielded his companion from a blow which might well have been fatal.

Subadar-Major Chethabahadur of the 2/9th was put in a small cage, starved, left for long periods in solitary confinement and beaten. He told the Japanese that they might as well kill him, for he would never submit. Subadar-Major Harisung Bohra of the 2/2nd was blinded and repeatedly beaten with bamboo poles; he died of internal haemorrhages in May 1944.

After brutality failed, the four surviving Gurkha officers were taken to Penang for treatment of a different sort. For ten weeks they were housed in a pleasant bungalow with Indian servants. They were offered commissions in the Japanese Army. When none accepted their holiday came to an end, and the efforts of the Japanese to woo them ended as well; but the stout stand of the Gurkha officers appeared to have impressed their captors, for when they were returned to normal captivity they were able to insist that the guards should stop abusing their men by hustling them about.

Sometimes when prisoners returning from work marched past Raffles Hotel in Singapore, Japanese officers would throw cigarettes at them and laugh to see the mad scramble. But Gurkhas, although noted for their love of tobacco, never scrambled. They kept their heads high and deliberately crushed cigarettes that lay in their path.

There were a few – very few – successful escapes from Japanese prisoner-of-war camps. Rifleman Chamansing Limbu of the 7th Gurkhas, who was put to work in a mine, escaped and managed to join up with a guerrilla force led by an American officer who had parachuted behind the lines. Bugler Randhoj Rai of the 2/7th was captured early in 1942 and worked for two years as a coolie on roads and railways. Then he and two others took advantage of the confusion created by an attack by Chinese troops to escape. He too joined up with an American force until he could rejoin his unit. Curiously, he had managed to retain his bugle, and when he returned to his battalion he still had it with him. It hangs today, inscribed with his name, in the officers' mess of the 7th Gurkhas.

Another Gurkha who ended up in an American unit was Jemadar Harkaman Limby of the 3/7th, who with five others was captured near Martaban, Burma. After being tied to a tree for two days and left without food or water, he was put in a Moulmein gaol, from which he escaped in March 1942. For two years he wandered about Burma dressed as a Burmese. He worked intermittently as a sweeper, railway porter and night watchman. In 1944 in northern Burma he fell in with a company of Merrill's Marauders and came out with them.

Rifleman Gangbahadur Gurung of the 1/7th and Havildar Dalbahadur Pun of the 1/3rd had the distinction of having been captured twice by the Japanese, and twice escaping. Gangbahadur was nicknamed 'Japan' by his comrades. Subadar Nardhoj Rai of the 3/7th was captured near the Sittang river in February 1942 and was put to work on the Japanese railway in Thailand, where torture was added to the common suffering from exposure, hunger and thirst. He escaped one night under cover of a torrential thunderstorm and made his way to China, where at first he was mistaken for a Japanese. Eventually he was passed through northern Burma by friendly Kachin tribesmen until he finally reached India, having travelled approximately 1,500 miles on foot.

The most remarkable escape story of all concerns Havildar Manbahadur Rai of the 1/7th. He escaped from a Japanese prison camp in southern Burma and in five months walked 600 miles until at last he reached the safety of his own lines. Interrogated by British intelligence officers about his remarkable feat, Manbahadur told them that the Burmese had not helped him. In any case he distrusted them, and he did not speak Burmese. But all that had not mattered, for he had a map, which before his capture had been given him by a British soldier in exchange for his cap badge, and he had marked his route every day with a pencil stub. He produced the much creased and soiled map. The intelligence officers stared at it in awe. It was a street map of London.

In south–east Asia it was, of course, more difficult for Europeans to escape than for Gurkhas; they could not blend with the local population, but Lieutenant John B. Goudge of the 3/7th kept his captivity brief. He had just been captured and was still being interrogated by a Japanese officer when he saw a party of some thirty Gurkhas unwittingly moving towards certain death or capture. Goudge coolly suggested that if permitted he would persuade them to surrender. Permission was granted, and he walked across to them. When he drew close, he yelled 'Bargo!' (the Gurkhali equivalent of 'scram') and scampered away with them to safety.

Escaped prisoners of war were welcomed back to their units and were usually given leave to recover from their ordeal and to spend time with their families. The experience of Lance-Naik Lokbahadur of the 2/5th was unique and there were unexpected complications. He was captured near the Sittang river, but managed to escape from a Rangoon gaol. Three years later he walked into the regimental centre at Abbottabad and immediately became a problem. He had been reported dead.

Any difficulties his reappearance created in the army were as nothing compared with the problems it raised for Lokbahadur in Nepal. News of his death had arrived at his village nearly three years before and the usual mourning ceremony had been carried out. In addition, the special Gurung rite which assures the passing of the soul had also been performed. It was therefore quite clear that Lokbahadur was dead. These religious rites were not to be lightly

dismissed as if they had never taken place. His reappearance among the living presented problems which had to be
solved before he could return home.

He was met on the path before he reached his village by
an uncle who took him to the house of another kinsman in
another village. There he was joined by his mother and later
his wife. All of the rites of passage in life had to be repeated.
He was reborn and renamed, becoming Chandrabahadur.
He was re-weaned and went through the Gurung ceremony
that is carried out when a boy has his first haircut. Finally,
he was remarried to his wife. All these ceremonies were
costly, to say nothing of the expense his family had incurred
in taking care of his soul after he was reported dead. When
Lokbahadur – or, rather, Chandrabahadur – returned to his
unit, he insisted, with some reason, that the government,
which had caused him so much trouble in the first place by
wrongly reporting his death, reimburse him for the cost of
all the ceremonies. The British officer at the depot agreed
and recommended that he be compensated from the regimental funds, but there is no record that it was ever done.

CHAPTER
19

World War II:
Italy

The 4th Indian Division, which had made such a splendid name for itself fighting in North Africa, moved to Italy to continue its service. There it was joined in August 1944 by 43 Lorried Infantry Brigade, consisting of the second battalions of the 6th, 8th and 10th Gurkhas. In all, battalions from eight Gurkha regiments fought in Italy as part of the British Eighth Army.

It was in the Arno valley that Lance-Naik Jitbahadur Rai, an ex-orderly in the reconstituted 1/7th, distinguished himself in his first battle. He was small even for a Gurkha, but he led his section in a charge and killed two large Germans. The bodies of both fell on him and he was pinned under them when a third German came at him. With a frantic effort he freed his right arm and his *kukri* from the tangle of bodies and with a wild swipe he nearly severed the German's arm.

Jitbahadur was extricated; the wounded German was taken prisoner and carried away on a stretcher. Jitbahadur was seen walking along beside it, his bloody *kukri* still in his hand, patting the terrified German on the shoulder and assuring him earnestly – in Gurkhali – that he was now perfectly safe.

Gurkhas are apt to obey orders literally, so that officers must exercise care if trouble, even tragedy, is not to result from a scrupulous obedience to the letter of their commands. After a hard-fought battle at Mozzagrogna, near the Sangro river, Major R.W. Morland-Hughes, commandant of the 1/5th, selected a battered house to be his new headquarters and ordered a detail of men to carry out nine German corpses from the cellar and bury them. They carried the bodies out and dumped them in a shell hole, but as they were carrying up the ninth, he suddenly sprang to life and leaped to his feet. *Kukris* were drawn and the screaming German, his hands over his head, was about to be dispatched when some English anti-craft gunners happened by and saved him. One called, 'Hey, Johnny! You can't kill him like that.' But the Gurkhas not only knew that they could, they were sure that they should. They had been ordered to bury *nine dead Germans*, and if one was not dead they had the means for making him so. Besides, they could not be expected to bury one alive.

During one battle in Italy, Rifleman Jagatbahadur, a runner for C Company of the 2/7th, passed a message through a hole to two soldiers in a cellar. When a voice thanked him in German he knew he had made a mistake, so he passed them a live grenade.

At the battle of the Sangro, Jemadar Ram Sing Rana, intelligence officer of the 1/5th, had just set up his section to work on maps in a deserted house when he heard sounds coming from the cellar. He and his men put down their pencils and drew their *kukris*. Downstairs they found and killed nine Germans. Ram Sing and his clerks then cleaned their *kukris* and picked up their pencils as calmly as if they had interrupted their work for lunch.

As the Germans slowly retreated up the Italian peninsula they fought tenaciously for every hill and ridge. In September 1944 the 2/10th had some of its hardest fighting at Passano Ridge. Held by the Germans, the ridge was dotted with farmhouses, each of which had been turned into a machine-gun post. The Spandaus traversed the front continually. In the capture of these positions there was some close in-fighting, which was graphically described by the official War Office observer:

Everywhere, out of the night, the little hillmen raced in upon the defenders with bomb and knife, for the hand-to-hand fighting in which they have no peers. Again and again a single Gurkha leapt into a group of enemies and destroyed them.

One Gurkha officer [Jemadar Bakhandhoj Rai of D Company] killed six Germans, another [Jemadar Harkajit Limbu of C Company] another five, in clearing farmhouses. Two German tanks, moving up in close support, were pounced upon, their crews slaughtered, and the tanks captured intact.

Colonel B.R. Mullaly of the 10th thought this account flamboyant, but said: 'Anyway, it was a good fight!'

Not long after the capture of Passano Ridge a group of 2/10th Gurkhas collided with a party of Germans. In true Gurkha style, Rifleman Ganjabahadur Rai charged with his naked *kukri* and engaged a six-foot-tall German who tried to fend him off with his rifle. Ganjabahadur broke through his guard and hacked him to death. (The German rifle with marks of *kukri* slashes on it was picked up and is still in the possession of the 10th Gurkhas.) Having killed one man, Ganjabahadur turned and sliced another from his neck to his hip before a party of Germans coming onto his flank killed him.

On 13 November 1944 Rifleman Thaman Gurung of the 1/5th won a posthumous Victoria Cross when, 'a lone figure on a bullet-swept hilltop', he fought to the death to save his platoon.

The 1/5th served for twenty months in Italy and suffered losses of more than a thousand men – more than its original complement. In addition to the Victoria Cross won by Thaman Gurung, officers and other ranks in the battalion earned two D.S.O.s, five I.O.M.s, one O.B.E., three M.B.E.s, seventeen M.C.s, twenty-seven I.D.S.M.s, six M.M.s, plus an American Silver Star and a Bronze Star.

The Gustav Line was one of the major barriers to an advance by the United States Fifth Army on the western side of the Italian peninsula, and the heavily fortified monastery at Monte Cassino was the chief obstacle in the drive to the Rapido River. All attempts to capture this key feature failed. An Allied aerial bombardment reduced the

The 2/4th Prince of Wales's Own Gurkha Rifles fight for and capture Point 132, near Pidvera, Italy, 18–19 December 1944. In this action Jemadar Dilbahadur Thapa won the Malay Cross. Watercolour by Harry Sheldon (*National Army Museum*)

monastery to rubble, but this actually improved the defensive capability of the place. It was here that the 1/9th endured a martyrdom, clinging for sixteen days to a position known as Hangman's Hill in the shadow of the monastery. The Germans tried to cut off all communications and supplies, and nearly succeeded. The troops there could only take out their casualties and bring in supplies at night; even then they were under shellfire. An attempt to airdrop supplies was only partially successful; half the containers rolled down the mountain out of reach. Men were killed trying to retrieve them. For a time Hangman's Hill became a focal point for the battle, both sides striving with all their strength for this tiny piece of terrain.

The Gurkhas' opponents were the German 1st Parachute Division, which has been described as 'one of the greatest fighting formations ever to take the field'. The Gurkhas were taking daily losses, they were on short rations, and it was obvious that they could not advance. Efforts of a New Zealand corps to relieve them failed. Even so, Gurkha morale remained high. When told that they were going to pull out, some asked, 'But who is going to relieve us?'

To effect a withdrawal, every effort was made to deceive the enemy. During the day an airdrop was made. With the help of a rum ration, the last to leave sang and played music while their comrades stole away. Then it was over. Only eight officers and 177 other ranks survived out of nearly a thousand. General Sir Francis Tuker said of this battle that it 'will go down to history as one of the most stubborn ever fought'. Today on a giant boulder near Hangman's Hill is carved the badge of the 9th Gurkha Rifles.

In Europe more officers than Gurkha ranks were able to escape. In Italy a number of captured British officers from Gurkha battalions were able eventually to regain their own lines or to cross into Switzerland. Many escaped in the interval between the collapse of Italian resistance and the German move to take control of the Italian prison camps. In some instances, Italian soldiers actually helped them.

Living in the hills and mountains, the escaped officers learned to select the safest houses at which to ask for food and shelter. Many Italian families risked their lives to help them. Some travelled only by day and some only by night. Captain N.D. Williams of the 4th Gurkhas, who escaped with others from the camp at Fontanellato, described the difficulty:

> To begin with we lay hidden by day and moved only at night, but village dogs and bright moonlight were apt to give us away. Concealment was next to impossible: whether we hid in the woods or in hedges, farmers or shepherds sniffed us out. We had no compass and no map and, in the early days, no knowledge of Italian or of the geography of the country and, worst of all, no inkling of the real sympathies of the people. We were nervous and imagined the enemy to be everywhere.

Williams concluded that travelling alone was unwise: men needed the moral support of at least one companion; without it, nerves frayed and resistance weakened. He found it better to keep moving; hiding was demoralizing. Parties of three or more were difficult to conceal in small peasant houses. Parties of two were preferable, even though they demanded a good deal of mutual tolerance, understanding and self-control.

Roger Werner and Ronald Smith were British Gurkha officers who escaped from Fontanello and travelled together over fields and across country. Werner brought with him a book from the prison library which he pulled out to read at every opportunity. This so annoyed his companion that one day in exasperation Smith said: 'Roger, if you flaunt that book in front of me again, I'll burn it!' The book was Richard Jefferies' *The Life of the Fields*.

Some escaped officers made their way north, hoping to find a way to cross the frontier into Switzerland; others went south, hoping to get through the combat zone to the Allied lines.

Captain Williams and some companions were among those who chose to make their way south through the country above Massa and Carrara, and along the way Williams had some interesting experiences. In March 1944 the group encountered an Italian who was an Allied agent, dropped in by air with enough arms, clothing and food to make him a local *capo*. He had, in Williams's opinion, distributed his supplies somewhat recklessly to young blades who strutted about the streets of the villages displaying their weapons. Nevertheless Williams, realizing that if a partisan force was to be formed this was the raw material for it, zealously set about organizing and training them. His success was only partial. Italian peasants were not Gurkhas. When the Germans decided to sweep the area with the Fascist Black Brigade and the Herman Goering Division, most of his partisans were rounded up and shot. Williams and some of his British companions struck out into the mountains where he made contact with other Allied agents, and by August he had organized an effective band of partisans in an upland valley. Then a group of trained British officers and wireless operators arrived to coordinate and direct the various partisan bands, and in November Williams joined a small party of other escaped prisoners which, led by an Italian guide, threaded its way south through the German lines.

When the Italians capitulated, German troops quickly surrounded the prison camp at Bologna, effectively preventing any escapes, and soon began moving the prisoners by train to a more secure location. At Modena the prisoners were transferred to some exceptionally filthy cattle trucks. In one truck, under the caked dirt of the floor, they found a defective board that they managed to prise up. With considerable effort they enlarged the aperture enough for young Lieutenant Peter McDowall, the smallest man in the group, to squeeze through.

It was dark and the train was in motion, but McDowall clambered along the undercarriage between the wheels, hoisted himself onto the running-board and then tried to reach the door, but the brake mechanism was in his way. He turned round and scrambled to the other side of the jolting, banging train. There the lock was secured by a wire too stout for him to break or undo. There was nothing to be done, so he crawled once more under the truck and squeezed back through the hole in the floor to report on the situation. Incredibly, one of the prisoners had a pair of pliers. Armed with these, McDowall once more made his perilous way under the truck and onto the running board. This time he was able to cut the wire. He unlocked the door and opened it – just as the train entered Verona. He was able to slip inside as the train was sliding to a stop.

German soldiers patrolling outside the train discovered the unlocked door. The men inside heard the lock being flipped down into position and a German laugh: 'These dumb Englishmen can't even discover that the door is open!' It was dark when the train pulled out of the station bound for its unknown destination. For the third time McDowall crawled out through the narrow hole and worked his way along the undercarriage and up to the door. Again he threw open the lock, the door was opened, and freedom beckoned to all with the courage to leap into the night from the moving train. McDowall was, of course, one of those who risked the leap, and he successfully made his way to internment in Switzerland. Regrettably, he died there of infantile paralysis, a disease he probably contracted while a prisoner.

On 2 May 1945 all German armies in Italy surrendered unconditionally to Field-Marshal Sir Harold Alexander, the Allied Supreme Commander.

CHAPTER

20

World War II:
Retreat from Burma

In November 1941 Mr Duff Cooper, in a minute to White-hall, wrote: 'I can find no support for the theory that war in Burma is imminent.' Two months later the Japanese Fifteenth Army under Lieutenant-General Shojiro Iida invaded Burma from Thailand and moved on Tavoy and Moulmein. The first shots fired at them came from the 1/7th Gurkhas. The British forces, amounting to the equivalent of two small infantry divisions, fought valiantly but were driven out of Moulmein with heavy losses in less than a month. By the end of January 1942 they were forced to withdraw across the Salween river. Thus began the longest retreat ever made by the British Army: It was longer than the retreat to Corunna in the Iberian peninsula in 1808–9; longer than the retreat from Mons in 1914.

In this bitter retreat – as, indeed, in the entire war in Burma – the Gurkhas played a prominent role. More Gurkha battalions were engaged in Burma than in all other theatres combined. War in this theatre, to which the British assigned the lowest priority for men, equipment and supplies, was nasty and brutish; the lives of those on active duty here were often short.

After the fall of Moulmein, the Japanese moved north-west, crossing the Salween in early February. Major-General John G. Smyth, V.C., commander of the soon-to-be-

famous 17th Division, urged a strategic retreat north to a
position where he could concentrate his forces and put up
a creditable defence, but permission was refused and he
was ordered to counter-attack. Smyth thought it was madness to fight under such conditions. His troops were near
exhaustion; the enemy was superior in numbers and in
arms; behind the troops was a single dusty road leading to
a single bridge over a broad river, the Sittang. However,
Smyth and his men obeyed their orders and the result was
the disastrous battle on the Bilin River, which was followed by a race to the Sittang, thirty miles north-west in
the British rear and only seventy miles from Rangoon.

In the weary, dispiriting retreat to the Sittang, men
became speechless with exhaustion but were given no rest.
Japanese aircraft bombed and strafed them daily. When
one day they saw British warplanes in the sky they roused
themselves to cheer – until the R.A.F. planes bombed and
strafed them, their pilots having been told that anything
east of the Sittang was fair game.

With the Japanese in hot pursuit, there was much confused and bitter fighting. Lieutenant-Colonel George Ballinger of the 1/3rd Gurkhas was with a group of his men
when they encountered nearly a dozen abject-looking Japanese soldiers who immediately raised their hands. When
Ballinger stepped out to accept their surrender, they threw
themselves on the ground and from behind them came a
burst of fire from light machine guns that ripped into the
group, killing Ballinger and three of his men. Gurkhas were
never enthusiastic about taking prisoners and in this battalion, for the rest of the war, no attempt to do so was ever
made again.

The fate of the small army in Burma, perhaps the fate of
all Burma, depended on a single bridge across the broad,
deep and swift-flowing Sittang river. It was a railway
bridge of eleven spans, each span 150 feet long. Planks
placed over the rails permitted vehicles to cross. At two
o'clock on the morning of 22 February the British started
to move vehicles across the river to the comparative safety
of the west bank. Two hours later a young Indian drove his

3-ton lorry off the planks and wedged it almost inextricably in the girders, delaying traffic for two precious hours.
All day long soldiers moved what could be saved over the
bridge. The eastern bridgehead was protected by seven
battalions of infantry, including the first and third battalions of the 7th Gurkhas, and three mountain batteries,
which were running out of ammunition and of mules to
pull their guns.

Preparations were made to destroy the bridge and at six
o'clock that evening Captain Robert Orgill of the Royal
Engineers reported it ready for demolition. Brigadier N.
Hugh Jones, commanding the all-Gurkha 48 Brigade (1/3rd,
1/4th and 2/5th) was left to hustle as much material and as
many men as possible across, and at the last possible
moment to blow it. If the Japanese captured the bridge
before it could be demolished, the route to Rangoon –
source of all supplies and reinforcements – would be theirs
for the picking. Hugh Jones asked Captain Orgill if he could
guarantee that the bridge could be successfully demolished
in daylight under observed fire with the enemy holding the
east bank. Orgill thought not. During the night Japanese
pressure became intense, and at three-thirty on the morning of 23 February they succeeded in placing a machine
gun within range of the bridge. All attempts to eliminate it
failed.

There were still thousands of men on the east side of the
river and Hugh Jones, understandably, did not want to take
the fateful decision to abandon them. He referred to his
superior, General 'Punch' Cowan: Should he blow now?
Cowan did not want to make the decision either, so he woke
up General Smyth and passed the decision to him. Smyth
made the decision that ended his military career. Later he
recalled his thoughts and emotions:

> He wanted a definite order from me as to whether he should
> blow the bridge or not. What a terrible decision to have to make!
> If we blew, it was in the knowledge that two-thirds of the divi-
> sion was left on the far bank. If we did not blow, a complete
> Japanese division could march straight on Rangoon. The deci-
> sion was one that had to be mine and mine alone, and having

made it I should, of course, take complete responsibility for it. It took me less than five minutes to make up my mind.... Hard though it was, there was very little doubt as to what was the correct course: I gave the order that the bridge was to be blown immediately.

Both the 1/7th and the 3/7th Gurkhas were among the troops still on the far shore. At the end, horns and whistles were blown, lamps were blinked, men even sang to help any last stray units find the bridge. However, no patrols were sent out. At 0300 hours the order was received to withdraw. B Company of the 1/3rd was withdrawn as the last rearguard. Then a hitch developed. Captain Orgill needed another fifteen minutes for his charges. B Company of the 1/3rd Gurkhas stood alone between the bridge and the Japanese. Finally, all was ready. B Company ran back over the bridge. Officers manning machine guns covered the sappers' withdrawal and the bridge was blown in three mighty explosions at about five-thirty in the morning.

One of the officers near the bridge on the west bank later said: 'Complete silence followed and the noise of all firing ceased.' An officer on the east bank wrote: 'The sound of the tremendous explosion had a remarkable effect. All firing ceased, and for a brief period complete silence reigned over the battlefield. Then the Japanese broke into excited shouts and chatter.'

Lieutenant V.K.S. Sundarum of the Indian Army Medical Service was at an aid station on the east side of the river. He had just finished giving morphine to five badly wounded Gurkhas of the 2/5th and 1/3rd when he heard the deafening roar. Captain Doyle, adjutant of the Second Battalion of the King's Own Shropshire Light Infantry, had been shot in the groin and was at the aid station, where he had just drifted off to sleep after an injection when he was roused by the blast. He opened his eyes and asked, 'What the hell was that?' Sergeant Dransfield of his battalion, slightly wounded, respectfully replied: 'Fuckin' bridge just gone up, sir.'

All, or most, understood the significance of the explosion. The Japanese realized that they had lost the race for the bridge. Those left on the east side of the Sittang knew that there was no longer a bridge to cross and that their army had abandoned them.

After a brief fight, most of the 1/3rd Gurkhas were captured in two parties. One surrender was without incident, but the other, under Major F.D. Bradford, was tragic. A Japanese officer came forward to accept the surrender, but old Subadar-Major Gagan Sing Thapa, a veteran of World War I, refused to lay down his arms, and instead shot at the Japanese officer and then shot himself through the heart. The officer, who had just received Major Bradford's pistol, shot and mortally wounded Bradford with it and was immediately shot through the head by a naik. It took some time for the Japanese to gain control; then officers were separated from their men and Major Bradford was carried off, never to be seen again.

Conditions on the east bank of the Sittang were chaotic. Most of the Gurkhas had not eaten for twenty-four hours, water supplies were low, communications with higher headquarters and with other units were erratic. Permission had been given to eat half the emergency ration, but of course the men were still hungry. Abandoned trucks were searched for food. A Japanese plane flew low and everyone fired at it. When it was seen to crash, there was jubilation – a good morale booster.

Lieutenant-Colonel R.T. Cameron, commanding the 2/5th, explained the situation to his men and told them what they must do: they were surrounded on three sides and would have to withdraw to the river. The withdrawal must be as rapid as possible, but no one was to run. He told them they would have to make bamboo rafts to cross the river and gave as a rendezvous point on the other side the town of Wau, eight miles back from the river, where there was a railhead. There was no sign of panic as the grim-faced soldiers swiftly moved out.

All along the east bank of the Sittang men looked longingly at the other side and devised ways to cross. Major S. Harvey-Williams of the 3/7th had a bullet in his right arm. With him were two mess orderlies who obviously looked to him to save them. Neither could swim. Harvey-Williams found some petrol tins and told them to bind them to their chests with their puttees, kick their feet and thrash their arms in the water and hope for the best. He tried to do the same, but with only one good arm it was quickly obvious he would never make it. He was in despair when a log floated near and he managed to grab and hold it. In spite of the pain of his wounded arm, he stayed afloat and two hours later was washed up two miles downstream on the west bank.

Neither Havildar Sherbahadur of the 2/5th nor the six men of his section with him could swim, but the havildar pointed to a huge log about as long as a telephone pole and ordered his men to put it in the river. This done, they slung their rifles, clung to the log and made it across with their weapons. Subadar Bombahadur Rai of the 3/7th also managed to get six of his men and their weapons over the river. He directed them in the construction of an excellent raft and they made the trip without difficulty.

Lieutenant Sundarum managed to get his wounded to the edge of the water, but he found only sodden bamboo to work with and the best raft he was able to improvise could carry only two men. However, a *bhisti* (water-carrier) from the 1/3rd provided some petrol tins to keep the raft afloat, and Sundarum calculated that his flimsy craft could now carry not only two severely wounded men, but that three men could cling to each side by resting their arms on its edge. They were on the verge of launching it when two British officers of the King's Own Yorkshire Light Infantry appeared supporting their severely wounded commanding officer. He was placed on the raft with a badly concussed rifleman. A Gurkha with a shattered right arm gave up his place; he could cling to the raft with his left arm. The *bhisti*, an officer of the 1/7th, a jemadar of the 2/5th, Lieutenant-Colonel R.T. Cameron of the 2/5th (the only swimmer), and Sundarum grasped the sides of the raft and they pushed off. About six o'clock that evening they reached the safety of the west bank. Sundarum wanted to return at once for other casualties, including two badly wounded Gurkha officers he had been forced to leave, but a superior officer ordered him not to make the attempt.

Captain Bruck Kinlock of the 1/3rd swam the river after dark and then came back with a boat. This enabled several wounded to be saved. Other men from the 1/3rd, together with some men of the 1st Duke of Wellington's Regiment, came to the demolished bridge and found that the gap made by the broken span was only about thirty yards. An officer and two N.C.O.s swam the river and brought back ropes for a lifeline. With this line non-swimmers could manage to cross and some 300 British, Gurkha and Indian soldiers made their way over.

Those on the western bank could see these attempts, and when men came ashore they were collected, dried, fed, and their wounds dressed. They were then sent back to Wau, where trains had been assembled. As the straggling survivors arrived, most with neither arms nor equipment, they were put aboard. At Wau, too, there were blankets, tea, beer and chapattis, but most men were too exhausted to eat; they simply slumped down and slept.

Of the Gurkha battalions which had crossed the Sittang before the bridge was blown, only the 1/4th survived reasonably intact as a fighting unit with twelve British officers, eighteen Gurkha officers and 650 other ranks. The remaining battalions were not fit to fight, their numbers hopelessly diminished:

	British Officers	Gurkha Officers	Other Ranks
1/7th	6	4	290
3/7th	5	5	160
1/3rd	3	4	100
2/5th	6	6	215

Survivors of the 1/3rd and 2/5th were temporarily amalgamated into a small battalion called the 5/3rd. Remnants of the 1/7th and the 3/7th were also temporarily amalgamated. When they were moved back to Pegu, a road and rail junction with a supply depot, the men were re-clothed,

re-equipped and re-armed as far as supplies allowed, but
there were serious shortages of Bren guns, mortars and sub-
machine guns; about 150 men were without personal
weapons for several weeks. There was no signalling equipment and there was a shortage of pots, pans, water containers, headgear and mules – all items a jungle army
needed desperately.

Most of the 2/5th Gurkhas and the other troops left on
the east bank of the Sittang were captured when the Japanese occupied the shore in strength the next morning, but
some forty men of the 2/5th, believed lost, rejoined weeks
later. In small parties they had moved northwards, looking
for a place to cross. There were many Burmese who had no
love for the British and, believing Japanese promises of
independence, actively worked against them. Knowing this,
the Gurkhas avoided villages and lived on roots, berries
and whatever they could find in the jungle. Some were
wounded; all suffered. One was killed by a Burmese. But
eventually these groups succeeded. One party, led by Naik
Kharku Pun, included a man who had been wounded in the
foot but who made his way for three weeks on improvised
crutches.

The Japanese were delayed by the lack of bridges over
the Sittang, but not for long; soon fighting patrols moved
forward to ambush and harass the retreating British. Lieutenant-Colonel R.G. Leonard of the 1/10th was in a vehicle
that was ambushed. All in it were killed or wounded. The
injured driver managed to turn round and drive to a brigade group headquarters, where the seriously wounded
Leonard was put in an ambulance and sent off to a field
hospital. But again his vehicle was ambushed and he lay
helpless for more than an hour while bullets struck all
around him, some even hitting his stretcher. He was rescued by Gurkhas.

In early March the Japanese surrounded Pegu. The British, in spite of reinforcements from the Chinese Sixty-sixth
Army, continued their retreat. Rangoon was abandoned and
when the Japanese marched in on 8 March 1942 they found
it in smoking ruins, filled with released criminals, lepers

and lunatics; even beasts from the zoo roamed the streets.
The refinery of the Burmah Oil Company, still throwing
black smoke into the atmosphere, had been completely
demolished by Captain Walter Scott of the Royal Engineers. (After the war, for reasons not readily understood,
the British government compensated the Burmah Oil Company to the tune of £11 million for its loss.)

Many men summoned reserves of extraordinary courage
and endurance during the retreat. One such was Rifleman
Bhojraj Pun of the 2/5th, severely wounded in the throat by
a mortar shell while his platoon was withdrawing during
an attack by a superior Japanese force. His platoon had no
way to carry him; he was unconscious and appeared to be
dying, so he was left behind. Not until the next day did he
regain consciousness. He was weak from hunger and loss
of blood, but he made his way to where his battalion had
been bivouacked. His comrades were gone. The Japanese
now occupied the area. That night he moved westward and
stumbled into a village where a Burmese family gave him
shelter and crudely dressed his wound. They offered him
food, but part of his tongue had been torn away and it was
difficult for him to eat anything. After resting a few days,
he moved on, making for Silchar. He reached it on 22 April,
eighteen days after he had been wounded.

In spite of some changes in command – Lieutenant-General Sir Harold Alexander replaced Hutton and Major-General William Slim took over 1st Burma Corps ('Burcorps') –
the British continued to suffer reverses. On 1 May Mandalay fell and the British left Burma, retreating across the
Chindwin river and into the border hill region of Manipur.

Both Slim's divisional commanders – Scott with 1st
Burma Division and Cowan with 17th Indian Division –
were former officers in Gurkha regiments. There were certain advantages to this. Telephone lines were sometimes
tapped by the enemy, but Slim could talk directly to Scott
and Cowan in Gurkhali, in which all three were fluent. Many
Japanese understood English, practically none Gurkhali.

Security and rest for the battered British, Gurkha and
Indian troops was represented by Imphal, capital of Mani-

pur state. It is located on a wide plain about 2,500 feet above sea level and surrounded by mountains, some nearly 10,000 feet high. It was then approached by a single road that climbed to the plateau from Dimapur. The foothills were pleasantly wooded and the Manipuri villages clean. It was to this haven that most of the battalions climbed. When they reached it they expected food in plenty, fresh clothing, new equipment and, best of all, time to sleep. Sadly enough, they were disappointed. There was neither clothing nor equipment available at first, and so little food that everyone was on half rations. Even sleep was in short supply, for the fierce local mosquitoes made the nights a misery.

All the Gurkha battalions who took part in the retreat had proven themselves in battle. They had behaved splendidly. The 1/10th arrived at Imphal with officers and men in rags, "but it marched in as a battalion with every man in possession of his weapons and equipment'. The same could not be said for all the units who took part in this long retreat from Burma, but praise for the Gurkhas was universal. Of all the Gurkha battalions, the 1/4th won the most praise. Compton Mackenzie wrote of the arrival of this battalion at Paleh, where motor transport was to carry them on the last stage to Imphal:

> One notable exception to the shattered appearance of a defeated army was the 4th Gurkhas, who marched in, C.O. and adjutant at the head and Second-in-Command in the rear, as if they were on parade.

In this incomparable battalion was a remarkable Gurkha officer, Subadar Agam Gurung, who, according to the regimental historian, 'brought his platoon out in a state with which no other could compare. It had sustained no avoidable casualties, no men were missing and it had its full complement of equipment, arms and stores. The platoon had been splendid in action and Agam always vigorous, watchful and self-reliant.' He received only a mention in despatches for this remarkable feat, though later he became a subadar-major and retired as an honorary lieutenant, sirdar bahadur, O.B.I., M.B.E.

The 1/4th suffered remarkably few casualties – 107 dead – considering the active part it had played in the fighting. One of the principal reasons lay in the exceptional abilities of the battalion commander, Lieutenant-Colonel W.D.A. ('Joe') Lentaigne, who, with glasses on his nose, looked more like a bank manager than the professional soldier he was. In a letter to Lieutenant-Colonel T.D.C. Owens, commanding the 4th Gurkhas Regimental Centre, Lentaigne outlined some of the reasons he thought his battalion had come through its ordeal so well and what it took to accomplish this feat. It was, he said, 'due to very rigid discipline and chasing all day and every day. Insistence on digging in; proper dispersion against air attack and shelling at all times; not allowing people to halt behind cover when under fire but push them on; strict water discipline; no fall-outs allowed and a little foresight in evacuating lame ducks; thinking cooking needs ahead so that the men were not hungry when others were; these are the sort of things that have kept down casualties.'

It had been a long, hard retreat and casualties overall had been high: 13,463 for the British and 4,597 for the Japanese. Now at the very door to India, the Japanese had to be defeated and pushed back along the same road they had taken on their victorious march through Burma.

CHAPTER

21

World War II:
Chindits

A *chinthe* is a half-lion, half-eagle figure often seen over the doors of Buddhist temples in Burma. Orde Wingate, World War II's most eccentric general, thought the *chinthe* was a good symbol for the air–ground cooperation required for the Long Range Penetration Force he raised in 1943 to operate behind Japanese lines in Burma, so he adopted it as his force's insigne. *Chinthe* became corrupted to 'chindit' and it was as chindits that his men were popularly known.

For his first expedition in 1943 he insisted that only British and Gurkha troops and Royal Air Force ground teams be included in his force. Wingate was an artillery officer unfamiliar with Gurkhas except by reputation and ignorant of the Indian Army and its peculiarities. The third battalions of the 2nd and 6th Gurkhas took part in both the first and the second chindit expeditions. Both of these were war-raised units, as were the Gurkha battalions that took part in the second expedition (3/4th, 3/9th and 4/10th); some of the soldiers serving in them were only sixteen or seventeen years old. Wingate believed that newly raised battalions could more easily be moulded to his ideas. This was an unfortunate conceit.

The Gurkha battalions were not kept as individual units but were broken up into sub-units and mixed with British troops. The 3/2rd was divided between four columns. Wingate either forgot or never knew that Gurkhas spoke little or no English, or perhaps he underestimated the importance of language and communication. Some Gurkhas were placed under officers who spoke no Gurkhali. Many Gurkhas were simply taken from their units and made muleteers, apparently under the mistaken notion that all Gurkhas understood the management of mules. Certainly Wingate did not understand that Gurkha soldiers required a special kind of leadership. In consequence, Wingate was the only officer in more than 130 years ever to criticize the performance of Gurkha soldiers, characterizing them as mentally unsuited for their role as chindits. Of course, the same might be said of Wingate.

Originally, the strategic concept of the first expedition was to distract the Japanese while the Chinese recaptured Myetkyina, a town regarded as the key to northern Burma. This made sense, as it was assumed that many more Japanese would have to be diverted from the defence of northern Burma to try to control the chindits. The columns, badly organized and conceived, had no mechanical transport and were supplied by air for three months. In the event, the Chinese attack never took place and Wingate knew that it would not when, with Wavell's permission, he launched his columns into Burma from Manipur. In February 1943 the first chindit columns crossed the Chindwin and Irrawaddy rivers. Some railway lines were temporarily cut, but no other damage of any importance to Japanese operations was effected. It required more than three months for the forces to extricate themselves. They lost a third of their men.

Gurkha soldiers suffered in ways which Wingate could never have conceived. One column, reduced to gnawing roots for food, came across a nilgai (blue bull), and an officer shot it. Although the Gurkhas were less particular than most Hindus about their food, they declined to eat it: it was too close to beef. The British and Karen scouts had, of course, no such inhibitions, but although the hungry Gurkhas, with great tact, looked away while others wolfed down a hearty meal, one young officer found himself quite unable to swallow his portion. 'The meat just stuck in my throat,' he said.

The first of Wingate's expeditions was badly organized, ineffective and bloody; in short, a disaster. Although he later argued that the experience gained was worth the cost, no strategic aim of any importance was achieved: the Japanese were warned of the danger from this type of operation; and the British learned mostly what they ought *not* to do. Nevertheless, journalists hearalded it as a success, and civilians in the Allied countries, unaware of the heavy cost in lives, were taken with the notion that their forces could operate for weeks, even months, behind the Japanese lines.

Orde Wingate was a curious man with a disturbed personality, but he possessed what few soldiers could claim: the power to convince politicians. Churchill was enamoured of Wingate, whom he called 'a man of genius and audacity'. He also believed in Wingate's long-range penetration schemes. He carried Wingate off with him to the First Quebec Conference, where he, Roosevelt and their military advisers met to make major decisions affecting the war. One of these decisions was to step up the war against Japan. Here the persuasive Wingate convinced all of the feasibility and importance of his strategies, and he received approval from the highest authority to execute a second, much larger, more ambitious penetration into Burma.

The second penetration by the chindits was made by five infantry brigades organized as the 3rd Indian Division, often called simply 'Special Forces'. For their mission, the troops were divided into two 'columns' and early in February 1944 were flown deep into north-central Burma. The plan was to cut the Mandalay–Myitkyina railway and generally disrupt the Japanese rear areas. The initial invasion was by glider at two isolated jungle locations code-named 'Broadway' and 'Chowringhee'. The main body moved to Mawlu and established a strong defensive position astride the railway. To assist him, Wingate had acquired not only his own private army, but an air force, called No. 1 Air Commando and commanded by Colonel Philip C. Cochran, a young American Air Corps officer.

One of the brigade commanders was Joe Lentaigne, who

had led his battalion of the 4th Gurkhas so brilliantly during the Burma retreat. He was now a brigadier commanding a brigade which included two British battalions and the 3/4th and 4/9th Gurkhas. Future novelist John Masters was his brigade major. When on 25 March word arrived that Wingate had been killed in a plane crash the day before, Lentaigne was flown out to become a major-general and take Wingate's place as commander of the chindits. His place as commander of 111 Brigade was taken by Masters.

The chindit columns did not accomplish enough to justify the effort. Once again casualties were high and the suffering of the troops was great. The 77 Brigade under Brigadier Michael Calvert became locked in a bloody battle to take Mogaung. A rifleman of the 7th Gurkhas who had escaped from a gaol in Mandalay joined up with the brigade there and provided unexpected and useful help. He had been supporting himself by selling milk to the Japanese, an enterprise that had given him access to a considerable amount of information about the Japanese and their positions.

It was in the course of this protracted battle that a Gurkha of the 3/6th, who for nearly three months had carried over hills and through jungles his heavy PIAT (projector, infantry, anti-tank) without ever having an opportunity to use it, thought he saw his chance when he spotted a lone Japanese soldier. The PIAT fired a 3-pound projectile capable of piercing four inches of armour and the Gurkha's aim was true. 'The result was remarkable and exceeded his wildest dreams,' said an eyewitness.

The strain on the men of all races in the chindit columns was intense. In 111 Brigade one young Gurkha terrified his companions when he broke under the pressure and began to howl like a dog and tried to eat his equipment. Considering the appalling experiences of the chindits, it is remarkable that 111 Brigade had only about a dozen psychiatric cases. Some thought that there was a psychopath directing these mad British expeditions behind the enemy lines: Orde Wingate.

The attention given in the press to the chindit expeditions distracted the public from the bitter Arakan campaign of 1943. Arakan, the western coastal strip in lower Burma, was an area with few roads and no railways: its only town of any importance was Akyab on an island of the same name. The British campaign which opened there late in 1943 was not a complete disaster; neither was it an overwhelming success. It was one of the bloodiest campaigns and Gurkhas were involved in its bitter battles, distinguishing themselves by their bravery and *élan*. An artillery observer with the 1/8th sent back a message to his battery commander: 'I am just witnessing one of the most glorious sights of the war, the Gurkhas attacking.'

Even defeat could be turned into a small victory of sorts. On 5 April 1944 at a place called Taung Bazaar, the Japanese attacked and overran British positions. After the battle all the members of the small guard of the 4/5th placed at the stores dump were reported missing. One week later seven of the Gurkha riflemen from the guard turned up – along with a five-year-old Bengali boy who had attached himself to them. They had fought their way free of the Japanese, killing five in a running fight with grenades, rifles and a light machine gun, and they had forced their way through the tangled jungle of the Mayu range. Through all their struggles with Japanese and jungle they had clung to the battalion's heavy treasure chest, taking turns carrying it on their backs.

There were many individual acts of great gallantry in Burma. Rifleman (later Havildar) Bhanbhagta Gurung of the 2nd Gurkhas won the Victoria Cross when his company attacked a hill the British had christened Snowdon East. When his section was pinned down by light machine-gun and mortar fire, a Japanese sniper in a tree only seventy-five yards away began to pick them off. He was too well concealed to be seen from where they lay, so Bhanbhagta moved to an exposed position and, standing in full view, took aim and killed him. The section was then able to advance, but twenty yards short of its objective it was again halted by intense fire from Japanese in trenches. Bhanbhagta leapt forward and threw a grenade into the first trench, killing two, and without stopping, dashed on to a second trench, where he killed two more with his bayonet. Heavy fire was coming from two other trenches, but he rushed on, clearing them both with grenades and bayonet. A Japanese machine gun inside a bunker opened fire, raking his own and another Gurkha platoon. Bhanbhagta ran towards it and leapt onto the roof. His supply of fragmentation grenades was exhausted, but he had two smoke grenades and he threw these into the bunker. Two Japanese soldiers staggered out, and he killed both with his *kukri*. One remained inside and valiantly continued to fire his weapon; Bhanbhagta crawled into the bunker and killed him.

Of the fifty-two Victoria Crosses awarded in 1944–5, twenty-seven were won in Burma. During the entire war only one hundred Victoria Crosses were awarded, of which thirty-one were given to men who fought in Burma.

CHAPTER
22

World War II:
Back to Burma

The decisive battles of the Burma war were fought at Kohima and Imphal. (The 2/5th Gurkhas alone lost 800 men in the fighting around Kohima.) The Japanese threw all their might against these strongly held positions and, in fact, laid siege to them. But supply by air and the advance by Slim's XXXIII Corps to relieve them resulted in a major Japanese failure, though more than once they came near to victory. It was a close thing. The fighting lasted from March until the end of June, 1944. The monsoons made the Japanese positions increasingly difficult; shortages of food and the inroads of disease impaired their fighting capabilities. Of their 65,000 dead, less than half were felled by British bullets and shells. British forces in Burma, organized as the Fourteenth Army, were now under the command of General Slim who, as soon as the Japanese had been beaten to a standstill, launched his divisions south, back to Burma.

The Japanese withdrew to Mandalay and Meiktila, and Slim's army followed. The British crossed the Irrawaddy and took Mandalay in March 1945. They raced to reach Rangoon before the monsoons and succeeded, arriving to find that the Japanese had already evacuated the town. By the war's end Slim had achieved the greatest land victory over the Japanese in World War II. It had not been easy.

The official *History of the Second World War*[*] described the
conditions under which Britain's troops fought to cut off
the retreat of the defeated Japanese Army:

> The main obstacle to the advance was the climate and coun-
> try. The columns, struggling through blinding rain, swollen
> torrents, deep cloying mud and along treacherous slippery
> paths on the mountain sides, were often hungry . . . The phys-
> ical effort of ascending and descending as much as 4,000 feet
> in a single march with the temperatures varying from the sub-
> tropical heat of the valley bottoms to the cold mists of the
> mountain tops, imposed a fearful strain on the fortitude of
> troops already beginning to suffer from undernourishment,
> exposure and fatigue. Dysentery, scrub typhus and skin dis-
> eases became rife and there was no comfort for the sick and
> wounded.

War is brutalizing and the war in Burma seemed to grow
ever more brutal. When a patrol of the 4/8th brought back
to camp the severed head of a Japanese officer, Lieutenant-
Colonel Walter C. Walker, the battalion commander, had it
nailed to the trunk of a tree near his bunker. The head had
a 'wispy beard and a drooping moustache' and it was, said
Captain Patrick Davis, 'a two-day wonder'. Gurkhas, many
of whom had never seen a Japanese soldier dead or alive,
crowded round for 'a rare chance for fraternization'. When
it began to stink, Walker ordered it to be buried.

The zest of the Gurkhas in their pursuit of the retreating
Japanese has been compared to that of terriers after rats.
One battalion commander offered a reward for each head
brought in, and one havildar returned with six bloody ears
in his haversack. These he placed in a neat row on the
ground. The commandant inspected them and asked what
had happened to the rest of the heads. 'Too heavy to carry,
sahib,' said the havildar.

At one point in the campaign British intelligence was
particularly anxious to obtain a Japanese prisoner and a

* *The War Against Japan,* vol. 3, H.M.S.O., 1962.

reward of Rs. 200 was offered for one. When a patrol of the
4/6th Gurkhas reported by radio that they had a slightly
wounded prisoner, an intelligence officer and an inter-
preter hurried to await them on top of a ridge. They heard
two shots below and not long afterwards the patrol arrived,
looking exceedingly tired. They had no prisoner. The havildar explained that he had unaccountably died on seeing
the steep hill he would have to be carried up. The offered
reward was perhaps too small.

There was certainly a reluctance on the part of the Gurkhas to take prisoners. When a patrol of the 1/10th brought
in word of some eighty Japanese with wounded about half
a mile away, a platoon under Jemadar Lalbahadur Limbu
was sent out to deal with them. Lalbahadur located them
and first put a section on the probable escape route before
attacking with his other two sections, using bayonets and
kukris. The Japanese were caught by surprise; those who
fled ran into the section lying in wait for them. At least
forty were killed. Lieutenant-Colonel D.D.M. McCready,
commander of the 1/10th, had this comment on the action:
'There was a great blooding of kukris in this small action
and significantly enough, in spite of the number of Japanese wounded, no wounded were brought back.' Lalbahadur Limbu received an immediate award of the Military
Cross.

During the fighting for the capture of Talingon in the
drive to retake Mandalay, two riflemen of the 4/10th sat in
a tree observing for the artillery. In the to-and-fro of battle,
they found themselves at one point on the Japanese side of
the conflict and they amused themselves by dropping grenades on unsuspecting Japanese who passed below. When
five officers assembled directly under the tree, they killed
them all – and themselves suffered some wounds from the
explosions 'in their nether regions', as the report put it.

There were many acts of gallantry. The best known to
Gurkhas – certainly to all non-commissioned officers, for
after the war the story was included in the Gurkhali reader,
required study for the educational examination that was
part of the qualification for promotion to corporal – was

the gallantry of Rifleman Ganju Lama of the 1/7th that won him the Victoria Cross.

Ganju Lama, a PIAT gunner, was with his battalion when it was ordered one rainy day, 11 June 1944, to relieve the 2/5th at the village of Ningthowkong. The 2/5th was under attack and two companies of the 1/7th, trying to go to its relief, came under the fire of three Japanese tanks. Ganju, who had already won the Military Medal by destroying two tanks, crawled forward with his PIAT to destroy these. Unfortunately, he was seen and caught in a crossfire. He was wounded in the arm and leg, and his left wrist was broken. Nevertheless, he crawled on through slick mud, bleeding profusely, dragging his weapon and ammunition. When he came within thirty yards of the first tank he set up his PIAT, fired, and saw the tank go up in flames. He somehow managed to load his weapon and fire again, and again accurately, destroying a second tank. As the tank crew survivors crawled out, he killed them with grenades. Then, his ammunition exhausted, he crawled back – for more projectiles. In spite of his wounds and loss of blood, he made his way forward again and knocked out a third tank.

Twenty years later, when Ganju Lama was serving as an officer in the Indian Army, a large boil developed on his leg. It swelled up and finally burst. Out came a Japanese bullet.

Another Gurkha who won the Victoria Cross during this phase of operations in Burma was Lachhiman Gurung, a rifleman in the 4/8th Gurkhas. He was a young soldier who had been in the battalion for only about two months when, on the night of 12–13 May 1945 at Taungdaw, twenty miles north of Pegu, he found himself in the forward trench of 9 Platoon, C Company. His battalion was then part of 89 Brigade in the famous 'Black Cat' 17th Indian Division engaged in blocking the Japanese escape route from Arakan.

Lachhiman's post dominated a jungle path which led into his platoon's area and was the key to his company's position. An hour and twenty minutes past midnight, some two hundred Japanese launched an assault on C Company's position. It began with a barrage of grenades hurled at close range. One grenade fell on the lip of the trench held by Lachhiman and two other riflemen. Lachhiman immediately seized it and threw it back. When a second grenade landed in the trench, he managed to throw this back as well. But when for a third time he attempted to return an enemy grenade it exploded in his hand, blowing off his fingers, shattering his right arm and severely wounding him in the face, body and legs. His two comrades, badly wounded, lay helpless in the bottom of the trench.

At this point the Japanese drove in their attack, screaming as they ran forward almost shoulder to shoulder. Lachhiman, in spite of his grievous wounds and the use of only one arm, wrenched his rifle into position and managed to fire, even to reload, with his left hand, calling out, 'Come and fight! Come and fight! While I live I will kill you!' The Japanese assault faltered but, despite heavy casualties, they pressed forward again and again in wave after wave of ferocious attacks. For four hours after receiving his wounds, Lachhiman remained alone with his wounded comrades, 'waiting with perfect calm for each attack', said his citation. Daylight revealed eighty-seven dead Japanese in front of C Company's position; of these, thirty-one lay in front of the trench held by Lachhiman Gurung. Later he said, 'I wanted to kill some Japanese before I died.'

After three days in a field hospital, Lachhiman was evacuated to a hospital in India. Doctors tried to save his right arm, but finally had to amputate it. He also lost the sight of his left eye. His recovery took five months. While he was in the field hospital he learned that he had been recommended for the Victoria Cross. When they told him, he thought there must be some mistake: 'I was not brave, but I saw all my friends wounded, and then I looked at my hand and I was very, very angry.'

Many are recommended for the V.C., but few are awarded. However, nine weeks after his recommendation had been submitted he received unofficial notification that the award had been approved, and on 19 December 1945, outside the Red Fort at Delhi, Lachhiman Gurung received his Victoria Cross from the hands of Lord Mountbatten. The V.C.

parade was the largest ever held in India; six Victoria Crosses and one George Cross were presented. Lachhiman was the only living recipient. All the other medals were posthumous awards. Lachhiman's brother and his parents were brought down from Nepal to see him honoured and to be guests at the garden party given by Lord Wavell after the parade.

Although Lachhiman never knew it, the Chief Commissioner of Delhi had begged Wavell not to hold the parade as he feared an anti-British demonstration, but Wavell noted in his diary that night, 'I absolutely refused to pay any regard to his protests. There was a large and orderly crowd, a very good parade and no demonstration of any kind.'

It was a grand thing for this illiterate boy from the mountains of Nepal to be so honoured by the Supreme Commander and the Viceroy of India. Years later he said, 'It was the proudest moment of my life.' In gaining the coveted V.C. he had also brought honour to his regiment and earned the admiration and respect of his officers and his comrades in the ranks. Patrick Davis, a junior officer in Lachhiman's battalion, wrote of their pride:

> It is a great thing for a unit to own a man who is awarded the V.C. The outside world thinks only of the individual; his unit regards the medal as partly theirs. . . . This was the first V.C. to be won by the 8th Gurkhas since 1904, and there was more than pride, there was a considerable dash of triumphant vanity that it should be a war-raised battalion, the youngest of the regiment, that had gained it.

The 8th Gurkha Rifles are now part of the army of an independent India, but Lachhiman's exploit has not been forgotten. Every year his battalion celebrates Taungdaw Day and on some of those days in the past Lachhiman has been an honoured guest, wearing his old uniform, one sleeve empty but still bearing the stripes of a havildar, the rank he attained before retiring on his pension and the £100 a year which Britain gives to living holders of the Victoria Cross.

Ganju Lama and Lachhiman Gurung well deserved their Victoria Crosses, but not all brave men received rewards commensurate with the valour they displayed. Rifleman Manbir Ale of the 4/8th Gurkhas was unable, because of the nature of the ground during one battle, effectively to fire his Bren gun, so he stood up to cover his section's attack on a machine-gun bunker; his right hand and forearm were shattered by Japanese bullets, but he supported his gun on his broken arm and carried on until mortally wounded. His gallantry earned him merely a posthumous mention in despatches.

General Tuker told of a platoon which had to cross a steep ravine with a stream flowing through it close against a Japanese position strongly defended by machine guns. Rifleman Jagaralhan Rai, small even by Gurkha standards, volunteered to cross and establish a bridgehead. He worked his way down the ravine and cautiously waded across the stream. Then, while his platoon waited and his jemadar fumed and cursed, he fumbled in his grenade pouch. It was strictly forbidden to carry anything but grenades in the pouch, but Jagaralhan pulled from his an assortment of stores, from cigarettes to rifle patches. When he at last extracted a grenade he expertly bounced it into a Japanese machine-gun post, then crept on and with equal skill and *sang-froid* knocked out the remaining machine guns. There is no record that little Jagaralhan Rai received anything but a cuff from his jemadar for failure to heed battalion orders concerning grenade pouches.

A curiosity of the war in Burma was the presence of American civilians, members of the American Field Service, in the combat zone. There were not many of them, but they earned a place in more than one Gurkha regimental history and in several memoirs. According to John Masters, these young men were 'the most popular and admired group in the Army'. They were all volunteers who either had been rejected as physically unfit by the American military services or had moral scruples about fighting. Masters described them as being 'pansies, Quakers, conscientious objectors and altruistic young men; but

damned near all heroes'. The history of the 5th Royal
Gurkha Rifles adds: 'Their courage and devotion were most
marked and became legendary.' They worked, usually in
two-man teams, with a jeep ambulance. The regimental
history of the 4th Gurkhas adds that 'the drivers showed a
most touching care for the comfort of our men'. Neal Gil-
liam, a Virginian, was mentioned in the histories of both
the 3rd and 6th Gurkhas, and the officers of the 3rd Gurkhas recommended him for the George Cross for bringing in
wounded under fire, but he received only the George Medal
because, it was said, he was a foreigner. Almost every
Gurkha regiment had some memorable experience with
these men. They were also welcome visitors to officers'
messes.

At least two Americans who had served in the American
Field Service were commissioned in the British Army and
served with Gurkhas. One of these was Captain A. Wright
of the 1/5th, who distinguished himself in the fighting in
the Marzena Valley in northern Italy in November 1944
and was seriously wounded there. Another was Lieutenant
Scott Gilmore of the 4/8th in Burma, who had served with
the American Field Service in North Africa. He was a large
man, casual in manner and a humorous extrovert. He never
learned to read a map and in a corps that prided itself on
its turn-out his dress was never up to standard. He was,
nevertheless, popular in the officers' mess and with his men,
who enjoyed his American-accented Gurkhali. It was soon
noticed that his Gurkha orderly affected an American
accent; shortly afterwards the contagion spread to his entire
company. Gilmore radically altered his colleagues' concep-
tion of Americans. Patrick Davis wrote: 'How could we
believe that all Americans were loud-mouthed, over-paid,
ignorant bastards when we had Scotty?' Gilmore saw much
fighting in Burma, including the fight at Taungdaw where
Lachhiman Gurung won his Victoria Cross.

In Burma the Gurkhas earned a high reputation for their
patrol work, which often carried them behind the enemy
lines. The 4/5th formed a 'guerrilla platoon', a picked body
of scouts. 'Tiger patrols' of two or four men used to gather

information or harass the enemy, and they sometimes remained out for several days. A portion of a patrol report of the 3/10th Gurkhas for 13 May 1943 illustrates some of the drama of these small actions:

> At 0830 hrs. to-day two patrols crossed from Tonhe to Intha. 1st patrol – L / Nk. and Rfn. – went towards Dokthida. One mile from village they came across 100 Japs. Having laid ambush they killed 10 Japs including officers. Rfn. was wounded with five bullet wounds but escaped. L / Nk. was about to throw grenade when Japs took him prisoner. They tied him to a tree and bayoneted him in the face, then they took him towards Intha. On the journey they treated him very badly, hitting him on the head. Near to Intha they were ambushed by second patrol of Hav. Dalbahadur and one Rfn. All the men escorting him and several more were killed. The remainder ran away. He then escaped into the jungle and returned by Dokthida to Tonhe.
>
> All the four involved returned though two were wounded . . .
>
> Casualties claimed inflicted on enemy by Hav. – 15 Japs killed, 4 wounded. By L / Nk. – 10 Japs killed, including 2 officers.

The war in Burma was ending; everyone was sure of that, some more sure than others. The 4/10th received an order to send an officer and eight men to take part in victory celebrations in Rangoon while the battalion was still actively engaged in fighting the Japanese. In fact, the battalion earned four more decorations for leadership and gallantry in battles fought after the parade.

The 4/6th, which had been among the chindits, knew that the war was almost over when they were reprimanded by the general commanding the 7th Division for not saluting him when he drove past in his staff car. Their commandant tried to soothe him by explaining that they had not saluted in the field under previous divisional orders, but he would have none of it. They must get rid of their 'commando habits', he told them. Says the regimental history: 'The insult was deeply resented.'

By the end of the war there were fifty-five Gurkha battalions serving in Britain's Indian Army, including more

Gurkha infantrymen than there are English infantry in today's army.

One of the most pleasant duties of all regiments was the release of prisoners of war. The 1/8th were able to release 600 men of their own regiment. Although most of the released prisoners suffered from the effects of disease – malaria, dysentery, scabies or beriberi – it was remarked that they were 'still bright and happy'. Lieutenant-Colonel Allsebrook, former commander of a battalion of the 9th Gurkhas, who had himself been a prisoner of war for three and a half years, spoke feelingly of his reunion with his freed soldiers:

> It was wonderful to see the men again and it was very touching to see their joy at seeing me. They were indeed a wonderful sight, all scrupulously clean and neatly dressed in ancient and patched clothes, sometimes in garments made by themselves . . .
>
> I held a parade to give the men a *sabash* (well done). To my amazement they marched as smartly as on a peacetime ceremonial. A picturesque sight they were. Their soldierly behaviour and appearance brought tributes from everyone . . . How proud I was of their loyalty and fidelity.

The end of the war brought many changes, but perhaps none was more of a bombshell to the Gurkha establishment than the request of the Maharajah of Nepal in 1946 that Gurkha soldiers be allowed to wear their hair long, that is, normal European length. For more than a century the heads of all Gurkhas serving in the Indian Army had been shaved except for a topknot. No one knew why. Nevertheless, it seemed sacrilegious to change this custom. There existed no good reason not to comply with the Maharajah's request, so the Gurkha ranks were allowed to let their hair grow.

For reasons not readily discernible – not discernible at all, in fact – military men have always had decided views about hair. These views have changed at different periods of history and in different armies – pigtails and shaved heads, for example – but nothing so raises a military rash as a change in hair styles. When the Maharajah's whim became an order, old soldiers were sure that the Gurkha Brigade was bound for hell. Colonel H.R.K. Gibbs of the 6th said that 'this departure from long-standing custom was an offence to the conservative eye'. Some never grew accustomed to Gurkha soldiers in front of mirrors with combs and hair oil. One officer, while reluctantly admitting that when the hair was 'kept well cut and brushed' the men looked quite smart, added ' – but oh! those combs!'

Perhaps the most important post-war change was the transformation of regimental centres formerly used for recruiting and training to their new role as demobilization and resettlement centres, a complete reversal of function. Unfortunately, the British in India were as slow to demobilize as they had been to mobilize when the war started. Wartime soldiers in Indian and British armies had enlisted for the duration of the war plus one year, but as soon as the fighting stopped most wanted instantly to be discharged. Although the official date for the end of the war was declared to be 1 April 1946, many soldiers were required to stay well beyond April 1947. In the administrative jumble, many who were anxious to remain in the army were discharged and many anxious to leave were retained. Failure to demobilize promptly and efficiently resulted in much discontent throughout the Indian Army and, indeed, throughout the entire British Army. There were cases of mass insubordination and a few cases of actual mutiny; Gurkhas were often employed to overawe this discontent.

British officialdom remained remarkably insensitive to the grievances of its veterans and seemingly unaware of its own inefficiency. It took the 5th Regimental Centre twenty-two months to release 6,389 men, but the regimental history says of this snail's pace operation that it was 'surely an achievement of which it may be proud'. One wonders why.

The United States Army, perhaps too hastily, discharged eight million men before the British decided the war was over; the British authorities, however, appeared unable to grasp the fact that the young men – British, Indian and Gurkha – who had so eagerly volunteered their services during the war were equally enthusiastic about returning to civilian life when the fighting ended. It was someone's curious notion that Indian and Gurkha soldiers about to be discharged should be 'trained' for civilian life. A gigantic scheme under Brigadier F.S. Brayne was put in motion. Courses were given to Gurkhas in pig-raising, bee-keeping, the rearing of guinea-fowl, design-printing on textiles, soap-making, calico-dyeing, embroidery, tailoring, cotton-spinning, basket-weaving, knitting and other skills. They were also instructed in hygiene, the use of manure, the conservation of savings, and anti-malarial measures. In many depots, schools and model farms were established. British officers knew little or nothing about most of these subjects themselves, but they struggled valiantly to teach them. This great 'resettlement' scheme was not popular; it was even less popular when it was discovered that men who volunteered for courses in cottage industries or farming had their release dates set back until they had finished their courses.

Even when discharged, it was not always easy for a soldier to return safely to his home with the wages due to him. Gurkha soldiers were paid in Indian rupees and the Nepal Durbar set an exchange rate which resulted in the ex-soldiers receiving far fewer Nepalese rupees when they exchanged their money. Ostensibly to alleviate this situation, the government of India allowed each man to purchase twenty-five yards of cloth and either a 'part-worn' greatcoat or an additional five yards of cloth, all of which the Nepal Durbar allowed to be imported duty-free. This operation enabled the Nepalese to continue bilking their own men and allowed the British to dispose of part of their immense and now completely useless store of greatcoats; it also assisted the sagging textile industry in India while enabling ex-soldiers to obtain cloth and clothing at cut rates. It proved popular with everyone.

The tiny kingdom of Nepal paid dearly in the blood of its young manhood for assisting the British: 7,544 were killed in action or died of wounds or disease, and another 1,441 were listed as missing, probably dead, making the total nearly 9,000. In addition, 23,655 were severely wounded or injured. Nepal's mercenary soldiers did, however, cover themselves with military glory, gaining 2,734 decorations, mentions in despatches and gallantry certificates.

Not everyone was pleased when the war ended. A jemadar of the 3rd Gurkhas came to Captain Tim Carew to complain that he had not had enough fighting. When Carew reminded him that in an action near Imphal he had distinguished himself, he protested: 'But I personally killed no enemy on that occasion . . . Also, there are new men in my platoon who have never seen battle, and they are very annoyed that the war is finished. They are asking me what they are wanted for.' But Gurkhas were still needed and there was to be more fighting for them in years ahead.

Military Occupations

For those content to give fighting a rest, the post-war deployment of the 2/5th seemed most fortunate. They were selected to be part of the Commonwealth Occupation Force in Japan. Britain wanted to make a good impression, not only on the Japanese but on her allies, who were also providing occupation troops, so it was decreed that all clothing, equipment and arms (except for American grenade launchers) would be of British manufacture. Supplies were issued on a lavish scale and no expense was spared. The battalion hired four tailors from Bombay and kept them busy for several weeks. New vehicles were issued, including 3-tonners and 15-kwt trucks, and there was even a real staff car for the battalion commandant. As one officer said, 'It was a dream come true.'

On 22 July 1946 the Second Battalion, 5th Royal Gurkha Rifles (Frontier Force) moved to Tokyo, where it found the guard for a number of posts, including the British and Canadian embassies and the Yakasami Shrine, and provided thirteen sentries for the Imperial Palace. The 8th United States Cavalry welcomed them with fifty gallons of ice cream, a luxury few had tasted, and Gurkhas and Americans became fast friends. For their part, the British put on for the Americans a ceremonial display involving massed bands of all British regiments. The American soldiers, at least half of whom came from southern states, listened politely to a spirited, if tactless, rendering of 'Marching Through Georgia'. The day closed with a ball at the Mitsui Hotel for 300 guests. Gurkhas in Nepalese dress presented each woman with a flower and a fan bearing the crest of the 5th Gurkhas.

Japan and Thailand were the only countries to which Gurkhas were sent in the immediate post-war period where no military action was required. In the great surge of nationalism that welled up and swept away the old colonial powers, communism often enough replaced colonialism – but not everywhere. In Greece the 1/2nd and the 2/7th were among the Allied forces supporting the government against communist rebels and the 2/7th fought a 'small but spirited' battle against E.L.A.S. forces near Patras.

After seeing service in 43 Gurkha Lorried Brigade in Italy the 2/10th sailed from Trieste on 11 July 1945 for service in Syria, where it acted to protect French lives and property from the wrath of Syrian nationalists. The 4/10th and the 4/2nd went to Indo-China, where the French were already at war with their former subjects who were disinclined to be ruled by their ex-masters.

In August 1945 the 4/5th, and later the 4/8th, 3/10th and 3/5th, went to Siam, where venereal disease, to which the Gurkhas fell victim in appalling numbers, was the only serious threat. Not without difficulty a volunteer from each company of the 4/8th was persuaded to act as demonstrator for the proper fitting of the army-issue condom.

During the Japanese occupation of the lands of southeast Asia, the doctrine of 'Asia for the Asians' had been preached and hatred of the European had been assiduously cultivated. Nowhere had this taken root more firmly than in the eastern possessions of the Dutch. Many inhabitants of the Dutch East Indies found Japanese rule no worse, perhaps even preferable, to Dutch rule. As at the war's end the Dutch had no army to send immediately to their former colony, the British sent troops to disarm the Japanese and restore order until the Dutch could take over. This proved a difficult assignment for the troops involved.

The situation, particularly in Java, was chaotic In the interior, Indonesians of different political factions had established their own governments irrespective of Allied military administration. In places the Japanese had handed over their arms to Indonesian nationalists, who then looted the homes of the Dutch and in some cases seized the internment camps, simply replacing the Japanese guards with Indonesians. In other places the Japanese had saved the lives of Dutch citizens threatened by bloodthirsty nationalists. Indonesians screaming 'Merdeka!' (Freedom) demanded immediate and complete self-government; a republic was declared on 17 August 1945. Indonesian factions then took to fighting each other and the British, who were trying to restore order.

In October and November a brigade of Gurkhas was sent to Java. They were not welcomed. The rules of engagement made operations difficult, frustrating and dangerous. They were not allowed to fight unless attacked; they were not allowed to impede the flow of inflammatory rhetoric on the radio or the violent propaganda in the press; they were forbidden to control the Dutch, who arrogantly attempted to reassume power; and officers found it difficult to explain the bizarre conditions in Java to their superiors in India, who did not appreciate the dangers and difficulties. The Indonesians were divided among themselves and it was often impossible to find someone with whom to negotiate during a crisis. Frequently there was no one in charge and those claiming to be leaders seemed usually to be ignored by those they claimed to lead.

In some cases the British re-armed the Japanese and used them as police. The Allied troops on the spot were more than a little perplexed. One officer said, 'Not only was it often impossible to know why fighting was going on, but to know who was fighting whom.' The war diary of the 3/5th for 9 December 1945 reads: 'Naturally enough the present situation is more than a little puzzling to all of us. Our policy changes as rapidly as the weather.'

The Indonesian rhetoric relied heavily on racist statements designed to pit Asians against Europeans. Some of it was directed towards the troops of the Indian Army, many of whose soldiers were already influenced by the highly emotional nationalist sentiments being freely expressed in their homeland, and 'appreciable numbers' deserted. It came as a shock to find that even a few Gurkhas were among them. In the 3/5th three havildar clerks deserted, changed their minds before the battalion left Java and returned to face court martial.

Few of the British, Dutch or French seemed to realize that the end of World War II marked the beginning of the end of Western imperialism – that in less than a quarter of a century all their great colonial empires would dissolve into dozens of independent states. Of these, the two giants to emerge in the East were Indonesia and India.

India, like Indonesia, was in turmoil. There were strikes by port and engineering workers, bank clerks, tram conductors and students. Stabbings, bomb and acid throwing, beatings – all were daily occurences. There was a continual succession of outbreaks; mobs grown out of control were frequently fired on by the police as Muslims, Sikhs and Hindus attacked one another. It did not take much to create an incident. A quarrel over a watermelon left several dead and injured. But the event, that, above all others, engaged the attention of Indians of all creeds as well as British, military and civilian, was the trial of three leaders of the Indian National Army (I.N.A.): prisoners of war who, induced by Japanese propaganda, changed sides and fought for the Japanese.

So many men (perhaps as many as 20,000) had deserted the Indian Army and joined the I.N.A. that it was impossible for the British to punish them all, but they did try to bring the main leaders to justice. At the first trial, held at the Red Fort in Delhi, three I.N.A. officers – a Muslim, a Hindu and a Sikh – were accused of desertion and of fighting for the Japanese. It was probably the British intention to demonstrate their absence of bias against any particular community by this selection of defendants, but the choice ensured that all three major religious communities would be antagonized and would unite in their vilification of the,

British. The Congress Party ecumenically took up the cudgels for all three. Jawaharlal Nehru and other prominent Indian lawyers joined the Defence Committee organized to give legal and financial support to the accused. Gandhi spoke in glowing terms of Subhas Bose, the plump Bengali Brahman who organized the I.N.A. and was subsequently killed in a plane crash, saying, 'His patriotism is second to none. His bravery shines through all of his actions.' Former I.N.A. men were honoured and fêted in their home towns and villages. Posters demanding the freedom of the officers on trial proliferated; some said that 'twenty white dogs' would die for every I.N.A. man harmed. There were huge demonstrations in the streets.

All three were convicted of 'waging war against the King' and sentenced to be cashiered and transported for life. General Auchinleck, Commander-in-Chief of the Indian Army, decided to commute their sentences and they were merely cashiered. His decision scandalized British officers. Lieutenant-General Sir Francis Tuker said: 'The leniency of the punishments handed out to these men was remarkable, especially to those who had committed acts of cruelty on our own soldiers, their brethren in captivity.' Auchinleck's leniency was seen as a sign of weakness by Indian politicians, as perhaps it was. Nehru later said: 'It became a trial of strength between the will of the Indian people and the will of those who held power in India, and it was the will of the people that triumphed in the end.' To have been cashiered by the British was not considered a disgrace by the Indian nationalists and indeed it came to be seen as a badge of honour. One of the three I.N.A. officers later became a junior minister in the government of India. Another, Captain P.K. Sahgal of the 2/10th Baluch Regiment, who had been captured by the 2/10th Gurkhas near Magyagan, Burma, on 28 April 1945, was apotheosized and later took as his wife the leader of an I.N.A. regiment of women (called the Rani of Jhansi's Regiment, after the only female ruler to rebel againt the British during the Mutiny of 1857–9).

Anti-army sentiment was whipped up by newspapers and

politicians and its extent could be measured by the number of army trucks attacked by mobs. Every accident involving a military vehicle was automatically blamed on the army. All attempts to appeal to reason were blown away by slogans and rhetoric. When General Tuker spoke to a group of university students he was bombarded by hostile questions. Why were British soldiers so sex crazy? Why were they so addicted to rape?

As it became apparent that the British were really going to leave India, nationalists tired of flogging a dead horse. In November 1945 there were forty-six attacks upon military vehicles; in February 1946 there were thirty-five; by August there were three, and then none. The storm of hate that had been whipped up turned to communal strife. Hatred of the British had, in a way, been a unifying factor for the Indians. When it became clear that Indians would have to learn to live with each other, people turned to look suspiciously at their neighbours and, where they were different, to attack them. Both the Hindu Congress and the Muslim League did their part in fanning the flames.

The winter of 1945–6 was pleasantly cool in northern India. February in Calcutta was remarkably comfortable, a good time for rioting. The Muslim League called for a demonstration to protest against a sentence of seven years' imprisonment for cruelty and abetment of murder given to one Abdul Rashid, late of the 14th Punjab Regiment and of the Indian National Army. On 11 February 1946, on a bright sunny morning in Calcutta, a large crowd gathered in Wellington Square. The inflammatory speeches began about one o'clock; by three o'clock the rioting had begun. The police arrived with brass-bound staves and by five o'clock the crowd had been generally dispersed – only to reappear after the evening meal for a night of rioting led by students. The police fired tear gas and towards morning had won a period of quiet.

Daybreak was followed by more rioting and the constabulary force of Gurkhas was called in. These were not Gurkhas such as the Indian Army customarily enlisted, but were so-called 'domiciled Gurkhas'. Most had never seen

Nepal, their families having lived in India for one, two or three generations; some were half Indian. They were made to pay dearly for doing their duty during the February riots: Bengali landlords turned them out of their homes, and they were boycotted in the food shops and generally reviled.

Even the constabulary was unable to control the mobs of Muslims who warred with the Hindus. Everyone blamed the British; each community accused them of being biased in favour of their particular enemies. Two battalions of British infantry and the 4/3rd Gurkhas were brought to Calcutta and they soon permeated the city and restored a degree of order. Roads were cleared, rioters were swept out and the dusty streets were left empty of all but soldiers, burning vehicles and the dead.

All this was but a prologue to the drama to come. On 29 July 1946 Mohammed Ali Jinnah, leader of the Muslim League, announced that 16 August would be Direct Action Day. People formed their own ideas about what this was supposed to mean, but it proved to be the beginning of what came to be called the Great Killing, the first of four days of savage slaughter and the bloodiest butchery since the Mutiny more than a hundred years earlier. Rioting, burning, maiming and killing raged unchecked. Weapons were iron bars, swords, firearms – anything that could hurt or kill. Water stopcocks were broken, vehicles and houses were set aflame, and roars of hatred welled up from screaming mobs of surging humanity. Babies and old men were slaughtered; women were raped and mutilated.

The speeches of irresponsible political leaders and inflammatory stories in newspapers added fuel to violence. According to General Tuker, who was in charge of Eastern Command, 'It was the press more than any other body which fanned disagreement into a flaming hatred and fanned it without pity, without scruple, without truth and without care for the consequences.'

Motor patrols of the 1/3rd and 3/8th Gurkhas, which had been added to the military force in Calcutta, drove into mêlées to establish order of a sort. When streets were cleared of the living, the results of their rage were all too apparent in the debris and the dead, many of whom had been horribly mutilated. Lieutenant-Colonel Rose of the 1/3rd Gurkhas described Calcutta in riot as 'a world suddenly gone mad; all the theatrical effects are there, corpses lying unburied in shops and streets, abandoned trams, houses in flames and sporadic firing'.

An officer described one gruesome sight:

> A man had been tied by the ankles to a tramway electric junction box, his hands were bound behind his back and a hole had been made in his forehead so that he bled to death through the brain. He was such a ghastly sight that it was a wonder that the soldiers who were ordered to cut him down and cover him with a nearby sack, were not sick on the spot.

But the soldiers were Gurkhas, who from this time until Independence Day were never off the streets of Calcutta.

Four days of rioting in Calcutta left an estimated 6,000 dead and 20,000 wounded, most of them Hindus. In November at Garhmukteswar during a fair, Jats massacred at least a thousand Muslims. Hindu mobs rampaged through the Muslim quarter of the town, slaughtering women and children. The hospital was attacked and a mob killed a Muslim doctor, the British district medical officer and his assistant. The wife of the Muslim doctor was raped and was paraded naked through the streets. News of this massacre went unreported in the United States and the United Kingdom; no official inquiry was ever held.

In December there was a recrudescence of rioting in Calcutta during the Muslim feast of Muharram, and by the end of the year there were outbreaks of violence throughout central and eastern India. Worse was to come . . . much worse.

CHAPTER

24

Independence and Partition

Independence Day, 15 August 1947, found the 1/5th Gurkhas at Fort Sitabaldi, an old Mahratta fort on a hill overlooking the city of Nagpur. It had long been regarded as a symbol of the strength of the ruling power. The military commander of the area, an Indian, had made elaborate arrangements for a ceremonial hoisting of the new flag of India over the fort, but all arrangements went by the board on the day itself as swarms of humanity swept past the cordons of soldiers, climbed over the walls and fences, and, wild with enthusiasm for their new government, celebrated the creation of a new country in their own way.

In Calcutta, mobs invaded Government House and stole all the silver, poured ink on antique tables and chairs, broke furniture, slashed pictures and broke glass. The large picture of Queen Victoria which hung in the ballroom seemed to attract the most violent attacks.

Things went off more peacefully in Shillong. The garrison engineer there prepared a beautiful Indian flag with gold toggles and cords, but at the last minute the premier of Assam insisted on raising a flag made of *khaddar* (homespun cotton) with curtain rods attached. The new government announced that it would feed the poor and all schoolchildren, but then discovered there was no rice with which to do this. On Independence night a banquet was held at

Government House for about seventy guests and all went peacefully, although as the strongest drink served was pineapple juice the British officers found it a long evening.

At Lucknow the battered buildings of the British Residency, preserved as a memorial to its occupants' stout defence during the long siege of the Mutiny, presented an attractive target to the nationalists. Over a tower flew the Union Jack, day and night – the only place in the Empire where this was authorized. Late in the evening of 13 August, Major-General C. Curtis and a few other officers went quietly to the Residency and watched while a warrant officer hauled the flag down. Sappers worked through the night cutting the steel flagstaff from its base and hacking out its masonry foundation. They cemented the hole flush with the floor and dragged the rubble down the steps and away. On Independence Day, as they had expected, a mob arrived to raise the Indian flag over the tower. Frustrated, they milled about uncertainly until they were quietened by the premier of Uttar Pradesh, who reminded them that this was a memorial to British dead and called upon them to disperse.

So it was that a new nation was born – two large nations, in fact, and subsequently made into three. So, too, was revived in a dreadful form the spectre of religious war, and for the first time since the middle ages religion became a major political factor. India was Hindu, and as Hindus no longer wished to associate peacefully with Muslim neighbours, another intensely nationalistic state was created, Muslim Pakistan: two new turbulent nations to flutter the peace of the world. Hindu and Muslim were at each other's throats instantly.

One of the most frightening aspects of this partition was the failure of the armed forces and the police to maintain order, a failure attributable in part to the political hatreds fanned by the turbulent times and in part to sheer incompetence. There was a serious mutiny in the Indian Navy and lesser mutinies in the Indian Air Force and the Indian Army. There were also mutinies among some police forces, notably that of the Bihar police. Muslim police refused to arrest Muslims and Hindu police refused to arrest Hindus. Only Gurkhas performed their duties impartially and with humanity in a raging sea of hate, fear and distrust.

In spite of the anti-British and anti-army sentiments of the political leaders, a considerable number of British officers were asked to stay on. The 'Indianization' of the army under the British had been too slow and the system had not yet produced enough Indian officers, particularly in the higher ranks. To keep the peace along the new frontier between India and Pakistan, Mountbatten had established the Punjab Boundary Force based on the excellent 4th Indian Division under Major-General T.W. ('Pete') Reese. Although this force contained 50,000 troops in all, including Gurkhas, it was not large enough to keep in check the chaos that followed Partition and it was disbanded on 27 August.

In his diary for 5 September 1947 General Tuker wrote: 'The sooner the British are out of Hindustan now, the better. We can't be responsible any longer for what these people do to each other.' What 'these people' were doing to each other was horrible.

Hysteria swept over literally hundreds of millions of people in India and Pakistan, a kind of madness in which mer appear to have lost all sense of humanity. More people were killed in a year than in all the battles fought by the British in World War II. Men, women and children were murdered wholesale; village wells were filled with the dead; women's bellies were slit and they were left to die slowly; children's hands were chopped off. Gangs of Muslims attacked Hindu villages; mobs of Hindus attacked Muslim refugees. Millions of people left their homes: Muslims to make their way, if they could, to Pakistan; Hindus to make their way to India – if they could.

Duncan Forbes has related how the followers of Gandhi, who would not eat meat or even swat a mosquito, 'went on a rampage in the greatest carnage since the Mongol hordes swept in from the steppes of Central Asia half a millennium before'. Hundreds of thousands were killed. Trains arrived in Pakistan filled only with corpses and on the side of the coaches was scrawled: A PRESENT FROM INDIA.

The 2nd Gurkhas were celebrating their regimental day, Delhi Day, at Dehra Dun when word reached the cantonments of a riot in the town. Someone near a mosque had thrown a stone at a Hindu religious procession. A mobile column of Gurkhas raced to the scene and cleared the street. An officer described what was now a familiar scene: 'The facts lay about the streets in the shape of dead Muslims, fire smouldering at the wooden doors of little shops, gutted and looted houses, the usual nauseating debris of Indian communal riot with a monsoon drizzle diluting the blood in the streets and washing it into the gutters.'

Railway trains filled with refugees were frequently attacked. The 2/1st Gurkhas left Peshawar for Allahabad by train on 31 August. All along the way they saw dead bodies. When, shortly before noon, they pulled into the station at Ambala, they found a train standing there with about 200 dead Muslims. Most had been killed with spear thrusts or sword cuts. Only seventeen of the victims were still alive, one, an old man, bleeding from sixteen spear wounds. One was a little girl of four or five whose legs had been hacked off above her knees. A pregnant woman was barely alive; her unborn baby had been ripped out of her womb and thrown in her face. Neither the Sikh police nor Sikh civilians would help the wounded. The commanding officer of the Gurkhas called the new Indian District Commissioner and described the carnage, but the commissioner was unable to come – he had not yet had lunch.

Hindus and Muslims alike behaved barbarously, but it is generally agreed – at least among the British witnesses – that the Sikhs were the worst. The Sikhs believed their ferocity was a sacred duty, for when Gobind Sing (1675–1708), the tenth and last guru of the Sikhs, was a boy of eleven, Muslims had cut off his father's head and presented it to him. Sydney Smith, correspondent of the *Daily Express*, stood on a street corner in Ludhiana while a Sikh mob, aided by Sikh police in uniform, attacked Muslim houses, dragged their occupants into the street and shot them while a superintendent of police watched. Asked by Smith what he intended to do, he replied, 'We are doing very well. We expect to exterminate every Muslim.' General Tuker said: 'Sikh savagery was appalling. Long after the victim was dead they would slash and slash away at the body, carving it up. They, and many Hindus, were like dogs that had taken to killing sheep – just an insensate devilish lust to wallow in the blood of helpless creatures.'

Major Clifford Williams, a staff officer with 11 Infantry Brigade, 4th Indian Division, wrote:

> I was driving down the Grand Trunk Road between Jullandar and Ludhiana when I came across the scene of a recent atrocity. By the side of the road were the naked mutilated bodies of about forty women, only one alive. The common mutilations were breasts cut off and stomachs of pregnant women slit open with their unborn babies beside them. While I gazed at this gruesome sight, a woman without breasts painfully sat up, saw me and sank back to die, and as she did so pulled a piece of clothing to hide her nakedness.

Most pitiable of all were those who tried to escape the massacre by fleeing to the land of their co-religionists. An estimated eight and a half million people crossed the frontier in one direction or the other. If they escaped death by the sword, they were herded into huge refugee camps with woefully inadequate facilities. There were fifty-six of these in India, the largest being at Kurukshetra, which held a quarter of a million. These wretched people, Muslims and Hindus, had no homes, no clothes and almost no food. Their plight was often made worse by politicians and bureaucrats: the East Punjab government, for example, forbade refugees to take food into West Punjab. People by the tens of thousands died of starvation, exposure, cholera, dysentery and other disorders.

At Partition the great Indian Army had not yet been divided into its three parts. The Pakistani and Indian governments-to-be established a Joint Defence Council on 11 August 1947, and under this Council Field-Marshal Auchinleck was to be the Supreme Commander. His headquarters was to continue to exist until 1 April 1948, by which time two armies were to be created. However, in November 1947 Auchinleck announced that his headquarters would close for lack of cooperation and goodwill on the part of representatives of the two countries.

Muslim units could not be trusted to guard Hindus and Hindu units could not be trusted to guard Muslims, while Sikh soldiers killed Muslims they were sent to protect. In this evaginated world, only the remaining British and Gurkha battalions could be relied upon. Gurkhas, although Hindus, dealt even-handedly and impartially with all, in spite of the tremendous pressures put upon them by their co-religionists and by national politicians, both Nepalese and Indian, and the many uncertainties created by British and Indian imbecilities.

D Company of the 2/9th was guarding a train loaded with Muslim refugees on their way from Ambala to Lahore when, passing through Patiala State (predominately Sikh), the train screeched to a halt in the countryside far from any station. The Hindu crew claimed that the fire-box had burned out and the train would not move. Terror seized the refugees. The Gurkhas were at once deployed into tactical platoon positions that gave the train an all-round defence. Luckily there were railwaymen among the refugees. They inspected the engine and found nothing wrong. The original crew, with rifles in their backs and Gurkha riflemen on the footplate, were ordered to get the train moving. As the engine gathered speed, the crump of a 3-inch mortar shell was heard behind them. The Sikh soldiers of the Patiala State Forces had arrived – only minutes too late.

Unfortunately, there were not enough Gurkhas to guard all the convoys of refugees and to quell all the riots. Captain W.D. Wells of the 7th Gurkhas wrote: 'We were at Dehra Baba Nanak [Gurdaspur District, northern Punjab] when the balloon went up. Murder, arson and loot [sic] ran riot. We were needed everywhere, and guarding, patrolling, escorting, investigating went on without stop twenty-four hours a day. There simply were not enough of us to cope with the outbreaks. They were terrible. Villages set on fire, whole families slaughtered in one room – their bodies still burning, women and children with their guts hanging out and slowly dying, heaps of dead feasted upon by pi-dogs and vultures. The smell of rotting flesh in the air.'

The Gurkha soldiers were ill-rewarded for their steadfast loyalty in those perilous days. For the first time since 1816 they were involved in a conflict in which their own interests were at stake. No one knew what was to become of the Gurkha mercenaries. Being Hindu, it was never contemplated that any of the Gurkha battalions would become part of the Pakistani Army: the question was how many, if any, would stay in the army of the new India, and how many, if any, would Britain retain. The divorce of Britain from its largest overseas territory was more complicated than anyone, British or Indian, had imagined, and all was done too hurriedly. General Tuker later complained: 'Whatever the reason, the anxieties of the trusting Gurkhas seem to have had little attention while the demands of the suspicious India held the field throughout.' Indeed, the Gurkha situation had of necessity to be subservient to the larger problems of Independence and Partition, but the Gurkhas ought not to have been lost sight of in the general reshuffle.

In his journal for 23 October 1946 Lord Wavell, then still Viceroy of India, wrote: 'A really bad day . . . Cabinet meeting considered Gurkhas, oil-seeds control, jute control and appointments of non-Indians. Nehru silent and sulky . . .' What was said is unknown. Although not forgotten, Gurkhas ought not, perhaps, to have been considered along with oil-seeds control.

Back in Britain there was some concern about the fate of the Gurkha regiments. Sir Arthur Salter, M.P., was assured by the government that an effort would be made to secure fair and just treatment for these gallant soldiers. On 10 July and again four days later, two Conservative M.P.s, both ex-officers, raised questions about the Gurkhas and were assured by Prime Minister Attlee that he regarded it as 'important that we should still have the use of Gurkha troops as in the past', and he added that 'there is no attempt to put Gurkhas under anyone whom they do not wish to serve'. Unfortunately, this was not true. Battalions selected for the Indian Army were turned over intact: the Gurkha soldiers had no opportunity to transfer to the British service.

Field-Marshal Montgomery, on his way to Australia, stopped off in India, arriving in Delhi on 23 June 1947. His purpose was to settle the programme for the withdrawal of British troops and 'to get agreement in principle for the continued use of Gurkha troops in the British Army after India had gained its independence'. In his talks with Indian leaders there was no disagreement on the withdrawal of British troops beginning on 15 August, when power was to be transferred to Pakistan and India. Montgomery discussed the Gurkha issue only with Nehru. In his memoirs Montgomery wrote that Nehru 'raised many objections and I did not get his final agreement till the evening of the next day, the 24th June'.

The details of this agreement are unknown, but shortly afterwards the commandants of the ten Gurkha regimental centres were called to Delhi and told that of the twenty-seven battalions still in being (constituting seven per cent of the total British Indian Army) only eight would remain with the British and the rest would be turned over to India. To the frustration and confusion of the commandants, they were still not told which battalions would go and which would stay. Not until 8 August 1947 – only one week before Independence and Partition – did a signal of decision go out from Army headquarters in Delhi: the first two battalions of the 2nd, 6th, 7th and 10th regiments were to become part of the British Army; all others were to pass to the army of the new India.

The reasoning that determined the selection of the four regiments to remain with the British is unknown, but it has been suggested that, as all four had battalions in Burma, the selection was made merely on the basis of administrative convenience – these battalions would not be required to return to India. However, the 7th and 10th Gurkhas recruited from eastern Nepal and the 2nd and 6th from western Nepal, and this may have influenced the selection. As the 7th and 10th were the only regiments recruiting Rais, Limbus, Sunwars and other *kiranti*, India raised a new regiment, the 11th Gurkhas, to recruit in eastern Nepal. Curiously, neither the British nor the Indians changed the regimental numbers; to this day they are numbered from one to eleven without regard to the nations they serve, as if all were still a part of the same army. Some Britons thought it particularly disgraceful that the 5th, a 'Royal' regiment, had been handed over to the Republic of India.

The British took the loyalty of the Gurkhas for granted and certainly imposed upon their patience. Neither the Gurkha ranks nor their officers knew what their future was to be. They were kept in suspense for so long that it created intense psychological stress, a stress made almost unbearable by the propaganda directed at them by Indians and 'domiciled Gurkhas'. There was a regrettable tendency on the part of the British to regard the Gurkhas' fidelity as, at least in part, a need for dependence on the part of the 'little men' (as they were perhaps too often affectionately called). This sometimes made the British forget that Gurkhas were in every sense *men* with responsibility for their families and concern for their careers and that these were responsibilities and concerns which equalled or exceeded their own.

Where accurate information was absent, rumours filled the vacuum. Among these was a rumour, reinforced by an article in the *Statesman* published in New Delhi on 13 June 1947, which reported that Indian officers would soon be posted to Gurkha battalions. Although they were a part of the Indian Army, officers and men in Gurkha regiments had always considered themselves something special and different – better than others. There was evidence to support this attitude. Gurkha regiments were not serially numbered with other regiments of Indian infantry and Gurkha battalions were exempt from the programme of 'Indianization' of the Indian Army which had begun in the 1920s. For any given military task, Gurkha and British troops were regarded as interchangeable. Gurkhas disdained Indian, or *'desi'*, regiments, 'which we of the Gurkha Brigade looked down upon as you look at a door-mat before wiping your feet', as Adrian Hayter put it. Indians, on the other hand, particularly Brahmans, looked down on the lower caste Gurkhas as barbarians. British Tommies and Johnny Gurkhas fraternized in a way that Indian and British troops never did. Rumours that they were to be treated like the rest of the Indian Army came as a shock. Gradually bitterness took root and distrust grew. Added to the soldiers' uneasiness was the rapid turnover of officers since the end of the war; there were fewer familiar and trusted faces among their regimental officers. Many Gurkhas began to feel, as one British officer expressed it, 'that we're all deserting them, like rats leaving a sinking ship . . . For the first time in my life I felt that the men distrusted us.'

Pressure upon the Gurkhas, who could get no answers from their officers to their anxious questions concerning their conditions of service, came in a number of different forms. In some places they and their wives found that merchants in the bazaars refused to sell to them; many were subjected to insults and molestation. In Calcutta after Independence Gurkhas were fined for carrying their *kukris*. On the other hand there was much anti-British propaganda from organizations such as the Nepalese National Congress (N.N.C.), a political body composed of domiciled Nepalese, many of them half Indian. According to General Tuker, whose views were conservative, members of the N.N.C. entertained extreme leftist or communist views and the organization 'attached itself to the Army and did no small measure of damage'.

Finally, after Independence, a referendum was held in each of the battalions selected to become part of the British regular army: each man in the eight battalions that were to be retained in the British service was called before a board consisting of a British, an Indian and a Nepalese officer and asked for his decision. He could elect to stay with his battalion, transfer to a battalion which would become part of the Indian Army, or take his discharge with some compensation. Probably few understood the implications of their choice. How could they? The British had not yet made up their minds what they would do with their Gurkha battalions, but it was obvious that they must serve outside India and Pakistan. What was to become of their families now that their traditional regimental homes were to disappear? What was to be the place of the Gurkhas as the only Asians and the only mercenaries in the British Army? Were the terms of service to be different? When it was learned that the Gurkha regiments' new homes were to be in Malaya there were further questions. Malaya was further away from Nepal and it was known to be more expensive than India. It would be some time before their families could join them there. There were schools for their children in India; would there be schools in Malaya? None were there now. The climate of Malaya was enervating and was thought to be unhealthy for those predisposed to tuberculosis. How would they get back to Nepal on leave, or return when they were discharged? Their British officers could give them no firm answers and, indeed, were themselves long kept in the dark concerning their own careers; they too were apprehensive.

India was familiar; Gurkha families were already there. India seemed to offer more opportunities. The Indian Army immediately gave regular commissions to sixteen Gurkha officers, leading others to think that they too might be commissioned. (India did not repeat this. As the Gurkha officers were phased out they were replaced by Indians and the Indian Army reverted to the British system, differing only in calling Gurkha officers Junior Commissioned Officers and generally keeping the old Indian Army names for ranks – see Appendix A.)

The inclination of many of the Gurkha officers towards Indian Army service undoubtedly influenced the other ranks. In the end, the majority of Gurkha soldiers elected to go with India's army. In the 2/7th only fifty-three men in the entire battalion elected to stay; in another battalion only one man volunteered for the British service – and he recanted when he discovered his lonely position. In battalions which had been serving in Pakistan and Burma and had not been exposed to the intensive Indian political propaganda, fewer opted for India. The 2/5th, while in Japan, had been out of touch with the turmoil in India. When it returned, just twelve days before Independence, its men were confused by the changes and by the sudden need to make decisions.

British officers were also confused – and angry. They directed their anger towards Indian politicians and, most of all, towards their own government for its indecision and for not dealing fairly and openly with the Gurkhas. The result was, as General Tuker said, 'our own British fault. We had hopelessly mishandled the whole business.'

Transition

If ever there was a time for British officers in India to display a stiff upper lip, it was during the last six months of 1947. If some of these lips quivered a bit it was certainly understandable. General Tuker summed up the British officer's position:

> At this time the British officer's greatest enemy was depression. This was born of a knowledge of failure – failure to produce anything of permanent value in India – the knowledge of a life wasted, the blank future before him; the detestable atmosphere of hatred about him; his own career and personal difficulties, particularly those of his family; difficulty of getting a passage for them and himself when he wanted it and packing up and despatching his recently opened household goods; apprehension of British customs duties on the little he possessed, and so on.

British officers in Gurkha regiments, particularly those who had served in Burma, asked why, having fought for so long and so hard to save India from the Japanese, they were now quitting it. No easy answer was available.

Hardest of all for the officers to accept was the decision of their men to serve under disdained *'desi'* (Indian) officers in the new Indian Army; it seemed like desertion to some, a betrayal as painful and personal as that of a faithless mistress. Before World War II Adrian Hayter's mother had instructed him: 'You must serve with Gurkha troops because they are so loyal.' Paternalism had always been a characteristic of the old Indian Army, and it was particularly strong among British officers serving with Gurkhas; British officers and Gurkhas had always seemed bound by the strongest ties of mutual loyalty, but now these bonds were sorely tested.

Major L.E. Pottinger transferred to the 6th Gurkhas when the 9th became part of the new Indian Army. Thirteen years later he wrote of the Gurkhas' feeling that their British officers had abandoned them:

> The worst thing was finding that the G.O.s [Gurkha Officers] and men did not understand, could not understand. They had served us, in our own few years of service during and after the war, with their accustomed loyalty, while their fathers had been serving our fathers for well over a hundred years in a spirit of brotherhood and trust that is peculiar to a Gurkha Regiment. Now their British officers were walking out and leaving them during conditions of near-chaos, leaving them moreover to be officered by Indians, in whose ability and integrity they had little confidence. They could not at first believe that the all-powerful British Raj, which had only recently beaten the Germans and the Japanese, could be so base as to abandon them. When they realized what was happening, they were resentful; and who shall blame them?

> We felt that we were a bunch of rats leaving our Regiment, and our own morale was as low as that of the men. A similar state of low morale prevailed to a greater or less degree in all the Gurkha Regiments which had not been chosen for the British Army, and everywhere there was a feeling of bitterness and frustration.

For British officers this was the 'time of the opt'. First, all were asked which British regiment they would prefer to join if there were no more Gurkha battalions or no vacancies in those that remained. Those for whom no places were available in the East were given surprisingly generous options. They could resign at once or within a year, and receive £3,300 in compensation for loss of career plus a pension of £330 per annum, or they could transfer to the British Army with a compensation of £725. It was less clear what was to happen to the officers who elected to stay but for whom there was no place. Major P. Richardson, then with the 2/9th, later wrote, 'The British officers felt bitterly disappointed at the loss of their regiments.'

Before Independence there had been an appeal to British officers in Gurkha regiments destined for the Indian Army to serve on for a year after Independence Day. Many did, with the consent of the British government, but this offer was soon withdrawn and nearly all were peremptorily ordered to quit their posts by the end of 1947. By the end of 1948 there were only 194 British officers in the Indian service; in October 1955 Major-General H. Williams, Engineer-in-Chief, was the last senior officer to leave.

In addition to anxiety about their own fate and that of their men -- or those formerly under their command -- there was also concern for the funds and properties of the officers' messes. What was to happen to the Mess Debentures, the Polo Debentures, the British Officers' Private Fund, the Regimental Mess Trust? And what was to happen to all that beautiful silver, not to mention the moth-eaten antelope heads, the chairs, the billiard tables, the trophies, medals and memorabilia? Were all these to be turned over to strangers, to Indian officers? And what of their battle honours, their proud traditions and cherished customs? Were they all to be jettisoned?

Before Independence and before the fate of individual regiments was known, the Commander-in-Chief issued instructions to all commanding officers of Gurkha battalions to turn over intact those units selected for the Indian Army, including the property of the officers' mess. At least one regiment, the 2nd Gurkhas, had no intention of obeying: all its silver was sent to silversmiths 'for repair and cleaning'. When the danger was past and the first two battalions of the regiment were selected for the British Army, the silversmiths were instructed to send the treasures to the regiment's new home in Malaya. In the 9th Gurkhas there was an attempt on the part of some British officers to smuggle regimental funds to the United Kingdom. Distrust and misunderstanding on the part of both British and Indian officers caused much bitterness on both sides.

The 4th Gurkhas managed to get some funds to England before Independence Day and these were used for various purposes: a part was earmarked for the War Memorial Fund, to which all ranks had contributed; part was spent on publishing the third, and last, volume of the regimental history; and Rs. 8,000 were paid for the re-erection in England of the memorial tablet which had been in St Oswald's Church at Bakloh.

Compliance with the Commander-in-Chief's instructions was not easy. Gurkha regiments, unlike other regiments in the Indian Army, where each battalion had its own treasures, held all their silver and trophies as the property of the regiments collectively; battalions were considered to have only 'field service messes', a custom that made turning over mess property a source of misunderstanding and suspicion.

Another source of contention was the disposition of Regimental Mess Trusts. These were funds put in trust in 1939 so that money would be available at the end of the war to refurbish the messes. At the same time the messes, with all their furnishings, silver and so on, were given on loan to the regimental centres. The British officers contended that the Regimental Mess Trusts should be transferred to the United Kingdom, where they could be used to publish regimental histories or turned over to regimental associations.

Most of the Indian officers who came to take over the Gurkha battalions could not understand why there was so little silver, nor could they understand or believe in the regimental system for messes. When Major D.K. Palit came to take over the 3/9th he and his officers had to dine off tin plates in the mess, even though the entire regiment had passed to the Indian Army. The Indian commanding officer of the regimental centre of the 9th and the battalion commander of the 2/9th charged that the British officers had stolen the silver and carried off the furnishings. It was in this unhealthy atmosphere that the 2/9th held one last great, wild party and destroyed much of the mess property.

Not all takeovers were marred by bitterness, spitefulness and distrust. A few battalions were handed over smoothly and amicably. In the 4th Gurkhas the British officers were impressed by the high quality and professional keenness of the Indian officers who took over from them. In the 6th Gurkhas the first two battalions were to remain but the Third Battalion, which was raised during the war, was handed over to India. Lieutenant-Colonel C.E. James, M.B.E., an Indian Christian, arrived from the 8th Punjab Regiment to assume command. According to Colonel H.R.K. Gibbs, he proved to be 'competent, sympathetic and popular'. As the Indian Army was to have no regiment labelled 6th Gurkhas, the 3/6th became the 5/5th.

The Indians appear to have chosen their officers for Gurkha battalions with great care. Nearly all were tactful gentlemen. (Indeed, former prime minister Lord Attlee once told the author that Indian Army officers were the 'last *pukka* Englishmen'.) Tact could and did ease the social strains, but for many the experience remained galling and not all British officers behaved decently. Major-General D.K. Palit, Vr.C., still remembers the time when he assumed command of the 3/9th as a 'painful and bewildering experience'.

One British officer tried to explain that 'the difficulty sprang from the suddenness, the haste and uncertainty of what was being done'. Years later, some achieved a better perspective, as did Major L.E. Pottinger:

> Looking back, we can sympathize not only with the Gurkhas but with the Indian officers who had the formidable task of winning the men's confidence, restoring morale and reshaping those battalions into loyal units of the new Indian Army. They succeeded, and they succeeded moreover in reviving and perpetuating the spirit and traditions of the Regiments . . . The Indian officers, particularly in the early days, did a magnifi-

cent job in the most discouraging circumstances. It is to be
regretted that in many cases there was little effort to make
them feel welcome.

The Gurkha battalions on the West Pakistan side of the
new frontier on Independence Day experienced special difficulties. The 1/4th, caught in Waziristan, sustained casualties when attacked by a Muslim mob. Gurkhas could expect
no help from the Muslim troops in Pakistan. The 5th and
6th Gurkhas had made their home in Abbottabad for ninety
years, but the Pakistanis ordered them to be gone within a
fortnight and the Gurkhas made haste to comply. In St
Luke's Church in Abbottabad were memorial tablets to
those officers of the 5th who had died in service. These were
taken down and shipped to England, where the regimental
association of the 5th Royal Gurkha Rifles (Frontier Force)
took charge of them and eventually arranged for them to
be installed in St Luke's Church in Chelsea. The regimental
memorials of the 6th Gurkhas were taken down and shipped
to the regiment's new home in Malaya. Left behind by both
regiments were their barracks, messes and clubs, the playing fields, the *Dashera* House, the little temple, and their
dead. The Gurkha Memorial Cemetery was turned over to
Pakistan's Frontier Force Rifles with the suggestion that
when they no longer had serving Hindus the cemetery
should be converted into a garden and children's recreational centre.

There was a general clean-out of the messes at Abbottabad and all that could be saved was packed up for the move
to India. The two regiments that had served together for so
many generations were to be parted for ever. The 6th
remained in the British service and it became (in 1959) the
6th Queen Elizabeth's Own Gurkha Rifles; the 5th lost its
'Royal' designation (but kept 'Frontier Force' in paren-
thesis after its name) in the Republic of India's army. Most
of the soldiers' families left together by train, but a group
of pregnant wives was left behind to follow after they had
delivered. One, however, refused to remain; her baby boy,
born on the train, was appropriately named 'Railbahadur'.

In the 1/6th all the clerks opted for the Indian Army. To prevent administration from collapsing an arrangement was worked out for the 1/6th to borrow them from the Indian Army, and they stayed at their old duties and moved with the battalion to Malaya. When replacements arrived a few months later the clerks had changed their minds and were eager to stay, but it was too late. They were dispatched to India. There were a number of other soldiers who, having declared for the Indian Army, later changed their minds. Colonel E.D. Smith described what happened:

> Some re-enlisted, others pretended to be part of our show and we sent them off to Malaya with new British Army numbers. We had no staff to check anything and eventually the Indian Army posted them as 'deserters, believed to be serving in the British Army'. They were – and most of them were given a nominal punishment and allowed to stay.

The turmoil in India during these post-war years spilled over into Nepal. Both the Nepalese National Congress and the Communist Party of India encouraged agitation. In the spring of 1947 a Dr R.M. Lohia of the Socialist Party of India instigated a strike at Nepal's newest and best industrial plant, a jute mill at Biratnagar on the Bihar border. Resentment of the ruling Rana family grew strong in the Katmandu Valley. Anti-Rana rumours swept through the bazaars of India. Indian newspapers featured stories of Rana oppression. In the Nepal Durbar there was fear of the new India.

Within two years of India's independence there was a violent revolution in Nepal, and the Rana family, which for 104 years had provided the country with hereditary prime ministers and commanders-in-chief, was overthrown. The head of the revolutionaries was King Mahendra, the titular ruler, who now became his country's ruler in fact.

This instability at home had its effect on the Gurkha soldiers, who tried to puzzle out a confusing situation amid the conflicting arguments of politicians. The unstable political atmosphere also made it difficult for Britain and India to conclude a tripartite agreement with Nepal on the employment of Gurkha mercenaries. Negotiations moved forward slowly in a climate of uncertainty and distrust. Both the British and the Nepalese feared that the Indians would exercise an undue influence on Nepal's affairs by propagandizing their Gurkha troops. India, fearful that Britain would draw off the best recruits by offering higher rates of pay, insisted that Gurkhas be paid the same (Indian rates) in both armies – about Rs. 350 for a rifleman (approximately £23 or U.S. $40). The British have since circumvented this agreement by paying generous 'allowances' which make the British service financially more attractive than the Indian. The Nepalese insisted that Britain and India should make a pledge never to use Gurkhas to fight Gurkhas. This has so far been honoured, but Britain and India also agreed that they would not employ Gurkhas against other Hindus or against civilians and both countries have violated these undertakings.

The customs, traditions and ways of doing things of the Gurkha regiments have largely been retained, no radical changes have been made. The initial bitterness has vanished for the most part. British and Indian officers wear the same Gurkha tie. Major L.E. Pottinger, writing in 1970, said: 'If you meet an officer of an Indian Gurkha regiment nowadays, you will find that he is as proud to be serving with Gurkha soldiers as we are, and if you are lucky enough to be offered the hospitality of an Indian Gurkha battalion, you will find that the men are as proud of their regiment and their officers as ever before.'

The new Indian Army changed the spelling of Gurkha to *Gorkha*, but retained all the old ranks with the exception of the title of jemadar, which became *naib subadar*. The uniform was hardly changed at all, but of course the badges of rank were altered, although keeping basically to the same system. The British crown was replaced by the three-headed Asoka lion; the *chakra* (wheel) replaced the four-pointed British star. Medals awarded for gallantry were also changed; there is none in the shape of a cross. Viceroy's Commissioned Officers became Junior Commissioned Officers. Those regimental days deemed repugnant to patriotic

Indians or to nationalistic sentiment, such as those commemorating Mutiny battles, were replaced by others commemorating engagements fought in other wars, or simply by a Raising Day, to recall the foundation of the regiment.

As there was no longer a viceroy the British no longer had Viceroy's Commissioned Officers, and all these became either Gurkha Commissioned Officers (G.C.O.s) or King's (later Queen's) Gurkha Officers (K.G.O.s or Q.G.O.s). The first of these had exactly the same status as British officers. Seeing how effective direct commissions were in luring Gurkha officers into the Indian Army, the British also tried offering them for a time. Both armies soon dropped the practice. Few G.C.O.s were created; none recently. The K.G.O.s were exactly like the old V.C.O.s and the Indian Army's J.C.O.s.

Perhaps the greatest change in the British service was in the names of the K.G.O.s' and the N.C.O.s' ranks. The old Indian Army names disappeared. The subadar-major became the Gurkha major; subadars became Gurkha captains; and jemadars became Gurkha lieutenants. For all non-commissioned officer ranks, the names adopted were those used in the British Army.

CHAPTER
26

The Savage Wars
of Peace

The first war fought by the new Indian Army was against
the new army of Pakistan, pitting against each other
men who had so lately served side by side. It began, almost
at the moment of Partition, in the beautiful lands of Jammu
and Kashmir. It was here that Gurkhas demonstrated they
could fight just as well, as bravely and as skilfully, under
Indian officers for India as they had fought under British
officers for the United Kingdom. Battalions of the 5th, 8th
and 9th Gorkhas took part in this inconclusive war. In 1948
Gurkhas also took part in India's invasion of the princely
state of Hyderabad and in the 1965 and 1971 wars with
Pakistan.

When on 14 July 1950 Trygve Lie, Secretary General of
the United Nations, asked all member nations for help in
Korea, Prime Minister Nehru explained that it was not in
keeping with Indian policy to send combat troops outside
the country as India's defence force was maintained solely
for internal defence. This policy was not long maintained.
On 14 March 1961 India dispatched a brigade group (5,650
men) under Brigadier K.A.S. Raja to be part of the United
Nations peace-keeping force in the Congo province of
Katanga. Included in this force were the 3/1st, 2/5th and
5/5th Gorkhas. In the fighting around Elizabethville on 5
December 1961 Captain G.S. Salaria of the 3/1st Gorkhas

earned a posthumous Param Vir Chakra, India's equivalent of the Victoria Cross, and two Gurkha riflemen were
awarded the Sena Army Medal for bravery.

The brigade group was withdrawn in March and April
1963. In the meantime, India was engaged in military
actions closer to home.

The first three battalions of the 9th Gorkhas were posted
in company strength positions along the peaks and valleys
of the Ladakh range in eastern Kashmir when at dawn on
20 October 1962 the Chinese launched an attack on them.
The 1/9th bore the first shock, although other troops were
quickly rushed to the area, including the 1/1st, which was
flown straight from its *Dashera* celebrations at Delhi. The
Gurkhas grimly joked that 'Mahakal'., nectar' (blood) was
still on the tongue of the goddess, but she thirsted for more.
Some of the fighting took place at elevations of 14,000 feet
and many men died of exposure in the bitter weather, as
did the battalion commander of the 8th Gorkhas. At Srijap
Post, Major Dhan Sing Thapa, one of the Gurkhas who had
been given a regular commission, distinguished himself in
hand-to-hand fighting and was awarded the Param Vir
Chakra.

Although Gurkhas make the finest infantrymen in the
world, and no one should know this better than the British,
almost from the moment they passed from the old Indian
Army into the British service efforts were made to put them
to other uses. The first attempt was the conversion to artillery of the 2/7th Gurkhas. Companies became batteries,
corporals became bombardiers, and Gurkha ranks learned
to man field pieces. The need for good infantry in the jungles of Malaya put an end to this ill-conceived experiment,
but later, units of signallers, sappers, truck drivers and
military police were created and for several years there was
even a Gurkha dog company with Alsatian security dogs
and Labrador trackers. Recruits do not always appear to
have been assigned to units where their best talents could
be used. In 1960, for example, recruit Jaganbahadur Limbu
proved himself the champion rifle shot, obtaining a score

of seventy-one out of a possible seventy-five points in classification. He was assigned, not to the infantry, but to the Gurkha Army Service Corps, where it was highly unlikely that he would ever need to fire his rifle in combat.

However, it was not a far-fetched idea to make paratroopers out of Gurkhas, paras being basically infantrymen trained to leap from aircraft and re-form as infantry on the ground. The first parachute unit was the 153rd Gurkha Parachute Battalion, raised in 1941 by Lieutenant-Colonel F.J. Loftus-Tottenham, former commandant of the 1/10th. This unit saw action twice. It distinguished itself at Shangshak in March 1944 when it played an important role in stemming the Japanese advance on Imphal, and again near the end of the war when two companies were successfully dropped on Elephant Point in May 1945, to silence guns commanding the river approach to Rangoon in advance of the seaboard assault.

There is a story, perhaps apocryphal, that a group of Gurkhas, when told that they might jump out of aircraft flying as low as 600 feet, looked worried and said that they thought 300 feet would be more reasonable. An officer explained that at this height their parachutes would not have time to open. 'Oh!' said one, surprised, 'then we will have parachutes?'

In the beginning, when officers were trying to obtain volunteers, it was necessary to explain parachuting – 'the second greatest pleasure a man can experience'. The recruiters were delighted to discover the existence of a training film. Without first being screened to assess its suitability, it was shown to the 3/7th Gurkhas. The film opened with a shot of a massive parachute drop and a voice-over narration that jolted the British officers to attention: 'Now, if you do your job well, there is no reason why ninety-five per cent of these men should ever reach the ground alive . . .' It was a film demonstrating techniques for killing parachutists. It proved to be a great success. As an officer explained later: 'All that the men saw was parachutists raining down from the sky and rolling about on the ground. There was plenty of fighting and they thought it tremendous fun.' The entire battalion volunteered.

The Gurkha Parachute Battalion was disbanded at Quetta in January 1947, just before Partition, but on 1 January 1963 a Gurkha Independent Parachute Company was raised in Malaya, from men in the 7th and 10th Gurkhas, for use in Brunei.

The principal arm for Gurkhas remained the infantry, in spite of all temptations to make other uses of them. Infantry was required in Malaya, where the Chinese communists' terrorist policy embraced the murder of the managers of tin mines and rubber estates (particularly Europeans), the destruction of machinery, the extortion of supplies and money from the civilian population, and the slaughter of anyone who resisted or who gave information to the security forces. The Chinese communists called themselves the Malayan Liberation Army, but the British usually called them communist terrorists (C.T.s) or simply 'bandits'.

Early in 1948 the depleted battalions of the British Gurkhas had reached Singapore and Malaya. Following the surrender of the Japanese, the Malay Union, comprising all the Malay states except Singapore, was formed and was given colony status and a British governor. In February 1948 the Union had been reorganized into the Federation of Malaya under a British High Commissioner.

The first Gurkha battalion to arrive in Malaya was the 1/6th, which sailed straight from Burma to Penang on the troopship *Dunera*. The other seven battalions were carried on P & O liners and arrived in Singapore in March. The battalions were easily brought up to strength by the abundant and eager reserves of manpower in Nepal, but there remained for some time a shortage of experienced officers and N.C.O.s to train them. All too many young, partially – trained soldiers had to go straight into the jungle where they learned their trade as they fought.

Following the murder of three British planters in Perak, Sir Edward Gent, the British High Commissioner, declared a state of emergency on 18 June 1948 (an emergency that lasted for nearly twelve years) and outlawed the Communist Party. Headquarters for the Brigade of Gurkhas was established at Sembilan, capital of the state of Negri, and six Gurkha battalions were stationed in Malaya with another in neighbouring Singapore. (The eighth battalion was sent to Hong Kong.) It took some time for the Gurkhas to settle down and to realize that Malaya was their new home. When at last the first units of the 2/2nd moved into their permanent quarters in Sirmoor Lines, Ipok, in 1953, an officer wrote: 'At last to have a permanent home again gave the men a great deal of pleasure.' A depot and training centre was established at Sungei Patani, consisting of an Administrative Company, a Boys' Company, and four recruit training companies, one for each regiment. Recruits for the Gurkha Signals and the Engineers did their basic training with the 2nd and 7th regiments' training companies.

The Gurkhas, working closely with the police, were soon engaged in 'jungle bashing'. Major P.R. Richards of the 7th Gurkhas was impressed with the numbers and kinds of leeches encountered: 'There were several varieties, including a green and yellow monster which I discovered one night on my leg and showed it to my orderly. He was neither sympathetic or impressed. In Nepal, he said, leeches were bigger, more prolific and much more colourful.'

On 20 October 1949 a patrol of the 1/10th stumbled upon a shack deep in the jungle and there found Naik Nakan Gurung of the 1st Gurkhas. He had become so weakened by malaria during the retreat from Burma in 1942 that he had had to be left behind with a pile of rations. He escaped detection by the Japanese and in a month had recovered sufficiently to look for a safe place to settle. He built the shack for himself and had been living on wild pig and fish. He did not know that the war was over.

The jungle patrols were trials of endurance, and often frustrating. In 1951 it was estimated that, on average, a soldier had 700 hours of patrolling before he saw a terrorist. Five years later, terrorists were even harder to find; an intelligence officer estimated that 64,400 man-hours were

.needed to kill each bandit. In 1955 a policy of 'shout before shooting' had come into being and most bandits, while declining to surrender, used the warning call as a signal to bolt, sometimes successfully.

On 10 October 1955 Nick Wibnes, an officer in the 2/10th, came upon three bandits making camp in an overgrown rubber plantation. *The Kukri*, the British Brigade of Gurkhas annual magazine, reflecting the prevailing attitude towards the new policy, reported: 'Creeping up . . . he asked them very very nicely if they would like to surrender. They said no thank you, they would much rather not, so he shot one and the other two escaped with their wounds into the undergrowth.'

In January 1952 Graham Greene visited Malaya. The 1/10th found him 'an easy guest to entertain' but noted, too, that 'he certainly kept us up late at night'. In spite of being out of physical condition, he insisted when with the 1/7th on going out with a patrol, 'a short strenuous one with every likelihood of meeting terrorists'. Greene found it more strenuous than he had imagined, but he gallantly kept up until he fainted from exhaustion. Brandy and ginger ale, dropped by air, revived him. He wrote an article about the conflict for the American magazine *Life*, and he told of his patrol in a book, *Ways of Escape*. Neither account mentioned the necessity for an airdrop of brandy and ginger ale.

Inevitably, perhaps, operations in Malaya took on the overtones of a cricket match. Battalions kept records of their kills, competed with each other and celebrated when they 'scored a century'. There were few captures. Although soldiers were not paid bounties, the importance of the slain was measured by the price placed on their heads by government. Some of the enemy were known by name. Rifleman Bharnabahadur Rai of C Company, 1/10th Gurkhas, won local fame and a full-page picture in *The Kukri*, the caption of which was 'Killer of Manap Jepun'. One notorious bandit chief, Ten Fouk Leong, was, of course, nicknamed Ten Foot Long.

The Kukri in the years of the Malayan operation took on

a sporting gloss. The following excerpts from issues of the 1950s are typical:

> In April, May and June [1955], A,B,D, and Support companies [of the 2/10th] killed five bandits between them, whilst their company commanders successfully reduced their handicaps on the Bahau Estate Golf Course.

> October 1952 proved to be the Battalion's best month since the beginning of the Emergency. Seventeen bandits were killed.

> [In the 2/6th] We rounded-off our 'rest and recuperation' by killing six-out-of-six terrorists whilst the Battalion cocktail party was in progress.

Civilians also counted the kills. When the 1/2nd killed its two-hundredth terrorist, the Johore State Counsellor, Dato MacKenzie, presented four silver beer mugs to the Gurkha Officers' Mess to commemorate the occasion. All took pride in the one thousandth kill made by the Brigade of Gurkhas. A patrol of the 1/6th accomplished this on 3 December 1952.

The Emergency in Malaya officially ended in 1959 and in 1963 Malaysia came into being, a country consisting of the former Federation of Malaya, Singapore, the colonies of North Borneo (re-christened Sabah) and Sarawak. Less than two years later Singapore seceded. Throughout the 1960s the Gurkhas constituted the principal weapon and instrument of British policy in South-east Asia. Organized into the 17th Gurkha Infantry Division (about one-third British), they formed the only major British fighting formation outside Europe that was maintained in a state-of-war readiness. There was still fighting to be done, and the next field of action for the Gurkhas was in Borneo.

CHAPTER
27

Borneo

The end of the Japanese occupation of Borneo left the island in chaos, economically and politically. Understandably, many of the inhabitants were confused. When the drum major of the 10th Gurkhas wandered into an out-of-the-way village, a shopkeeper welcomed him effusively. He was delighted, he said, to see that the Japanese were back again. It was a time when new political entities were formed, political slogans were bruited and untried politicians appeared on the scene. Perhaps there were many who wished to return to the stern but more stable government of the Japanese.

Labuan and North Borneo merged to become first the crown colony of North Borneo (later renamed Sabah) and finally a part of Malaysia. The rule of the white rajahs of Sarawak ended and it, too, joined Malaysia. The only former British dependency inhabited by Malay people that did not join in 1963 was the Sultanate of Brunei, and the Sultan had good reason to be grateful for British bayonets.

On the night of 7 December 1962, the anniversary of the Japanese attack on Pearl Harbor, several officers of the 1/2nd Gurkhas in Singapore, looking for diversion, went to the cinema to see *The Longest Day*. The battalion was undergoing its Annual Administrative Inspection and there were difficulties; all had not gone well that day.

Later the same night, in London, the duty officer in the War Room was searching for a country called Brunei on a large map that would be used at the morning briefing. He had an 'incident pin' to stick there.

At two o'clock in the morning, Brunei time, the Sultan's palace, the prime minister's house, the police station and other places of importance in the capital city of Brunei (population 56,000) had been attacked by revolutionaries bent on creating an independent state, Kalimantan Utara, from the three North Borneo territories. Although largely unsuccessful, the rebels had managed to seize the power station and to take some fifty Europeans as hostages. The Sultan called for help, but the nearest British troops were 800 miles away in Singapore.

At five o'clock in the morning the brigade major called the adjutant of the 1/2nd Gurkhas and ordered the battalion to stand-to and be ready to send two companies and a tactical headquarters to Brunei as soon as possible. No one was excited because all thought it was merely a test of the administrative procedures and that the troops would go no farther than the airport.

Gradually a sense of reality emerged as reports of the fighting came in: there were casualties; the whereabouts of the Sultan was unknown; communications with Brunei became tenuous. The situation was serious, but Singapore on a Saturday morning was unprepared for the distant crisis. Trucks sent to the storage depot for ammunition were told to come back on Monday. The officer in charge of the maps at brigade headquarters was swimming; no one knew at which beach. Transport to carry the troops to the airfield would be available only in the early afternoon, after schoolchildren had been taken home. The Royal Air Force had no aircraft available at the moment, but hoped some might return late in the afternoon.

In spite of all these difficulties, one company and a tactical headquarters arrived at the airfield about noon and the second company soon after. They had to wait more than four hours for aircraft. It was five o'clock in the afternoon before all were airborne in an assortment of planes. Some,

too large for the Brunei airport, put down at Labuan and
Jesselton, from which the men had to be ferried to Brunei
town by civil aircraft. Nevertheless, by the end of the following morning the small Gurkha force under Major Lloyd
Williams had set up headquarters at the police station and
sent out patrols. More Gurkhas arrived, the Sultan was
found and protected, the hostages were freed, and the
uproar subsided.

The Brunei revolt finally collapsed completely when the
last hard-core rebels were killed or captured by the 2/7th
Gurkhas in a fight on 18 May 1963 in a swamp a few miles
outside Brunei town. However, a month earlier Indonesia
had begun its 'confrontation' with Malaysia by an attack
on a Sarawak police post. Hostile activities on the part of
the Indonesians kept British Gurkhas and Commonwealth
troops on active duty in Borneo for nearly four years.

In general, the British officers enjoyed their tours of duty
in Borneo, particularly when they were stationed at Seria,
where the Shell Oil Company worked the oilfields (discovered in 1929) which provided the Sultan of Brunei with
most of his wealth. At their camp on the seashore there was
plenty of sport, and officers were welcomed at the splendid
Panaga Club, Shell's social and recreational club for its
executives, where they were free to use its lavish facilities;
those provided for the Gurkha ranks were less alluring, and
prices in the bazaar were considerably higher than in
Malaya or Hong Kong.

It was in Borneo that 21148786 Lance-Corporal Rambahadur Limbu won a Victoria Cross, the thirteenth awarded
to a Gurkha and the first to a Limbu. The official citation
for the medal begins: 'On 21st November 1965 in the Bau
District of Sarawak, Lance-Corporal Rambahadur Limbu
was with his Company when they discovered and attacked
a strong enemy force located in the border area.' This was
true, as far as it went. Not revealed was the fact that the
attack was part of a planned raid across the border and
that Rambahadur won his Victoria Cross fighting Indonesian troops on Indonesian territory. It speaks well for the

British authorities that they did not deny a brave man his medal because the facts, if discovered, might prove embarrassing.

Rambahadur's unit, C Company of the 2/10th, had found the Indonesians strongly entrenched in platoon strength on top of a steep hill on their own side of the frontier. The only approach to the position was along a knife-edge ridge that would allow only three men to move abreast. Leading his support group, Rambahadur could see a sentry and a machine gun in the nearest trench. He inched forward until about ten yards from the trench when the sentry saw him and fired, hitting his friend, Bijuliparsad Rai, who was on his right. 'I saw blood on his face,' said Rambahadur later. 'As soon as I saw his blood, my own blood began to boil. I swore that the enemy would pay for this with their blood. Blood for blood and nothing but blood would settle this account. For a few moments I could think of nothing else.'

Running forward, Rambahadur jumped into the trench and killed the sentry, but the enemy was now alerted and concentrated a heavy fire by automatic weapons on the attackers, particularly on the trench held alone by Rambahadur. Realizing that he could not support his platoon from this position, he left the comparative safety of the trench, collected his fire group, and led them to a better position forward. He then tried shouting and making hand signals to indicate his intentions to his platoon commander, but the clatter of machine guns and the roar of exploding grenades made this impossible, so he again moved into the open to report.

It was while reporting to his platoon commander that he saw two young riflemen of his platoon lying seriously wounded in an exposed position. He began his rescue attempt cautiously, at a crawl, but on coming under extremely heavy fire from two machine guns he decided that only speed would succeed; he jumped to his feet and ran. Hurling himself on the ground beside one of the men, he called for support from two light machine guns. When they came up on his right, he picked up the wounded man and carried him to safety, then turned back into heavy fire to bring in the second. The enemy were obviously making a concerted effort to stop him and it seemed to those who watched that he had no chance of coming through alive. His citation says: 'That he was able to achieve what he did against such overwhelming odds without being hit, was miraculous.' Said Rambahadur modestly: 'A man with small stature like me has some advantage . . . It must have been my lucky day.'

Reduction in Force
and Retirement

On 3 January 1963 the *Daily Telegraph* published a long article by its military correspondent, Brigadier W.F.K. Thompson, expressing alarm and indignation over a proposed cut in the number of Gurkhas in the British Army. The announcement that the Brigade of Gurkhas would be reduced from 14,600 to 10,000 set off alarm bells throughout the British Army and the Nepal Durbar. There were rumours that the government wanted eventually to reduce the Brigade still further, to a mere 4,000.

It was difficult for military men to understand the government's logic. Gurkha infantry was not only among the best, it was also the cheapest, yet the government pleaded economy as its reason for the reduction. India had expanded her seven Gurkha regiments to five or six battalions each; Britain reduced its infantry battalions to five. Three field-marshals – Slim, Harding and Templer – protested at the reduction. Nevertheless, at the request of the government, Slim flew to Nepal to convince the king of its necessity. Privately he wrote to Lord Harding, giving his personal view: 'I told the Secretary of State for War [John Profumo] that I thought anyone who reduced the Gurkhas in the present world situation was "crackers", and I still believe that. The amount we shall save out of a £1,700 million Defence Budget is not worth it. We would do better to cut one rocket!' There were many who agreed with Slim.

Former British Gurkha officers and old comrades' associations set off the cry: 'Save the Gurkhas!' Leading the pack was a serving officer, Major-General Walter Walker, whose title was Major General of the Brigade of Gurkhas (M.G.B.G.). Walker had never been a popular officer and had a reputation as a hard-nosed disciplinarian. Even more than most British generals, he was convinced that his own views on any subject were the correct ones. However, no one ever accused him of lack of courage, even of that rare variety, moral courage. His vigorous efforts to save the Gurkhas went so far beyond the boundaries set for protests by British officers that even those who, like Lord Slim, agreed with his sentiments and logic expressed disapproval of his conduct. Walker went to Nepal and warned the king of the danger to Nepal's economy of Britain's reduction in her forces. He even convinced the United States ambassador to Nepal that the retired Gurkhas constituted a stabilizing influence and that the United States would have to provide more aid to Nepal if the British Brigade of Gurkhas was reduced. Walker was right, but for his pains he was relieved of his post as M.G.B.G. and was treated to a chilling interview with the Chief of the Imperial General Staff.

All efforts to prevent the reduction in force failed and the shrinking of the Brigade of Gurkhas began, ending only in 1971 when a Conservative government came to power and Lord Carrington, the new Minister of Defence, 'halted the rundown of the Gurkhas'. By this time there were only about 7,000 men left and all the infantry regiments except the 2nd had lost their second battalions. Carrington permitted this regiment to be the only two-battalion Gurkha regiment in the army. The Gurkha signal, engineer and transport regiments were also reduced. The Brigade then remained stable until 1975, when another cut was ordered that would reduce the Gurkhas to 6,000 men by 1 April 1979. The two battalions of the 2nd were to be amalgamated. This rundown was halted just in time, and the Brigade of Gurkhas was ordered to be augmented. The 2/2nd was saved and in 1982 a second battalion was added to the 7th Duke of Edinburgh's Own Gurkha Rifles.

During the reductions, very few men volunteered to leave the army: many were forced to retire before they wished, and before they had earned an adequate pension. Retirement was usually a sad time in any case – in spite of the many farewell parties.

A typical send-off was that given to Gurkha Major Harke Thapa of the 2/10th when he retired in July 1952. There were parties for him at the Officers' Mess, the King's Gurkha Officers' Mess, and the Sergeants' Mess. At each he was given a present – a shooting stick, a Parker pen, a gold watch. He left, garlanded in flowers, in the commanding officer's car and the roads in the barracks were lined with cheering men of all ranks.

What then?

An old soldier in the hills of Nepal once told Philip Mason that when he first returned to his village he thought only of his life in his battalion – the sports, the companionship, the sense of purpose. His heart would flutter with excitement when he learned that a British Gurkha officer was in the area and he would hurry to meet him and talk of times past. Gradually, though, he settled down. Now, he said, his thoughts were only about the crops and the children. He had adjusted.

Soldiers could usually retire on a pension after serving for only fifteen years, but some served much longer. Singbir Thapa had been among those gallant defenders of the fort at Kalunga who fought the British; but when he retired as a subadar-major in Britain's Indian Army, he had served for fifty-three years – and he lived on for another twelve years on land purchased for him by the East India Company. Of his long regimental service it was said that 'he had showed an example of good conduct and soldierly qualities seldom equalled'.

Most of those who returned to Nepal went back to the village of their birth and worked, as of old, on the land. Their pensions made them men of some substance and their army service commanded respect, so that former officers and senior N.C.O.s often became village headmen, chairmen of local school boards, officers in veterans' organizations, sometimes even provincial governors. When on 16 November 1952 a fifteen-member national cabinet was formed for the first time in Nepal, two of the ministers were ex-Gurkha soldiers: Honorary Captain Narbahadur Gurung, formerly of the 4th Gurkhas, became Minister of State for Health, and Naradmuni Rai, formerly of the 7th Gurkhas, became Minister for Local Self-Government. A few took up new work, sometimes using skills acquired in the army, though during and after World War II the army generally produced more technicians than Nepal could absorb.

Gurkha soldiers often founded elementary schools in their own villages, and even today in remote hill villages groups of children can be seen learning by rote from a retired soldier. John Morris once found such a school near Pokhara. Each child was intently executing army drill while the instructor shouted commands and railed against laggards. What about reading and writing? asked Morris. The ex-soldier stared at him. 'That sort of stuff is no use here,' he said. 'All these children need is discipline.'

In addition to regular pensions, holders of the Victoria Cross are awarded £100 a year. This amount does not go far in Britain, but it is more money than most Nepalese hillmen see in a year. Because of some bit of bureaucratic bungling, Lachhiman Gurung, who lost an arm but won a Victoria Cross near Taungdaw, Burma, in 1945, did not receive his V.C. pension for a decade. Finally, in 1969, he was given £1,000 in rupees – after he had walked several days to reach the depot to receive it. A thousand pounds buys a lot of rum and Lachhiman was sent reeling home under the protection of two armed guards.

In 1972 Brigid Keenan, a journalist, journeyed to Nepal, obtained permission to go into the hills, and made her way to the village where Lachhiman had retired. (He was then one of only eight living holders of the V.C.) The reporter had a short and easy trip by Nepalese standards: twelve hours by jeep north-west from Katmandu, and then a six-hour climb on foot.

Keenan found Lachhiman asleep – or pretending to be – on the veranda of his house. He was then about forty-nine years old, but the young reporter described him as 'a toothless old man with watery eyes and a grizzled military moustache'. Word of the journalist's coming had, of course, preceded her and the villagers squatted round silently to watch and listen. Lachhiman was asked how he had won the Victoria Cross, but at first he merely muttered that he had been wondering the same thing himself. Finally he consented to tell his story once more. Settling himself comfortably, he spoke fluently, pausing from time to time to wave back the crowd, clear his throat and heave a satisfactory spit.

Lachhiman also told of returning a hero to his village, of the drinking, the singing, the dancing. He told, too, of how hard it had been to put his army life behind him. The V.C. had not made him rich, he said, and he still worked. As proof, he exhibited his calloused left hand. But the army had made him wiser: 'I was a simple man. I knew nothing. But now I have travelled and met people and I can talk and think and understand better.' What makes the Gurkhas so brave? Lachhiman's answer was: 'It is only that we have such bad tempers when something makes us angry.'

The government of Nepal, which for more than a century has depended upon the allotments and pensions of its mercenary soldiers as the principal source of foreign currency, has always taken a dim view of ex-soldiers who fail to take their money and their skills back to their homeland. Yet some men preferred not to return. Reluctant to give up the comforts to which they had grown accustomed, they chose, where this was possible, to remain in India, where they could earn more money than they could in Nepal. Because of their reputation for honesty and reliability, many found jobs as watchmen or policemen.

Soldiers also came to value education and to want their children to grow up literate; the rough-and-ready schools of Nepal could not compete with those to be found on the plains of India.

Hospitals, sanitation and welfare schemes also gained the

soldiers' respect. Since 1950, however, Nepal has allowed foreigners to enter the country and the British Army to extend its medical and welfare services as well as recruitment inside Nepal. Health facilities and welfare have expanded dramatically. Today the British military hospital at Dahran sees 30,000 out-patients and admits 1,200 in-patients each year, mostly pensioned Gurkhas and their families, and this has proved an inducement for discharged soldiers to return to Nepal.

In 1967 the Gurkha Welfare Appeal was launched to help former soldiers and their families. The sudden reduction of the Brigade of Gurkhas threatened to swamp the existing welfare services and many felt that India was doing more than Britain for its pensioners. The appeal produced a million and a half pounds sterling which, invested, has brought in more than £100,000 per year. Most of this is spent on families in distress and the rest goes to widows, for whom the British government makes no provision, pensions ending with the death of the pensioner. The government, whose policies created the need for the appeal, then generously agreed to pay the costs of administering the programme, which is managed by a brigadier at Dahran.

Officers and other ranks in the Brigade of Gurkhas contribute one day's pay each. Canadians have contributed most generously, the Canadian government adding two dollars for every one raised by the Canadian International Development Agency. The Gurkha Appeal in Canada was started by ex-soldiers of the Canadian Army who had fought beside Gurkhas in two wars. Most of the Canadian money is used for major projects such as the construction of schools and hospitals.

Gurkha pensioners receive their pensions in cash. There are several permanent paying stations, but the practice was, and in some areas is still, for officers to set off with bags of rupees and a small staff to set up camps where old soldiers and their families can come down from the hills to be paid. It once took several months for all to be paid and it still takes several weeks. In 1980 Britain paid about 16,000 pensioners who had retired since 1948; India pays the pensions

of those who retired earlier. These pensions, though meagre
by British standards, make a soldier with fifteen or more
years of service a prosperous man in a mountain village.

There are old comrades' associations both in Nepal and
in Britain. In England there are regimental associations of
former officers, most of which were instituted about the
time of Partition. There is also a Gurkha Brigade Association. On 11 June 1965 the Association, to commemorate the
150 years that Gurkhas have served in Britain's armies, held
a formal reception in London that was attended by the
Queen, the Duke of Edinburgh, some 900 past and present
members of the Brigade and dignitaries from Nepal.

In addition to these formal organizations there is, or was
in 1956, an informal meeting place in London for Gurkha
officers, retired and serving, at Hatchett's Men's Bar ('half
way down the stairs and turn right from the Piccadilly
entrance'). A book was placed there for names, addresses,
notices of dinners and reunions, and for the results of annual
Gurkha sporting events.

The clubs and associations provide occasions for former
soldiers to renew old acquaintance as they once did on regimental days when the regiments had their homes in India.
In the Indian Army today a regimental reunion is held every
five years at regimental centres; old soldiers wear their
medals and are waited on by the serving soldiers. On 14
September 1907 the 2nd Gurkhas celebrated the fiftieth
anniversary of the capture of Delhi with a parade and a
feast for some 700 veterans, nine of whom had served there.
John Masters has told of the regimental day of the 4th
Gurkhas in 1936 when a veteran said to be 108 years old
attended. Complaining that neither the regiment nor the
whisky was as good as it once was, he drained two full tum-
blers of Scotch and slowly, uprightly, marched off.

Since Nepal has been open to tourists, officers and former
officers frequently tour the hills from which their men are
or were recruited. There they always meet old soldiers, some
of whom served in their regiments. In September 1981,
when John Nott, Britain's Defence Minister and a former
British Gurkha officer (1953–7) who had commanded a sig-

nals platoon in the 2nd Gurkhas in Malaya, visited Nepal, he encountered ex-Corporal Mankaji Gurung, who had been his driver, and other old soldiers he had known, assembled at a 'Gurkha Soldiers Evening' at the British Gurkha Centre in Pokhara; some had walked for days to see him once again.

The 'old and bold' were always ready to serve again if asked. During the Indian Mutiny some fifty pensioners heeded the call of Major Charles Reid and came down from their hills to man the depot at Dehra Dun after he had marched his Sirmoor Battalion off to Delhi. And in World War II, when many Gurkha officers and N.C.O.s were asked to come back and help train recruits, they did so with obvious relish.

CHAPTER
29

Today and Tomorrow

All old soldiers are dissatisfied with, and contemptuous of, soldiers who joined more recently. In 1975 retired Lieutenant-Colonel Andrew Mercer, age eighty, was asked his opinion of the modern Gurkha soldier, for he had served for more than thirty-three years in the Indian Army, mostly with Gurkhas. While admitting that the Gurkha of today is better educated, he averred that 'the modern Gurkha has not got any power in his legs. Anything over a two-mile march and he has to have a motor vehicle to carry him. This is progress!'

Much that has here been said about the Gurkhas, their officers and the *kaida* (the way of doing things in Gurkha regiments) has remained unchanged, but the Gurkha recruit and the composition of Gurkha battalions has not remained the same. Training depots still get a few recruits who are totally illiterate, but they are now rare. The army provides a considerable amount of education and, although the working language of the regiments is still Gurkhali, the educational programmes in the British Brigade of Gurkhas places heavy emphasis on English and an N.C.O. must be fluent before he can become a Queen's Gurkha Officer. Drill commands, given in Urdu in the Indian Army, are now given in English in the British Gurkhas.

Each year's intake of recruits (now selected three times

a year) is more self-confident, articulate and literate. The once despised line boy is now more readily accepted in an army where the tools of soldiering grow ever more complex.

The British Forces Broadcasting Service, which began transmitting programmes in English and Gurkhali in 1971, is now on the air for sixteen hours a day in Hong Kong. In 1980 it sponsored a short-story contest for Gurkhas and six of the best were read on the air. Gurkha officers and other ranks are encouraged to contribute to *The Kukri* in the British Army and to *The Gorkha* in the Indian Army, and there are even publications in Gurkhali.

The *pani patiya* ceremony after crossing the 'black sea', which seventy years ago seemed so important, has now fallen into disuse and buffalo are no longer slaughtered during *Dashera*, but each battalion still has its *bahun*. Professionals now educate children, care for the sick and advise young wives, but the *bahun* is still needed. In 1980 the 7th Gurkhas planned a 'Charity Fête and Tattoo' in Hong Kong, the money raised to go to local and Nepalese charities. For two days before the event, rain fell in torrents. The *bahun*, appealed to, prayed for fair weather; the rain stopped, the sun came out and the 7th basked in two dry days during their fair.

It is expected that the Sultan of Brunei's contract with Britain for a battalion of Gurkhas will be renewed in 1984. For this, the Sultan pays about one and a half million pounds annually – plus the cost of accommodation, food, petrol, hospitalization and schooling – but then, he has plenty of oil money and he has envious neighbours. He gets good value: a battalion of what is still some of the world's finest infantry.

Recruiting areas have been expanded in recent years. Where formerly few recruits came from the lowland Terai, considerable numbers now come from there, for that is where most of Nepal's schools are located. Within regiments there is no longer the strict division by tribes which once prevailed. The 2nd Gurkhas, which was traditionally almost entirely composed of Gurungs and Magars, took in

Limbus and Rais in 1971 and now about fifteen per cent of its strength are *kiranti*.

In 1971 the British Gurkhas left Malaya for Hong Kong; their training centre moved from Sungei Patani to Sek Kong. It was generally felt with some bitterness that the Gurkha successes in Malaya had not been properly appreciated by the Malaysian authorities. Just before the Gurkhas left, the Family Welfare Centre went up in flames. 'This mishap,' blandly reported *The Kukri*, 'was apparently due to carelessness soon after negotiations for its purchase by the Malaysians had fallen through.'

On 2 October 1972 direct airtrooping between Nepal and Hong Kong began. Now a young man who perhaps saw his first road and first wheeled vehicle at the British Gurkha Depot in Dharan can within a year be in Kowloon, driving a lorry through some of the densest traffic in the world.

There is still not enough family accommodation in Hong Kong, but there is more than there was thirty years ago in Malaya, and of far better quality. In the 10th Gurkhas in 1978 there were 935 men, 398 wives and 721 children. Gurkhas place a high value on education and in Hong Kong their children can be educated. The Gurkha High School provides instruction leading to the Nepalese School Leaving Certificate.

As may be expected in the army of a welfare state, there is a heavy emphasis on the provision of social services to serving and retired soldiers and their families. The Gurkha Welfare Trusts now provide nearly £100,000 per year. In addition, each soldier in the Brigade of Gurkhas contributes one day's pay per year, generating an additional £8,500. There are also a variety of scholarships for Gurkha children both in Nepal and abroad.

Aid to soldiers and ex-soldiers sometimes comes from unlikely individuals. Sir Horace Kadorie, an immensely wealthy resident of Hong Kong, has given tens of thousands of dollars for a wide variety of schemes in which he has taken a close personal interest. Ellice and Rosa McDonald, Americans described as 'great *aficionados* of Gurkhas and Scottish bagpipe music', founded the Gurkha

Welfare Trust Foundation in the United States. In 1980 they gave the Brigade of Gurkhas a magnificent solid silver Revere Bowl mounted on a polished mahogany plinth, to be awarded annually to the most outstanding piper in the brigade.

In 1975 a Canadian from Victoria, British Columbia, sent his contribution to the Gurkhas with a note: 'Since my church here has decided to sponsor U.S. draft-dodgers in this country, I have severed my connections. I can think of no more appropriate place to send my collection money than to the men who will walk a hundred miles to get on a draft.'

The bands, pipers and drummers are always popular with soldiers and civilians of all ages, so they are sent to play in many lands. Three pipers and two drummers who took part in a Highland Gathering in Djakarta, Indonesia, in 1978 won fourteen medals among them. In addition, Sergeant Meherman Tamang of the 7th Duke of Edinburgh's Own Gurkha Rifles won the Cathay Pacific Trophy for the 'Best Dressed Scotsman.'

The Gurkhas' principal task in Hong Kong is guarding the border with China, where tens of thousands of Chinese try to cross over to the freedom offered by the last vestiges of British colonialism. In just one three-week period in 1979 the 7th Gurkhas caught 2,200 illegal immigrants, and in one three-year period (1978–81) the 2/2nd Gurkhas caught 21,671 people. There is always a great deal of 'healthy competition' between companies and battalions about these arrests. In 1967 and again the following year, there were nasty riots fomented by Red Guards on the border. These have stopped, but now there are refugees from Vietnam, many of whom are not, strictly speaking, political refugees, but simply people who want an opportunity to make a better life for themselves.

Because of the shortage of land, Hong Kong is far from an ideal training area. Still, British troops stationed there do the best they can. Anti-insurgency exercises are practised and when it is the turn of the Gurkhas to play the role of enemy they have been known to dress their *marunis* as gun-toting women guerrillas. Gurkhas have in recent years taken part in military manoeuvres in Cyprus, Canada, Jamaica, Germany, Australia, Malaysia and New Zealand.

The day is probably not far distant when most British officers in Gurkha battalions will be replaced by Gurkhas. More and more hold the Queen's commission. In 1958 Second Lieutenant Chandrabahadur Rai, the first Gurkha ever commissioned at the Royal Military Academy, Sandhurst, was assigned to the 1/10th. Others followed, and as we have related earlier, in 1981 Lieutenant Bijay Rawat is credited with being the first Gurkha (although by heritage a Garhwali) to win the Sword of Honour at Sandhurst. The highest ranking Gurkha now serving is Lieutenant-Colonel Lalbahadur Pun of the 2nd Gurkhas. He is a staff college graduate who won the Military Cross as a captain in 1966; in 1982 he was in command of the Training Depot at Sek Kong.

Four battalions, with the headquarters of the Brigade of Gurkhas, are stationed in Hong Kong, together with the Gurkha Signals, Engineer and Transport regiments. One battalion of infantry is regularly sent on duty to the United Kingdom, and another to Brunei. However, Gurkhas are also stationed in other parts of a troubled world. The 10th Gurkhas and some Gurkha Signals were in Cyprus in 1974 when President Makarios was forced to flee and the Turks invaded. In 1973 Gurkhas from the 7th took over frontier guard duties in Gibraltar, the first to do so, and 'the diplomatic wrangling between Gibraltar, Rabat and Tangiers over getting visas for Nepalese citizens was something which had to be seen to be believed', reported one officer. Gurkhas have also been used in Belize to keep an armed watch on the greedy Guatemalans.

When Britain decided to recapture the Falkland Islands in 1982, the army sent in its first team, its finest, which included, of course, a battalion of the Gurkhas – the First Battalion of the Duke of Edinburgh's Own Gurkha Rifles, which was on duty in England at the time. The 1/7th formed part of 5 Brigade with a battalion each of the Scots Guards and the Welsh Guards, all under the command of Brigadier M.J.A. ('Tony') Wilson.

It was Wilson who, leading his men cautiously toward Port Stanley, hit upon a novel time-saving notion. He had reached Swan Inlet, a small hamlet about thirty miles from Port Stanley, and had found that the telephone lines were still operational. He stopped at a house and telephoned ahead to Fitzroy, the next hamlet. 'Any Argies there?' he asked. Ron Binnie, a farmer, told him that the Argentines had been there but had gone. 'In that case,' said Wilson, 'I think I'll join you.' Mr Binnie assured him that he would be welcome. Wilson then swiftly pushed a hundred of his soldiers ahead in helicopters.

Argentine troops were apprehensive about the Gurkhas, and they had many misconceptions about them, some of which were encouraged by the locals. An Argentine captain inquired about the Gurkhas of Eric Goss of Goose Green: 'What do you pay them?' 'Oh, a handful of rice a day,' said Goss. 'We will pay them three handsful if they will fight for us,' said the captain.

A general on Buenos Aires television reported that his men were eager to come to grips with these famous fighters. However, at one point in the fighting some three hundred Argentines were retreating before the Scots Guards when they encountered an advanced patrol of the Gurkhas. They at once reversed direction and surrendered to the Scots Guards.

It was widely believed by the Argentines that the Gurkhas killed their own wounded. Father Vicente Martinez, an Argentine chaplain, was reported as saying that Gurkhas had slit the throats of some forty Argentine soldiers at a place called Moody Brook, near Port Stanley. These false stories of their prowess amused the Gurkhas, who delighted in their bloodthirsty reputation. 'They knew we were coming and they feared us,' said Lieutenant-Colonel David Morgan, Commandant of the 1/7th Gurkha Rifles. 'Of course, I think they had every ground to fear us,' he added.

Major-General John Jeremy Moore, the commander of the land forces on the Falklands, planned a two-stage

The 1/7th Duke of Edinburgh's Own Gurkha Rifles training on the
QE II. Sketch by Linda Kitson (*Imperial War Museum*)

assault on the Argentine troops dug in on the so-called Galtieri Line around Port Stanley. At dawn on 14 June 1982 he
decided to pause and consolidate, for his men had been
fighting incessantly for the past seventy-two hours. Then
he received word of the successful assault of the Gurkhas
on Mount William, a key position. The Galtieri Line had
cracked.

5 Brigade was sent to the Falklands to be the reserve force
for 3 Commando Brigade, composed of Royal Marines and
paratroopers, and the Gurkhas did not think they would be
thrust into the battle so soon. But after twenty-one days at
sea, the Gurkhas landed at San Carlos, the first of 5 Brigade
to go ashore, and the entire battalion, except for D Com-

pany, was sent at once to Goose Green. On 2 June they relieved the exhausted Second Battalion of the Parachute Regiment.

D Company, left behind to help 40 Commando hold the high ground overlooking San Carlos, was later ordered to catch up by walking, each man carrying 120 pounds. This they did, marching to Goose Green, a distance of thirty kilometers, in less than two days – and this included a six-hour wait for helicopters which never arrived.

The full battalion then went to Bluff Cove and from there it was ordered to take up a position under the lee of Mount Harriet, which the Argentines then occupied. Here the Gurkhas were heavily shelled and sustained four casualties. Lieutenant-Colonel Morgan planned an ambitious patrol programme, but this was cancelled and on 12 June the 1/7th received orders for an attack, as part of 5 Brigade's assault on Mount Tumbledown and Mount William.

The plan was complex and dangerous, for it called for the 2nd Scots Guards to take Tumbledown and then for the Gurkhas – at night – to pass through the Guards and march to the eastern end of Tumbledown and across a spur leading north to Mount William. However, in the event, the Scots Guards encountered considerable difficulty in achieving their objectives: they sustained a number of casualties and did not secure Mount Tumbledown until dawn. So it was in the early morning light that the Gurkhas moved forward on a six-and-a-half-kilometer march along the northern slope of Tumbledown.

The first objective of the 1/7th was easily taken: there were no Argentines there. As the Gurkhas were deploying for an assault on their second objective, the enemy suddenly bolted for Port Stanley, leaving behind their guns and throwing away their rifles. The 1/7th rapidly advanced and captured Mount William, finding only three live Argentine soldiers there. It was an easy victory, but during the approach march the Gurkhas were shelled by accurate enemy artillery fire and suffered eight men wounded, two seriously. There was a further loss of two more men wounded to make a total of fourteen: all recovered.

The Argentines fled when they realized that they were being outflanked and that those outflanking them were Gurkhas. In a letter to the author, Lieutenant-Colonel Morgan, who strode through the entire campaign armed only with a silver-headed rattan cane which his grandfather had carried in the Boxer Rebellion in China, wrote that 'it was desperately frustrating and exasperating for us to find no enemy on an objective, but when all is said and done, if we can win by reputation, who wants to kill people?'

The only Gurkha killed by the Argentines was twenty-four-year-old Lance-Corporal Buddhaprasad Limbu, a signaller in the 1/7th. He was killed after the battle while engaged in removing the many mines which the 'Argies' had indiscriminately laid in the area. Many civilians attended his funeral in the local cemetery at Darwin, some coming in on tractors and Land Rovers to mark their appreciation of his sacrifice.

The two reductions in force suffered since the end of hostilities in Malaya shook morale, and for a time there were fears that a new Labour government might again reduce the strength of the Brigade. Before the Falklands War there were also fears that the Brigade might degenerate into a mere Hong Kong *gendarmerie* and that the lack of activity in the shrunken empire would make a career in the Gurkhas unattractive to bright young British officers. Still, the future of the Gurkha battalions looks promising at the moment. The newly raised, or re-raised, Second Battalion of the 7th, which became fully operational in 1982, and the brilliant feat of arms of the First Battalion of the same regiment in the Falklands, would seem to assure that there will continue to be a place for these Nepalese mercenaries in the British Army. It seems most unlikely that there will be a time in the foreseeable future when there will be no role for them to play in a world unwilling to abandon war as a means of settling disputes.

APPENDIX A

Ranks in Gurkha Regiments

After the demise of the Honourable East India Company in September 1858, all British officers carried the sovereign's commission and were King's or Queen's Commissioned Officers. From the 1920s an increasing number of Indian officers were also commissioned, but except for doctors seconded from the Indian Medical Service they were never assigned to Gurkha regiments. Ranks of non-commissioned officers and what are known as warrant officers in the British Army had their equivalent ranks in the Indian Army. However, throughout the Indian Army there was, and is, a three-tier system of ranks. Between non-commissioned and warrant officers, and officers holding the sovereign's or president's commission, there is a three-tier line of authority not found in other armies. Members were originally called 'native officers', but as the word 'native' took on pejorative connotations, the term was changed and these became Viceroy's Commissioned Officers (V.C.O.s).

When India became independent and there was no longer a viceroy, commissioned officers held their appointments from the president of India. In the Gurkha battalions remaining in the Indian Army a handful of former V.C.O.s were given direct commissions, an experiment that was not repeated. Most former V.C.O.s became Junior Commissioned Officers. When the four regiments passed into the

British service in 1947 the British also gave direct commissions to a few former V.C.O.s; again, this was never repeated. Most former V.C.O.s became King's (later Queen's) Gurkha Officers. The only serving soldier holding the Victoria Cross is Lieutenant (Q.G.O.) Rambahadur Gurung. There is no equivalent for the Gurkha officer ranks in any other part of the British Army.

The table below shows the various ranks beneath that of a second lieutenant holding a president's or a British sovereign's commission. The ranks in the British Indian Army have been retained in the present Indian Army, except that the rank of jemadar has been replaced by the rank of naib subadar.

In the British Army chaplains wear uniforms and have ranks, but Hindu priests in the Indian Army do not. Each Gurkha battalion has its *pandit* or *bahun*, but he is a civilian.

British Army Infantry	Indian Army Cavalry	Indian Army Infantry
major (Q.G.O.)	rissaldar-major	subadar-major
captain (Q.G.O.)	rissaldar	subadar
lieutenant (Q.G.O.)	jemadar	jemadar
sergeant-major	daffadar-major	havildar-major
sergeant	daffadar	havildar
corporal	naik	naik
lance-corporal	lance-naik	lance-naik
private	sowar	sepoy

APPENDIX B

Hindu Religious and Social Divisions

There are four main castes or *varnas*:

Brahman – priests, advisers, ministers of state;
Kshatriya (or *Rajput*) – rulers, warriors, landlords;
Vaisiya – traders, artisans, cultivators, herdsmen;
Sudra – menial workers (mostly conquered aborigines).

In each *varna* there are many sub-castes, including, for example, seven classes of Brahmans. Below all these are the outcasts, untouchables, or, as they are politely called today, the scheduled castes. There is a vast social and religious gulf between the first two *varnas*, who wear the Brahmanical thread, and other castes.

Among tribes of different origins in Nepal there are eleven main socio-religious divisions. In descending order of social standing, these are:

> Brahmans
> Thakurs
> Chhetris or Khas
> Gurungs
> Magars
> Newars
> Limbus
> Rais
> Sunwars
> Muranis
> Tharus

Progressive Title Changes in Gurkha Infantry While in British Service

1st Gurkha Rifles

1815 1st Nasiri Battalion; 1823 5th, 6th, or 1st Nasiri Local Battalion; 1826 4th, or Nasiri Local Battalion; 1843 4th, or Nasiri (Rifle Battalion); 1850 66th or Goorkha Regiment, Bengal Native Infantry; 1858 66th or Goorkha Light Infantry Regiment, Bengal Native Infantry; 1861 11th Regiment of Bengal Native Infantry; 1861 1st Goorkha Regiment (Light Infantry); 1886 1st Goorkha Regiment (Light Infantry); 1891 1st Gurkha (Rifle) Regiment; 1901 1st Gurkha Rifles; 1903 1st Gurkha Rifles (the Malaun Regiment); 1906 1st Prince of Wales Own Gurkha Rifles; 1910 1st King George's Own Gurkha Rifles (the Malaun Regiment); 1937 1st King George V's Own Gurkha Rifles (the Malaun Regiment); 1947 left the British service.

2nd Gurkha Rifles

1815 Sirmoor Battalion; 1823 8th (or Sirmoor) Local Battalion; 1826 6th (or Sirmoor) Local Battalion; 1850 Sirmoor Battalion; 1858 Sirmoor Rifle Regiment; 1861 17th Regiment of Bengal Native Infantry; 1861 2nd Goorkha Regiment; 1864 2nd Goorkha (the Sirmoor Rifles) Regiment; 1876 2nd (Prince of Wales's Own) Goorkha Regiment (the Sirmoor Rifles); 1886 2nd (the Prince of Wales's Own) Goorkha Regiment (The Sirmoor Rifles); 1891 2nd (the Prince of Wales's Own) Gurkha (Rifles); Regiment (the Sirmoor Rifles); 1901 2nd (the Prince of Wales's Own) Gurkha Rifles (the Sirmoor Rifles); 1906 2nd King Edward's Own Gurkha Rifles (the Sirmoor Rifles); 1936 2nd King Edward VII's Own Gurkha Rifles (the Sirmoor Rifles); 1947 to British Army.

3rd Gurkha Rifles

1815 Kumaon Battalion; 1816 Kumaon Provincial Battalion; 1823 9th (or Kumaon) Local Battalion; 1826 7th (or Kumaon) Local Battalion; 1860 Kumaon Battalion; 1861 18th Regiment of Bengal Native Infantry; 1861 3rd Goorkha Regiment; 1864 3rd (the Kumaon) Goorkha Regiment; 1887 3rd Goorkha Regiment; 1891 3rd Goorkha (Rifle) Regiment; 1901 3rd Gurkha Rifles; 1907 3rd The Queen's Own Gurkha Rifles; 1908 3rd Queen Alexandra's Own Gurkha Rifles; 1947 left the British service.

4th Gurkha Rifles

1857 Extra Goorkha Regiment; 1861 19th Regiment of Bengal Native Infantry; 1861 4th Goorkha Regiment; 1891 4th Gurkha (Rifle) Regiment; 1901 4th Gurkha Rifles; 1924 4th Prince of Wales's Own Gurkha Rifles; 1947 left the British service.

5th Gurkha Rifles

1858 25th Punjab Infantry, or Hazara Goorkha Battalion; 1861 7th Regiment of Infantry (or Hazara Goorkha Battalion), Punjab Irregular Force; 1861 5th Goorkha Regiment, or Hazara Goorkha Battalion; 1886 5th Goorkha Regiment, the Hazara Goorkha Battalion; 1887 5th Goorkha Regiment; 1891 5th Gurkha (Rifle) Regiment; 1901 5th Gurkha Rifles; 1903 5th Gurkha Rifles (Frontier Force); 1923 5th Royal Gurkha Rifles (Frontier Force); 1947 left the British service.

6th Gurkha Rifles

1817 Cuttack Legion; 1823 Rangpur Light Infantry Battalion; 1826 8th (or Rangpur) Local Light Infantry Battalion; 1828 8th (or Assam) Local Light Infantry Battalion; 1844 1st Assam Light Infantry; 1861 42nd Regiment of Bengal Native Infantry; 1864 42nd (Assam) Regiment of Bengal Native (Light) Infantry; 1885 42nd (Assam) Regiment of Bengal (Light) Infantry; 1886 42nd Regiment Goorkha Light Infantry; 1889 42nd (Goorkha) Regiment of Bengal (Light) Infantry; 1891 42nd Gurkha (Rifle) Regiment of Bengal Infantry; 1901 42nd Gurkha Rifles; 1903 6th Gurkha Rifles; 1947 to British Army; 1959 6th Queen Elizabeth's Own Gurkha Rifles.

7th Gurkha Rifles

1902 8th Gurkha Rifles; 1903 2nd Battalion, 10th Gurkha Rifles; 1907 7th Gurkha Rifles; 1947 to British Army; 1 January 1959 7th Duke of Edinburgh's Own Gurkha Rifles.

8th Gurkha Rifles

1824 16th or Sylhet Local Battalion; 1826 11th or Sylhet Local (Light) Infantry Battalion; 1861 48th Regiment of Bengal Native Infantry; 1861 44th Regiment of Bengal Native Infantry; 1864 44th (Sylhet) Regiment of Bengal Native (Light) Infantry; 1885 44th (Sylhet) Regiment of Bengal (Light) Infantry; 1886 44th Regiment, Goorkha (Light) Infantry; 1889 44th (Goorkha) Regiment of Bengal

(Light) Infantry; 1891 44th Gurkha (Rifle) Regiment of Bengal Infantry; 1901 44th Gurkha Rifles; 1903 8th Gurkha Rifles; 1907 became the 1st Battalion. 2nd Battalion raised at Gauhati: 1835 Assam Sebundy Corps; 1839 Lower Assam Sebundy Corps; 1839 1st Assam Sebundy Corps; 1844 2nd Assam Light Infantry; 1861 47th Regiment of Bengal Native Infantry; 1861 43rd Regiment of Bengal Native Infantry; 1884 43rd (Assam) Regiment of Bengal Native (Light) Infantry; 1865 43rd (Assam) Regiment of Bengal (Light) Infantry; 1886 43rd Regiment Goorka Light Infantry; 1889 43rd (Goorkha) Regiment of Bengal (Light) Infantry; 1891 43rd Gurkha (Rifle) Regiment of Bengal Infantry; 1901 43rd Gurkha Rifles; 1903 7th Gurkha Rifles; 1907 became the 2nd Battalion, 8th Gurkha Rifles; 1947 left the British service.

9th Gurkha Rifles

1817 Fatehgarh Levy; 1819 Manipuri Levy; 1823 1st Battalion, 32nd Regiment of Bengal Native Infantry; 1824 63rd Regiment of Bengal Native Infantry; 1861 9th Regiment of Bengal Native Infantry; 1885 9th Regiment of Bengal Infantry; 1894 9th (Gurkha Rifles) Regiment of Bengal Infantry; 1901 9th Gurkha Rifles; 1947 left the British service.

10th Gurkha Rifles

1890 1st Regiment of Burma Infantry; 1891 10th Regiment (1st Burma Battalion) of Madras Infantry; 1892 10th Regiment (1st Burma Rifles) Madras Infantry; 1895 10th Regiment (1st Burma Gurkha Rifles) Madras Infantry; 1901 10th Gurkha Rifles; 1947 to British Army; 1949 10th Princess Mary's Own Gurkha Rifles.

APPENDIX D

The Gurkha Tribes

Magars form the largest tribe in Nepal and constitute about one-third of the population. They are an agricultural people, cultivating their small holdings in the temperate region just north of the foothills, in the shadow of Annapurna and Machhpuchare. They were described by Lieutenant-Colonel Eden Vansittart, who wrote the old Indian Army's handbook on Gurkhas in 1895, as 'the basic Mongolian peasant of Central Nepal' and the *beau idéal* of what a Gurkha soldier should be.

Socially, Magars are divided into two major classes, *charjat* and *solah-jat*. The *char-jat* is the aristocracy and is subdivided into four kindreds; the *solah-jat* is subdivided into sixteen. There are also seven clans, of which the Thapa is the largest and the Pun the second largest. Three clans – Thapa, Ale and Rana – are regarded as superior in physique and breeding, Ranas being the elite group. Among themselves, the *char-jat* and some others speak their own language, called Magarkura.

As one might expect, most Magars in the Indian and British armies are and have always been Thapas and Puns. Puns, although lower on the social scale and unable to speak Magarkura, have always been noted for their cheerful disposition. All Gurkhas are noted for their broad, happy grins, but most would agree that none grins more broadly and is

more irrepressibly cheerful than a Pun. The regiments welcome him as a recruit.

The Gurungs, living to the north of the Magars, are a more
pastoral people. Like the Magars, they are divided into *char-
jats* and *solah-jats*, and they are much alike in their customs and character. The Gurungs have their own language,
Gurungkura, which is more closely related to Tibetan than
any other Himalayan dialect. Colonel William Brook
Northey thought the Gurungs more intelligent and quicker
in learning. They have been considered less Hinduized than
the Magars, although the Ghales, one of the four *char-jats*
will not touch goat or eggs and they place some restrictions
on mutton. Buddhist influence is still strongly felt among
the Gurungs and in time of trouble they are more likely to
call in a lama than a Brahman.

Eden Vansittart, speaking of Magars and Gurungs in
1894, said:

> They are intensely fond of soldiering. They are very hardy
> and extremely simple-minded. They are kind-hearted and gen-
> erous and, as recruits, absolutely truthful. They are very proud
> and sensitive, and they deeply feel abuse and undeserved cen-
> sure. They are very obstinate, very independent, very vain, and
> in their plain clothes inclined to be dirty. They are intensely
> loyal to each other and their officers in time of trouble or dan-
> ger.

Much the same might be said of the *kiranti:* the Rais and
Limbus. The Rais are said to be generally smaller and
quicker than the Limbus, who are slightly taller, slower
speaking and have broader features. The differences in
temperament between the *kiranti* of eastern Nepal and the
parbatiya of western Nepal are believed to be related to the
differences in their life-styles. The *parbatiya* live grouped
together in villages in the west; they are accustomed to
communal life and to meeting with friends in the evening.
The *kiranti* in the east live in scattered homesteads, neighbours divided by land. Regiments which recruited Magars
and Gurungs were therefore thought to be more sociable
than those recruiting Limbus and Rais.

Although they are much alike in manners and customs, there are differences between Limbus and Rais. The Rai is somewhat more Mongolian in appearance with a fairer, more yellowish complexion and eyes set far apart, and he is considered to be less quarrelsome and more amenable to discipline than the Limbu. The Rais are divided into many sub-tribes and have no common tribal language; instead there are ten separate languages and some seventy dialects. It is a Nepalese joke that every Rai has his own language.

Among the *kiranti*, nestled between the Rais and Limbus, is a small tribe, the Sunwar, which also contributes its quota of recruits. Like their neighbours, they are of Tibetan origin. They are generally smaller than other Gurkhas, with prominent cheekbones and reddish complexion. They are divided into many tiny sub-tribes, but all are reserved and have attractive manners. Unlike most other tribes, they are rarely found outside their own tribal areas.

Another small tribe from eastern Nepal from which some recruits are drawn is the Thamang (also called Lama, though not to be confused with Buddhist monks or priests; unlike other Gurkhas, they are more likely to be Buddhists than Hindus). They are generally industrious and amenable, but are classed below the other *kiranti* tribes in social status. Other Mongolian races living in the highlands of Nepal include Tibetans, Lepchas, Bhotes and, of course, Sherpas. Occasionally some were recruited from these racial groups, but not often.

When tourists visit Katmandu, the people they see there are likely to be Newars. Few have Mongolian features, and no one ever regarded them as Gurkhas. The Newar language is distinct from that spoken in other parts of Nepal, and their Hindu religious practices and rituals are inextricably mixed with Buddhist rites. They are the merchants, traders and artisans of Nepal, and at one time they had a strong artistic tradition. No effort is made to recruit Newars, but from time to time one is enlisted.

The 9th Gurkha Rifles is the only regiment to recruit the higher-caste Rajputs: Chhetris and Thakurs, whose manners, customs and religious observances are radically different from those of the other groups. They are below the average European in height, but taller than most Nepalese. They are slightly built and generally sharper featured, and as hirsute as other races. It is believed that Chhetris and Thakurs, who are found throughout the country, are the result of miscegenation between immigrants from northern India and the more Mongolian hill people. They are *ksatriyas*, of the warrior caste, and thus of a *varna* entitled to wear the sacred thread; among the mercenary soldiers, they are the most orthodox Hindus. They are regarded as intelligent (a quality not generally included in the list of Gurkha virtues), possess clean habits, and as soldiers present a smart appearance. In Nepal's own army, Chhetris constitute the largest class.

Select Bibliography

In addition to the books and articles listed here, I also relied upon personal correspondence and upon copies of *The Kukri* and *The Gorkha* issued since 1950.

Ashmead-Bartlett, E., *The Uncensored Dardanelles*, Hutchinson, London, n.d.

Adshead, Robin, *Gurkha: The Legendary Soldier*, Asia Pacific Press, Singapore, 1970.

Anon., *The Brigade of Gurkhas*, booklet, *c*. 1978.

Anon., *Frontier and Overseas Expeditions from India*, vols. 1 and 2, Government Monotype Press, Simla, 1907 and 1908.

Anon., *History of the 5th Royal Gurkha Rifles (Frontier Force)*, vol. 1 (1858–1928), Gale & Polden, Aldershot, 1930.

Anon., *History of the 5th Royal Gurkha Rifles (Frontier Force)*, vol. 2 (1929–47), printed for the Regimental Committee by Gale & Polden, Aldershot, 1956.

Anon., *Nepal and the Gurkhas*, Ministry of Defence, H.M.S.O., London, 1965.

Anon., *The Tiger Kills: The Story of the Indian Divisions in the North African Campaign*, H.M.S.O. for the Government of India, 1944.

Barclay, C.N. (ed.), *The Regimental History of the 3rd Queen Alexandra's Own Gurkha Rifles*, 2 vols., London, 1953.

Bernstein, Jeremy, *The Wildest Dreams of Kew: A Profile of Nepal*, Simon & Schuster, New York, 1970.

Birdwood, Field-Marshal Lord, *Khaki and Gown*, Ward Lock & Co., London and Melbourne, 1941.

Bristow, Robert C., *Memories of the British Raj*, Johnson, London, 1974.

Candler, Edmond, *The Long Road to Baghdad*, 2 vols., Houghton Mifflin, Boston and New York, 1919.

Carew, Tim, *All This and a Medal Too*, Constable, London, 1954.

——*The Longest Retreat: The Burma Campaign, 1942*, Hamish Hamilton, London, 1969.

Davis, Patrick, *A Child at Arms*, Hutchinson, London, 1970.

Fleming, Peter, *Bayonets to Lhasa*, Rupert Hart-Davis, London, 1961.

Forbes, Duncan, *Johnny Gurkha*, Robert Hale, London, 1964.

Gibbs, H.R.K., *Historical Record of the 6th Gurkha Rifles*, vol. 2, Gale & Polden, Aldershot, 1955.

Gould, Tony, 'My Army Life', in *New Society*, 25 November 1976.

Greene, Graham, *Ways of Escape*, Simon & Schuster, New York, 1980.

Hart, B.H. Liddell, *History of the Second World War*, Putnam, New York, 1970.

Hatch, Alden, *The Mountbattens*, Random House, New York, 1965.

Hayter, Adrian, *The Second Step*, Hodder & Stoughton, London, 1962.

Huxford, H.J. (compiler), *History of the 8th Gurkha Rifles, 1824–1949*, Gale & Polden, Aldershot, 1952.

The Indian Armed Forces Year Book for various years.

James, Harold, and Denis Sheil-Small, *The Gurkhas*, Macdonald, London, 1965.

—— *A Pride of Gurkhas: The 2nd King Edward VII's Own Goorkhas (The Sirmoor Rifles) 1948–1971*, Leo Cooper, London, 1975.

Karan, Pradyumna P., and William M. Jenkins, *The Himalayan*

Kingdoms: Bhutan, Sikkam and Nepal. Van Nostrand, Princeton, New Jersey, 1963.

Lewin, Ronald, *Slim: The Standardbearer*, Leo Cooper, London, 1976.

Longer, V., *Red Coats to Olive Green: A History of the Indian Army 1600–1974*, Allied Publishers, Bombay, 1974.

Macdonell, Ronald, and Marcus Macaulay (compilers), *A History of the 4th Prince of Wales Own Gurkha Rifles, 1857–1937*, 2 vols., William Blackwood, Edinburgh and London, 1940.

Mackay Col. J.N. (compiler), *A History of the 4th Prince of Wales's Own Gurkha Rifles*, vol. 3 (1938–48), William Blackwood, London, 1952. (Edited and illustrated by Lt.-Col. C.G. Borrowman.)

—— *History of 7th Duke of Edinburgh's Own Gurkha Rifles*, William Blackwood, Edinburgh and London, 1962.

Mains, Tony, *'Joining the Ninth Gurkhas in the Thirties'*, unpublished manuscript.

Mason, Philip, *A Matter of Honour*, Holt, Rinehart & Winston, New York, 1974.

Masters, John, *The Road Past Mandalay*, Michael Joseph, London, 1961.

—— *Bugles and a Tiger*, Viking, New York, 1956.

Merewether, Lt.-Col. J.W.B., and Sir Frederick Smith, *The Indian Corps in France*, John Murray, London, 1917.

Moorehead, Alan, *The March to Tunis*, Harper & Row, New York, 1941.

Moraes, Frank, *Witness to an Era*, Holt, Rinehart & Winston, New York, 1973.

Morris, John, *Hired to Kill*. Rupert Hart-Davis in association with The Cresset Press, London, 1960.

—— *A Winter in Nepal*, Rupert Hart-Davis, London, 1963.

Mullaly, Col. B.R., *Bugle and Kukri: The Story of the 10th Princess Mary's Own Gurkha Rifles*, William Blackwood, Edinburgh and London, 1957.

Neild, Eric, *With Pegasus in India: The Story of the 153 Gurkha Parachute Battalion*, Jay Burch, Singapore, n.d.

Nicholson, J.B.R., *The Gurkha Rifles*, Osprey, Reading, Berkshire, 1974.

Nicholson, Nigel, *Alex: The Life of Field-Marshal Earl Alexander of Tunis*, Atheneum, New York, 1973.

Northey, W. Brook, and C.J. Morris, *The Gurkhas: Their Manners, Customs and Country*, Cosmo Publications, Delhi, 1974 (original published 1928).

Owen, Frank, *The Fall of Singapore*, Michael Joseph, London, 1960.

Pal, Dharm, *Traditions of the Indian Army*, National Book Trust, Delhi, 1961.

Palit, Lt.-Col. A.N., *'With the 5th Gurkhas, 1910–11'*, unpublished manuscript.

Pearse, Hugh, 'Goorka Soldier (as an Enemy and Friend)', in *Macmillan's Magazine*, July 1898.

Pemble, John, *The Invasion of Nepal: John Company at War*, Clarendon Press, Oxford, 1971.

Pocock, Tom, *Fighting General: The Public and Private Campaigns of General Sir Walter Walker*, Collins, London, 1973.

Rambahadur Limbu, V.C., *My Life Story* (as told to Warrant Officer Kulbahadur Rai), The Gurkha Welfare Trusts, London, n.d.

Thompson, Edward, and G.T. Garratt, *Rise and Fulfilment of British Rule in India*, Central Book Depot, Allahabad, 1962.

Simpson, Colin, *Katmandu*, Angus & Robertson, Sydney, 1968.

Shakespear, Col. L.W., *History of the 2nd King Edward's Own Goorkha Rifles (The Sirmoor Rifles)*, 2 vols., Gale & Polden, Aldershot. (Vol. 1 first published 1912 and reprinted 1950, vol. 2 published *c*. 1924.)

Slim, Field-Marshal Sir William, *Unofficial History*, David McKay, New York, 1959.

Smith, E.D., *Britain's Brigade of Gurkhas*, Leo Cooper, London, 1973.

Smyth, Brigadier The Rt. Hon. Sir John, *Great Stories of the Victoria Cross*, Arthur Barker, London, 1977.

Stanhope, Henry, *The Soldiers: An Anatomy of the British Army*, Hamish Hamilton, London, 1979.

Tamplin, J.M.A., and P.E. Abbott, *British Gallantry Awards*, Doubleday, New York, 1972.

Tuker, Sir Francis, *Gorkha: The Story of the Gurkhas of Nepal*, Constable, London, 1957.

—— *While Memory Serves*, Cassell, London, 1950.

Woodruff, Philip, *The Men Who Ruled India*, 2 vols., Jonathan Cape, London, 1954.

—— *A Matter of Honour*, Holt, Rinehart and Winston, New York, 1974.

Woodyatt, Nigel G., *The Regimental History of the 3rd Queen Alexandra's Own Gurkha Rifles*, Philip Allen, London, 1929.

—— *Under Ten Viceroys: The Reminiscences of a Gurkha*, Herbert Jenkins, London, 1922.

Index

MORE ABOUT PENGUINS, PELICANS, PEREGRINES AND PUFFINS

For further information about books available from Penguins please write to Dept EP, Penguin Books Ltd, Harmondsworth, Middlesex UB7 0DA.

In the U.S.A.: For a complete list of books available from Penguins in the United States write to Dept DG, Penguin Books, 299 Murray Hill Parkway, East Rutherford, New Jersey 07073.

In Canada: For a complete list of books available from Penguins in Canada write to Penguin Books Canada Ltd, 2801 John Street, Markham, Ontario L3R 1B4.

In Australia: For a complete list of books available from Penguins in Australia write to the Marketing Department, Penguin Books Australia Ltd, P.O. Box 257, Ringwood, Victoria 3134.

In New Zealand: For a complete list of books available from Penguins in New Zealand write to the Marketing Department, Penguin Books (N.Z.) Ltd, Private Bag, Takapuna, Auckland 9.

In India: For a complete list of books available from Penguins in India write to Penguin Overseas Ltd, 706 Eros Apartments, 56 Nehru Place, New Delhi 110019.